Shadowing Fame

by

Robert Keith

To the memory of
a truly honorable man,
whose lifetime of achievements
might have otherwise been unknown.

For Judy, my partner in life,
the only one who still believes
I can actually write.

Acknowledgement

A little over a year ago I had just finished my second book, which, like my first book, was based on my father's ancestors. Over supper, on a visit to my sister in Phoenix, my niece, an accomplished attorney, insisted that my next book, I'm not sure how she knew there would even be a *next*, needed to follow one life, from beginning to end. On my return home, I dutifully turned my attention to the family tree I had assembled on my mother's side of the family in search of a person as the launching pad for book three. I followed that tree from its roots that included two, more *traditional* ancestors of *proper* English descent, who arrived in America within a decade or two after one group of our founding fathers and mothers left their footprints in the sand around Plymouth Rock.

I started an electronic climb up the tree and landed on a branch that I remembered had a limb connected to a twig supporting a great-great uncle. A Kentucky born man that was an early attorney and judge after immigrating west to Illinois. In fact, I had earlier located an article originally printed by the Illinois State Historical Society in 1908, written by Dr. John Francis Snyder, entitled, *The Forgotten Statesman of Illinois,* about that man, James H. Ralston[1]. After conducting some additional research, I reckoned I would give Judge Ralston a try to see if it would be possible for his lifetime achievements to be featured as the subject of a book; they were, and then some.

Dr. John F. Snyder [1830 -1921]

In the spring of 2014 while conducting more online research, I ran across the name and email address of Martin Hansen who had posted some recent information about Judge Ralston. After emailing him, I discovered that "Marty" was not only a direct descendant but he had an interest in genealogy. He had collected and committed to memory a great amount of information over the years about the judge and his descendants some of which was supplied by Merle Harris and Walter Vernon. Furthermore, he was in touch with family cousins who also had, at one time or another, contributed to the knowledge base. Since that first contact, Marty and his band of cousins, graciously allowed me to open many heretofore-curtained windows into the life of the judge. This included one-of-a-kind correspondence, pictures, and remembrances; items that only family would save and treasure.

Along the way there were others who contributed to this project; the Nevada State Historical Society in Reno, NV, the good citizens of Austin NV, and several internet sites, some of them well known and some not, some free and some not. Included in the dot coms are ancestry.com, newspapers.com, the terrific map collection of cartographer David Rumsey at davidrumsey.com, The California Digital Newspaper Collection hosted by the University of California at Riverside, cdnc.ucr.edu, The Maritime Heritage Project, maritimeheritage.org, and the burgeoning daily effort to place searchable old books online at archive.org and books.google.com; the last five are free. Additionally, there are various federal and state genealogical and historical sites who do a wonderful job of making available online records, including the Bureau of Land Management, the National Archives and Records Administration [NARA], and the Illinois State Archives just to name a very few that I used. Like most of my other books, I have provided endnotes further explaining a person, place, or thing of some interest. Please read them!

Lastly, someone other than me has to closely edit everything I write, give me a swift kick in the *toosh* when my nose strays too far from the grindstone, and, being *somewhat* aged, keeping me healthy and above ground. That someone is my wife, Judy, and without her, this hobby would not be near as much fun or, for that matter, at all possible.

Foreword

Few names in American history in the second half of the 19th century garner more attention than Abraham Lincoln, Stephen Douglas, Robert E. Lee, Horace Greeley, William Tecumseh Sherman, *Mark Twain*, and John C. Fremont. In addition to the high marks these men received for their diverse accomplishments, they also had a little-known common thread; they were all close friends, colleagues, or acquaintances of J. H. Ralston.

A rare biography of Judge Ralston characterizes him using the word, *forgotten,* meaning that at one time a subject was well in mind, and now it is unremembered. It is almost a certainty that the name James H. Ralston was never the correct response to a history question. Therefore, rather than *forgotten,* I believe *unknown* is the better word. However, *unknown* does not in the least equate with a lack of success. The central theme of this book is to entertainingly create and preserve a memory of the judge's significant contributions to the history of his time.

Ralston was only 29 years of age when he was appointed to the

Judge James Hervey Ralston
Courtesy of the Nevada State Historical Society

judgeship of the Illinois 5th Judicial Circuit in 1837. A young man of striking personality, a little over six feet tall, straight, and thinly formed. With auburn hair, blue eyes, and faultless features. He was polite, agreeable, and as courtly and dignified in bearing as a Virginia gentleman of the colonial days. He had a sociable, kind, and generous disposition, though impulsive-spirited and extraordinarily ambitious. The judge was driven in life by a high sense of honor and strictly honest in personal affairs and the discharge of his public duties. In some instances his judgment was no doubt at fault. Though in the main his motives were pure and he never willfully violated his conception of right and justice. One of his favorite quotations was from Sheridan's adaption of Pizarro[2]; *Should the scales of justice poise doubtfully, let mercy touch the beam and turn the balance to the gentler side.* The judge was persuasive and showy in public, entertaining in conversation, and an impressive impromptu speaker though his rudimentary schooling in his formative Kentucky years was occasionally evident in his grammar.

A prominent characteristic of James Ralston was his firmness and determination of purpose with the explicit exclusion of his children, who wanted for nothing. Yet, he was weak in resisting flattery and was easily influenced by those in whom he had implicit confidence. To an unrecognizable fault, he was politically an ardent Jacksonian democrat. He was a member and four-time lodge founder in the Masonic Order, though not attached to any religious denomination. He had liberal views on the subject of a man's spiritual nature. James was fond of music, of gay and lively society, enjoyed the occasional use of tobacco, and he had quite a self-taught interest in literature and poetry.

Enjoy reading about a life filled with accomplishments, rubbing elbows with the rich and famous, experiencing unbounded joy, and deep sadness, a man who lived his life *shadowing fame*.

Table of Contents

Chapter 1

The Old Kentucky Home

The serenity and pastoral beauty of Bath County's lush green rolling hills in 1819 Kentucky belied the daily hardscrabble existence facing the eight members of the John Ralston family who lived there. John brought his bride, Elizabeth *Betsy* Neely[3] Ralston, to this land near the Licking River in north central Kentucky[4]. They arrived shortly after their marriage in Mercer County, near Lexington, twenty-one years earlier. The two of them settled on their farm they called *Hope Springs*. The name was not derived from any natural springs on the land previously owned by some fellow named *Hope*. Rather, it originated from the work of the English poet, Alexander Pope, who declared that *hope springs eternal in the breast of man*; the couple's favorite mantra. The centerpiece of their well-kept 120-acre farm was a 20 by 24 foot two-room solidly built log cabin that Betsy wistfully referred to as *the manor house*. Most of the indoor family activities took place at a small oak dining table adjacent to an unusually large stone fireplace. A fireplace used not only as the source for the cabin's warmth but also Mother's kitchen stove. The children's sleeping quarters were in a loft above the larger of the two ground floor rooms. The area was only accessible by a ladder that was put in place in the evening and removed in the morning. A Ralston child knew a rite of passage was realized with that first climb to the loft. That sacred place where, with selected siblings, countless whispered plots were hatched, dreams for the future were shared, and perhaps above all else, lifetime bonds were formed.

In the forest just behind the cabin was a meager lean-to enclosed by a split-rail fence that accommodated the family's collection of common livestock. The menagerie included a milk cow, four goats, two horses, and two roosters. The latter frequently engaged in non-life-threatening skirmishes to impress the harem of uncounted laying hens. Though their farm was in the neighborhood of what would eventually become the thoroughbred racehorse capital of the world, the Ralston horses were not of that lineage. Named by a family vote, *Giddy* and *Yup*, the horses were solidly rooted in a long line of sturdy and steady plow and wagon pullers that managed their top speed when they meandered to the feed trough.

Occasionally a panhandling covey of quail, squirrel, rabbit, and deer wandered through the area for a free meal. If any one of them failed to respond appropriately after being

noticed, it was usually enjoyed as dinner's main course. Raccoon, possum, and thankfully only on rare occasions a skunk curried the favor of the Ralston's mixed breed, floppy-eared nearly blind hound, *Nosey.* The dog still had a keen sense of smell, could tree its quarry, and proudly announce the deed to anyone in the vicinity. Every Ralston male had a coonskin cap just like the

Ralston Kentucky Home

one rumored to be worn by Kentucky's much admired legend in his own time, frontiersman Daniel Boone.[5] The Ralston children seldom tired of hearing their father's favorite bedtime story he titled *Dan'l the Great.*

Before John married Betsy, on one of his regular visits to Lexington in the fall of 1795, near his small farm in Fayette County, he saw a notice on the wall of the town's post office. The notice read that Captain Daniel Boone seeks a company of able-bodied woodsmen who, under his direction, will widen the Wilderness Road[6] to allow wagon travel. Interest, it read, should be shown in person by attending Miller's Station, 28 miles up the Maysville Road at 12 o'clock noon on the 26th day of September, 1795. John was single and if the money was right, he might be interested in the work. In the least, it was worth a long day's trip just to see and meet the man known far-and-wide for his exploits as an Indian fighter, hunter, and trailblazer.

A short distance from Miller's Station, John began to see a crowd of fellow Kentuckians. The men, women, and children shared his interest in seeing the one and only Daniel Boone. Shortly after noon, a tall, aging, stout, rugged, yet kind looking man clad in buckskin stooped through the cabin door to the front porch of Millers Station and stood erect in front of the quieted and eager assembly.

In as loud as voice as he was able, he introduced himself as Colonel Dan'l Boone long of *Virginny* and *Kintuckee*; his words were greeted by loud *hurrahs* and applause. For the next few

Daniel Boone 1734 - 1820

minutes, Boone talked about the 20-year history of the Wilderness Road and about his role in *gittin' it a goin'*; there was more applause. He shared a story about getting *caught up* by the Shawnee *twiced over* and still *livin' to tell the tale* as muted *oohs* and *aahs* arose from the multitude. John noticed Boone showed little emotion or change in voice as he spoke. Yet with his mannerisms and overall demeanor, the crowd hung on every *countrified* word. He ended his speech by telling the gathering that he had written a letter to *old Isaac*, Governor Isaac Shelby of Kentucky. *I have sum intention of undertaking this road … and I think My Self intiteled to the ofer of the Bisness, as I first Marked out that Rode … and never Re'd* [received] *anything for my truble*. Dan'l walked toward the cabin to a nearly overwhelming amount of shouting and applause, acknowledged by the Colonel with a smile and a repeated wave of his hand. The fact that Colonel Boone was without a coonskin cap did not escape John's attention, and he assumed he left it in the cabin.

The station's owner, John Miller, told the gathering that interested and able men should come in the cabin, sign up for the work, and shake the Colonel's hand. When the work was given to *Dan'l*, he would send word to each of them along with the amount of pay for the work. Father said that after separating the women and children, about 200 men, including him, stood in a line that stretched a good distance from the cabin door. When it came his time to shake the hand of *Dan'l the Great*, all he remembered was he had never before or since, experienced such a firm grip or looked in the eyes of a man so determined. Father always ended the story with a frown saying that he never heard another word from Miller or Boone, though he knew the road was widened two years later in 1797.

There was another story that fascinated the Ralston children. Though the basis in fact of most of his stories was never questioned, there was suspicion on the part of the older siblings. Their father occasionally interlaced his accounts with what the more worldly offspring politely called *tall tales*. The story of *the bush that ran away* was just such a story. The account was set in wilds of the English colony of Upper Canada to the north where, truthfully, their father, among a large number of other horse-mounted Kentuckians, had gone in the fall of 1813. Their task was to fight off an invasion of America from the north by the red-coated English soldiers and their Indian allies.[7] It seems there was one Indian chief in particular who led a notably savage group of angry bloodthirsty Indian braves. According to their father, the chief was named *Tocomesee* by his father because he was such a large baby at birth that the rest of the Indians had *to come see* the baby to wonder at his size. At any rate, the Indian braves of *Tocomesee* had

Tecumseh 1768 - 1813

fought valiantly but the Indian's bows and arrows and spears were no match for the long muskets of the Kentuckians. Soon, the few remaining Indians were surrounded by their foes and they waved a white flag and put up their hands in surrender. Father recounted that he and several of his friends came closer to the red men to take away their weapons. He noticed a very large bush near the base of a tree seemed to be ever so slowly moving away from him toward the dense forest. John was the only one who saw the bush moving. He sat down on a fallen log after everyone else had gone and stared at the bush to make sure his eyes were not deceiving him. Soon the bush started to move again very slowly, then faster and faster. John jumped up and chased the bush. Near a small river called the Thames, the fast moving bush collided with a large tree and stopped moving. Father told his children that he went up to examine the bush more closely. He soon noticed that there was a very tall Indian carefully wrapped in the branches of a bush that was killed when he hit the tree. John took his friends to see the Indian and one of them recognized him as Chief Tocomesee, and they all called their father a hero of the battle.

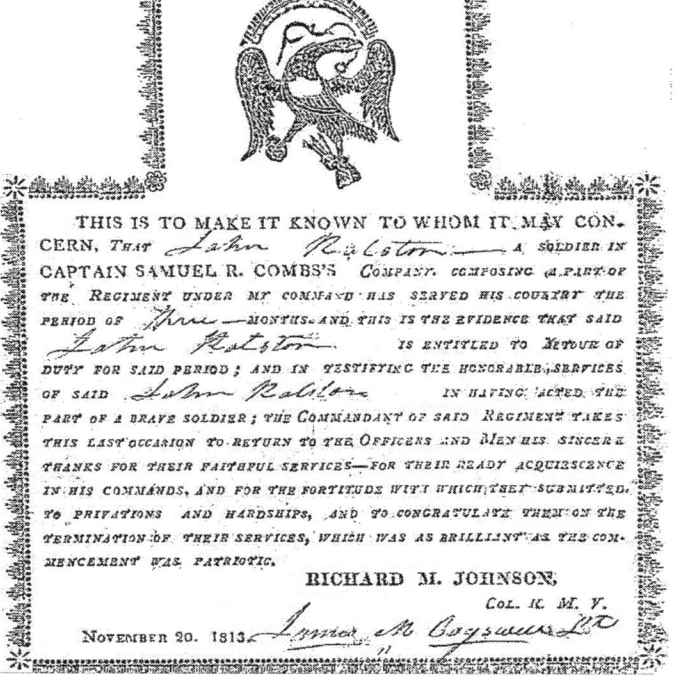

Certificate of Service, John Ralston, War of 1812
Courtesy of Martin Hansen

John Ralston's cash crops were tobacco, corn, and hemp. They were successfully grown when Mother Nature smiled and with the help of every available able-bodied family member. This growing season, a pregnant Betsy, with son William Henry Hervey, had more than her hands full with *manor house* chores and the large and bountiful family garden. On the Kentucky frontier, a distance of anything less than five miles was considered nearby. Therefore, when the *nearby* one-room *fits all* school adjourned for the growing season, John's full and part-time labor force blossomed. Assisting their father was the tall and handsome son, 18 year-old Joseph. A seventeen year-old *tomboy* called Sarah for a reason no one remembered because her given name was Nancy. Fifteen year-old playful Polly, born Mary, and thirteen year-old bookworm Thomas. The youngest member of the troupe was the scheming, impetuous, thin, and auburn-haired

12 year-old James. At harvest time, Father enlisted additional help from his son-in-law, Henry Sanders, who had a small farm a *stone's throw* down the road where he lived with his bride, the oldest Ralston offspring, 20 year-old Patsy aka Martha. The Sanders' had two young children Lizzie and infant son Josiah.[8]

One day while cutting the hemp during harvest, James had a question for his father. Holding up the hemp plant he had just cut, he wanted to know what would happen if a piece of rope made from that very plant was used for a hangman's noose. With no hesitation, his father panned a reply that with the quality of the hemp grown on their farm, the guilty rascal would surely die. Laughter could be heard in the next row where brothers Joseph and Thomas were at work. Father smiled and added that he clearly understood that was not what his son intended with the question, however, James did need to realize that the hangman's noose does not end a criminal's life. Rather, it is the judge and a jury of his peers that decide the punishment that is then carried out. The satisfied look on his son's face ended the matter. This may well have been one of James earliest discussions on the subject of the law though it would be far from his last.

After harvest, the tobacco made its way for a time to the drying barn of a good friend, Samuel Graham, then sold at auction in Paris, Kentucky about 18 miles distant. The hemp would be hauled by wagon some 30 miles to Cynthiana where it was loaded on a flat boat at the Licking River landing. The flat boat followed the river's twists and turns on its way north to the Ohio River and to the markets in Cincinnati and beyond. The corn stayed home to be used for a number of purposes, primary of which was food for the livestock and the family.

In many ways, Joseph and Betsy Ralston were cut from the same cloth as most of their neighbors on the Kentucky frontier in the early 19th century. Their ancestors immigrated to America from Europe for the promise of a better life and survived unimaginable hardships in making the journey. They had a large family, for sadly, with the toll taken by disease and very limited access to medical care, there was still a need for many working hands. The success of a frontier family was in its numbers. They had little monetary wealth or formal education yet a strong religious faith and an even stronger work ethic. They homesteaded in the midst of numerous frontier perils because the land was affordable. In short, these rural farming families were the cornerstones to the success of building a young country. However, the genetic threads of the Ralston cloth set the family apart from their neighbors; it was woven for notable success. After all, hope springs.

Chapter 2

The Illinois Frontier

Winter announced the first signs of an early arrival as a few flakes of light snow began to fall in Quincy, Illinois. The year was 1828. James Ralston, who recently celebrated his 21st birthday, had just arrived in the village on the limestone bluffs overlooking the Mississippi River. With a sense of accomplishment, he slowly lowered his tall, thin, and aching body from the saddle. He had spent the most part of the last three days riding west on the overland trail from Springfield, Illinois. He had not faced any real adversity during the journey across the grassy plains, other than picking his way through the swamps near Jacksonville. It was the greatest distance he had ever ridden alone. He tied his horse to a rail in front of Rufus Brown's two-story log and wood-framed building that served as Quincy's tavern, general store, and only hotel. It was locally known as the *bed bug* inn and humorously as the *dew drop inn.* James' mentor in Springfield, Squire Pugh, recommended Mr. Brown's establishment if a body ever needed at least a night's stay in Quincy. The story of why James was now at an obscure village of *maybe* 150 souls on the western frontier of Illinois is of noteworthy interest and hereafter summarily described.

Six months earlier, James could not mask his heavy-hearted disappointment when it was confirmed by his father that he would not be next in line to attend the hallowed log halls of Transylvania College in Lexington. Or, the lesser-known halls of the nearby faith-based Rittenhouse Academy in Georgetown or any halls of formal learning for that matter. Two years earlier his oldest brother Joseph earned a Doctor of Medicine degree from Transylvania, the highly regarded *Harvard of the West* and his brother Thomas had begun a course of study in religion at Rittenhouse. His father told him that the money the family had so frugally set aside for so many years for the education of the Ralston family males was completely exhausted. Further, with the death of his wife and James' mother, Betsy, the year before, there was no real hope for any additional funds.

James viewed his limited options and concluded there was really only one available. Their mother had been the glue that held the family together for longer than anyone could have ever imagined and she was unexpectedly gone. Now, Joseph had left the farm to start his medical practice as was *want to be reverend* Thomas. The absence of four strong hands and two strong backs was critical. Despite his lack of agricultural fervor, James' foreseeable future would be spent farming. He would help his father simply try to maintain what was, in good growing years, a meager existence. Just when James thought he was going to have to postpone his dreams of doing something, just anything but being a farmer, he received help from a most unlikely source.

For as long as James could remember, just a few long steps short of five miles south on the Mt. Sterling road, as that time-honored crow flies, lived his Uncle William, Aunt Nancy[9], and a cabin full of Ralston cousins. He remembered that he had once called his uncle by the name of *Willie*, a nickname he often heard at school for *William* and that error resulted in his inability to sit comfortably for a week. Uncle *William*, a few years older than his father, was also a farmer. James had two particularly vivid memories as he was growing up of the times his father and his uncle were together in the same room. The seemingly never-ending arguments about the best way to grow tobacco and hemp, and the highly interesting discussions about which of them was the better soldier. William was at Yorktown when Cornwallis surrendered and John in the recent conflict with the British and the Indians in Canada. The one subject on which there was absolute and unconditional agreement was how crazy England's King George III really must be. James had also spent more than his fair share of time rousting about with his male cousins then ganging up and relentlessly teasing the cousins of the fairer sex. For several years, his mother's sister, Aunt Patsy, had lived with his family and he remembered attending her marriage to his cousin, Andrew, the oldest son of Uncle William. James still smiled when he recalled his mother tirelessly trying to explain to him just how Andrew and Patsy were not really related when it seemed to him they just had to be.

Uncle William and Aunt Nancy made a special trip to the John Ralston farm. They announced they were planning to leave Kentucky and settle on some never before tilled river-bottom land in a valley near a town called Springfield in Illinois. James would never forget the look of astonishment and then abandonment on his father's face when he heard the news. All of the Ralston's knew something about this place.

A good friend of both Ralston families, the former sheriff of Bath County, Tom Iles, had a son Eli[10], who had left Kentucky a few years ago to seek his fortune near St. Louis. The accounts sent home described Eli's moderate success in his ventures there, but that he had done particularly well as a merchant in Springfield, 90 miles north and east of the gateway to the west. Uncle William produced a letter written to him by Eli that described land that he could find for William. Eli guaranteed it would be *the best 160 acres of farming soil your eyes will ever have the pleasure to gaze upon.* The letter included instructions on the best way to travel from Bath County to Springfield.

John Ralston did not want to understand why his brother was so willing to pick up and leave the place where he married, built a home, and reared his large family; James, on the other hand, could. For nearly a decade the Ralston farms, and those of their neighbors, had consistently yielded less crops per acre. The years of not rotating crops in favor of repeatedly planting badly needed money crops in the same soil was coming home to haunt them. Those that stayed in Kentucky would pay the price. Uncle William may not have had many planting seasons left in his old bones but he, like James who had plenty of seasons remaining, were both planning to make the most of them. James petitioned his father to let him accompany his uncle to Illinois. Though he felt betrayed, his father fully realized that James was nearing the age of adulthood. John Ralston's heart and mind did not agree with the decision, but he had no choice other than to let his son go.

The members of the families that planned to stay on their farms in Kentucky gathered for a tearful farewell for the members heading about 450 miles to the north and west to central Illinois. Promises of love and the writing of letters were made by everyone but nothing was ever mentioned about their possible return to Kentucky. In fact, that would never happen. As was often the case with the families who originally arrived by ship on the American east coast, those that chose to continue an ever westward migration, rarely returned from whence they came.

Three wagons full of the William Ralston family possessions and with nephew James driving the third wagon, the convoy struck out on their journey. The trip would take them through Lexington, Frankfort, and Louisville, Kentucky, where they would cross the Ohio River to New Albany, Indiana. They would continue through the Indiana towns of Paoli, Hindustan[11], and the former Indiana Territorial capital of Vincennes where they crossed into Illinois. From there they would travel to Lawrenceville, Edwardsville and north to the Sangamon River valley and Springfield. The road they used from Louisville to Edwardsville was the route taken by the Louisville, Vincennes, and St. Louis stagecoach line. It was a well-traveled route with an abundance of merchants providing the goods and services needed by the emigrants riding on wagons. In earlier years this road was known as the Goshen trace with its origins as an Indian and bison trail. Now, among the many other purposeful voyagers, this was a road to adventure and discovery, though it also held some trepidation for the members of the Ralston clan. They sought a new beginning in a place they knew by name only.

The Ralstons expected to have encounters with hostile Indians. But, the road they used was a busy thoroughfare for the white man, the Indians knew it, and they avoided the area at all costs. They expected axle-deep quagmires of mud, but they wisely departed after the spring rains and their route remained high and dry. They expected a treacherous crossing of the mighty Ohio River, but the ferrymen below the rapids had been at their appointed post for more than a score of years. Whether in periods of high or low water, they knew their work well. They had expected at least one of the storied plains storms. Strong winds, rain, and hail that howled unchecked across the gently rolling treeless prairie of knee-high tall wild grass. On this count, they were not disappointed. At a point about midway between Vincennes and Edwardsville, the ominous dark billowing clouds accentuated with lightning bolts

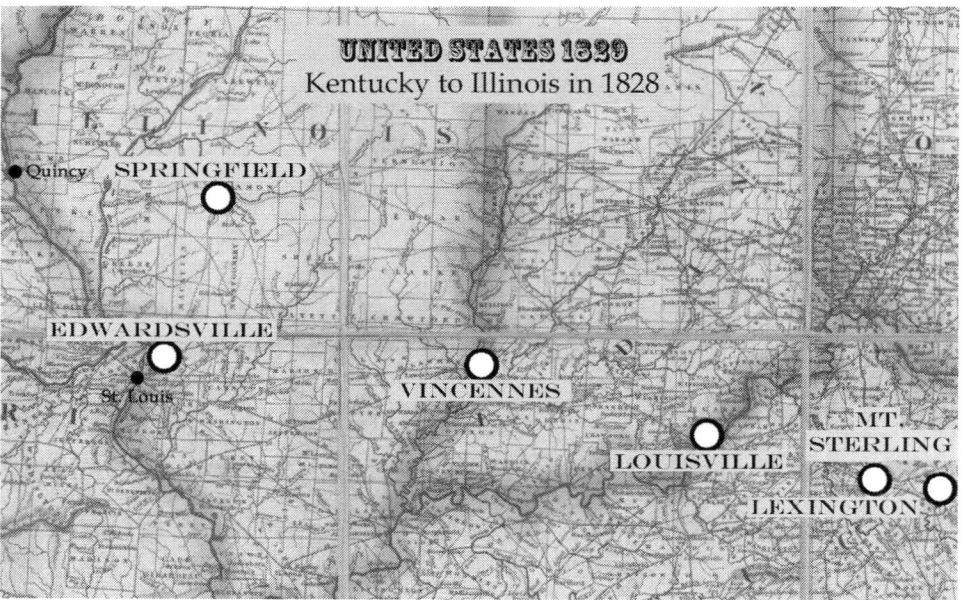

and thunder claps bore down. The three Ralston wagons formed a small circle to help protect the precious cargo against the buffeting winds. The family huddled closely together for safety beneath them. In less than 5 minutes, the roaring storm had passed and continued to share its pent up energy with the helpless flora, fauna, and humankind to the north and east. No harm was readily visible to any clan member other than James' left eye. It was nearly swollen shut by a small hard object of unknown nature. It struck him full-force in the face when he unwisely lifted his head to view the wrath of the storm first-hand. However, the same could not be said for the family's belongings. They had been carefully tied down in each of the three wagons with suitable heavy hemp rope that the storm's high winds had broken like string. The belongings could now be viewed strewn on the prairie in a line that followed the storm's exact path nearly as far as the eye could see. A full day of recovery, inspection, and periodic crying over beyond repair and lost treasures ensued. Each family member realized full-well that God's blessing had spared them. They were in much better condition than the fury of the storm intended as they resumed their journey.

James was caught unaware when Uncle William directed the wagons to the left at a major crossroad in the middle of the village at Edwardsville. Thankfully for the troupe, James brought this to his uncle's attention. The driver of a passing stagecoach confirmed the error and the correction was made. The trail rather than a road they followed north from Edwardsville was less traveled by far than the stagecoach road. The family viewed fewer and fewer homesteads and settlements. Game of many kinds appeared in abundant numbers and James smiled. He thought to himself about the ease of securing a meal of rabbit, venison, or wild turkey in this location compared to hunting in the dense forests of Kentucky. The fear of Indian encounters in this sparsely populated place came to the fore of everyone's attention and they made sure their weapons were loaded, kept high and dry, and near at hand. What the travelers did not know was that the Indians of this region did not farm as a means of subsistence. They preferred the more abundant lakes and game-filled forests about two hundred miles to the north as the place for their riverbank villages.

After three weeks on the road and trail, the Ralston wagons cleared the rise of a hill. Below them was a panorama of a lush green valley cradling a river shimmering like a golden ribbon in the reflected light of the sun. Along the banks of the river they saw two or three dozen log homes and some larger framed structures they assumed contained the wares of a merchant or perhaps the boarding rooms of a hotel. The driver of a wagon heading in the opposite direction confirmed that they had arrived at the village of Springfield on the banks of the Sangamon River in the Illinois County of the same name. As he passed, he heartily welcomed them to town. The weary travelers agreed that the first order of business was to establish a camp for the night and, in the morning, they would ride to town and find family friend Eli Iles.

Eli kept the promise he made by letter to his Kentucky friends. The 160 acres of land that he found for them just west of Springfield on Spring Creek was the most fertile William Ralston had ever seen. With the help of his sons, his nephew, and several of their new neighbors, William quickly constructed a handsome two-room cabin near the creek, and the Ralston males plowed 20 acres of the family's land to get in some crops before winter. James remained at his uncle's farm until the last of the tilling was done and then he went to Springfield looking for a job that did not directly involve working the soil.

He quickly found employment in the store of the clan's benefactor, Eli Iles, working as a stockman, salesman, and clerk. He boarded in a small storeroom attached to the side of the store. Not long after his new career as a merchant's clerk began, he assisted a tall-distinguished looking gentleman who needed a proper sized dress shirt for courtroom attire. One discussion led to another and James and his new friend discovered that, in addition to the store's owner, they too had common roots in Bath County Kentucky. James, and the older Jonathan Pugh , a Springfield attorney and part-time justice of the peace, talked for over an hour about their experiences of growing up in the Kentucky back woods and about their aspirations for the future. Pugh asked James if he had ever considered the law as a profession. James replied that he had no knowledge of the subject and did not hold an opinion on the question. Squire Pugh suggested that his new friend come around to Pugh's office when he was not working for Iles. That way he could at least find out what the study and practice of the law was all about. James agreed he would very much like to do that.

To make a longer story shorter, James found the law to be a calling for which he was aptly suited. Attorney Pugh was well considered and respected in central Illinois law circles. He soon found a position for his younger Kentucky friend as a clerk in the law practice of attorney George Logan, in Quincy, Illinois about 100 miles to the west. Attorney Logan held a position similar to that of Pughs. In addition to his own practice he was on call as the Illinois states attorney in the circuit district court whenever the circuit judge was in town to hear cases. With Pugh's letter of introduction in his coat pocket, James bid farewell to Uncle William and his family. He thanked them for kindly allowing him to *hang on to their coattails* for the trip from Kentucky. He reined his horse to the west where he hoped to begin a new chapter in his life as an attorney on the Illinois frontier.

James had three reasons to enter the Quincy establishment of Rufus Brown; he needed a room, a hot meal, and directions to locate Squire Logan. He removed his coat, shook off the light snow, and stooped to enter the low front door of Brown's Tavern. He already felt warmer by the time he ran the gauntlet through the half-dozen or so patrons in various stages of inebriation. James purposefully sat at a table near the fireplace warming his hands. He was soon joined by a plain unkempt auburn-haired woman. Her hard life had unforgivingly made what remained of her looks twenty years older than she likely was. She asked James in a barely understandable Irish brogue what he wanted. He decided to avoid any language difficulties and he simply asked for Rufus

Brown. The *experienced maiden* pointed to a short and stout elderly full-bearded man behind the bar, and she ambled back to wherever it was she had come. James stood up, to the extent the low ceiling allowed, and made his way to the bar where he introduced himself to the bar keep owner. He was greeted as if he was Mr. Brown's prodigal son. Both men knew James had never been *in this neck of the woods* before but they also knew the frontier code of hospitality, *a stranger is a friend well met.* Brown asked James what he could do for him and the visitor repeated his three reasons for being there. Brown maintained his broad smile and told James he could help with all three of his requests. The owner gave him a free pint of ale to boot as a token of welcome to Quincy. A pint of ale, a full stomach, and a restful night would set James Ralston right with his world, for now. Tomorrow he would again take up the subject of his future.

A week later, James wrote his first letter[12] home since leaving Bath County.

31st October, '28
Quincy, Adams County, Illinois

Dearest family,

Firstly, I must apologize for not writing at an earlier date but perhaps the following report will explain the reason.

Secondly, I am glad to say that Uncle William, Aunt Nancy, my cousins, and I arrived in Springfield in safety and the best of health after about three weeks' time. The oxen, horses, and wagons served us well the entire trip and we encountered no trouble with either disease or Indians. With one notable exception, the weather did not delay or disparage us in our trip.

Just west of the half-way tavern and inn on the Louisville to St. Louis stagecoach road in the state of Illinois, a great storm came upon us. It protruding the darkest possible clouds of gray and green I have ever seen. Just as we circled the wagons and tied off the horses hail the size of a walnut drove us to shelter under the wagons. A very short time later a wind blowing with a force beyond description and blinding rain were on us but not for more than at most five minutes. It seemed much longer at the time. The storm succeeded in scattering nearly all of Uncle William's possessions over a good extent of the Illinois countryside and we all spent a full day recovering what could be found that was undamaged and again loading it on the wagons. I believe we were all thankful the storm spared our lives though from its ferocity that was not likely its intent.

When we arrived in Springfield, we took little time in finding and reaquainting [sic] ourselves with Eli Iles. He made good on his promise to find Uncle William 160 acres of fertile ground all of which could be used for planting if that was Uncle's wish. I will tell you that I saw only one or two small groves of trees on the entire acreage and there is a wide and clear stream running through his land! Father, were I the farmer you wished for me to be and according to Uncle William, this land appears to be the best land possible for farming.

Eli also hired me on as a clerk in his store in the village. From what I saw and from what he told me, I sermise [sic] that he is more than properly well off in terms of his wealth and high esteem. The job in the store although providing meeger [sic] income did provide an opportunity to make aquaintences [sic].

Among them was Mr. Jonathan Pugh who is a few years older than I am, from the Pugh family I recall hearing about that lived east of Owingsville [Kentucky]. He came to Springfield five years back and he is now an attorney and justice of the peace. When I was not working at the store, Jonathan allowed me to spend time at his office learning about the law. I will readily admit that I found the work to be enjoyable, understandable, and perhaps much more suited to my disposition than regretably [sic] farming. With no disrespect in any way intended, I know for certain the possible financial benefit from following the law profession will exceed that of a farmer.

Jonathan provided me with a letter of introduction for Mr. George Logan and [sic] attorney here in Quincy (about 100 miles do [sic] west of Springfield) with whom I have found an apprenticeship position. The initial pay is merely room, board, and a new suit of clothes but that is quite agreeable given that I am learning the trade and not contributing income to Squire Logan's practice, a fact I hope to change in time. Mr. Asher Anderson, a merchant in Quincy, has provided me a comfortable room above his store with a goose down bed and a small fireplace! Though I am still penniless I believe I am living as royalty and perhaps happier than I have been for some time.

I promised Uncle that I would give you all his best wishes for continued health and happiness and I remind each of you of my deep and abiding love. Write me when you can and I promise I will do the same.

Your son and brother, always, [signed] James

As John Ralston read the letter from his son, tears formed in the corners of his eyes and slowly made their way down his cheeks. His tears were of sadness for a son no longer at home and happiness that the absent son was faring well. They reflected the fond memories of his own youth, when first he was on his own. He softly whispered to his departed Betsy that the two of them had done well by this son, and he told her how much he missed her and loved her.

Chapter 3

Learning the Trade

James was settled for the evening in the warmth of his small rented room above Asher Anderson's general store. There would be no study of the law or mulling over a legal decision this night as James chose to bask in the sublimely quiet solitude marking the end of a full day. He sat comfortably in his oversized cushioned rocker with his feet resting on a matching ottoman. Both handmade furniture items were given him in trade for his work by a grateful but cash poor client; he closed his eyes and took a deep relaxing breath. In the distance, he could hear the crisp and clear tolling of a steeple bell calling the faithful to Christmas Eve worship, 1831, that he knew would be held in candle light replete with joyful caroling. He let his mind wander, reflecting on some of his more memorable moments since he first arrived on the Quincy bluffs three years earlier.

He thought back to the endless hours of tutoring seated next to his dear friend and mentor, George Logan, learning to understand the rudimentary aspects of federal and state law. He remembered closely following along behind his teacher, like the young novice he was, to the 24 x 12 foot log courthouse watching and listening in wonderment as the practical application of the law took center stage. He recalled that shortly after he began his apprenticeship, Squire Logan asked him to be on that glorious stage for the first time to take a leading role in what James called, *the case of the wayward steer*.

Three stray cattle wandered onto the farm of Solomon Wigle, Sr. and the law-abiding farmer and miller penned the animals and advertised them in the local paper, the *Illinois Bounty Land Register*. One of the three was a steer unable to be restrained in any ordinary enclosure. It roamed the countryside creating riotous havoc among the people in the area. When the actions of the steer finally exhausted the neighborhood's patience, the time for action had come.

Believing in the value of justice, a trial to determine the steer's fate was called. Judge Logan presided, James Ralston for the defense, Archibald Williams for the prosecution and Sheriff Earl Pierce, the bailiff. It was decided the expense would be too great for such a nonsensical affair to assemble a panel of the *steer's peers* to pass judgment. So, four or five of the townspeople, including the local newspaper reporter, each donned a full buffalo robe and properly sat in the juror box. The charges brought against the animal ranged from disturbing the peace to murder. The steer had intentionally caused the death of one of the neighbor's prized sheepdogs ending its life with a swift kick to the head.

After much discussion, mock hair pulling by the defense about the *trumped up charges*, and no deliberation in the least by the jury, a verdict of guilty was rendered. Judge Logan sentenced the steer to death by slaughter, with the properly dressed beef to be divided among the neighborhood, and the hide converted to a leather belt for Wigle's one horse powered gristmill. The sentence was executed to the letter of the law, thus becoming the first and only case of bovine capital punishment in Adams County.

George Logan's patience resided at the exact opposite end of the scale from his impetuous young apprentice. James remembered one event that unquestionably proved that point. He and the Squire were walking from the office toward the courthouse when a group of over a dozen townspeople people, mostly women, suddenly appeared from behind the courthouse. They positioned themselves between the two men and the courthouse door. George wondered aloud if this congregation, given the number in its membership appeared close to twelve, was perchance a jury from one of his recent trials seeking to change their collective verdict. After this much too subtle attempt at levity completely missed its mark with the impromptu gathering, George muttered something about the lack of the gathering's sense of humor.

Leading the group, James recognized Mrs. Jabez Porter, a local minister's wife and likely the self-elected spokesperson. She indignantly asked Logan if he knew why the good citizens of Quincy should be exposed to such outrageously blatant heretical behavior. Ever the gentleman, George politely asked Mrs. Reverend Porter if she would be so kind as to explain what event had taken place that prompted her concerned inquiry. She responded that the previous evening nearly everyone one in town had personally witnessed Mr. Pierson, and that *touched* man who calls himself a hatter, prancing half-naked down main street. The drunken sots had placed lighted candles all over their body including the top of their head, repeatedly chanting *we are the light of the world* in their loudest voice possible.

It was all James could do to choke back his laughter. However, without so much as a hint of a smile, Judge Logan told Mrs. Porter and the others, the evidence of this indecency deserved to be as quickly as possible heard before a proper judge for a verdict and possible sentencing. The delegation all emphatically nodded their heads in agreement with the Judge and Mrs. Porter asked how swiftly justice could be served. There was an intentionally long pause while the judge stroked his chin seemingly to consider his options. Then he authoritatively told the group that he, being the only proper judge in Quincy at the present, had considered the evidence on that very spot. In his carefully considered opinion, Mr. Pierson and the *mad hatter*, were guilty of disturbing the decency of some of the most upstanding town citizens. He added the sentence would be one session in his personal chambers to counsel the two men against ever repeating this activity if they were NOT inebriated. Quincy's impromptu decency committee applauded Judge Logan and profusely thanked him for his thoughtful decision and sound judgment in the matter. The judge doffed his hat to the petitioners and both he and James continued their walk to the courthouse. The group had nearly dispersed when George whispered to James, ***what*** *a person says can be well hidden by* ***how*** *it is said.*

The memory of that valuable whispered advice faded to an image of Squire Logan announcing that although James was not yet officially an attorney, it was time for him to take on his first real client. The local chapter of the American Temperance Society, the Red Ribbon Club, had twelve founding members. Based on the advice of the national organization, the membership wanted to draft a constitution and by-laws at the outset of the group's formation that would be in  strict accordance with Illinois and U. S. laws governing the matter. This step would assure that the activities of the group could not be legally challenged or that any of its members individually would face legal action. George asked James to meet with the group and help. After a week's time, he and the temperance members finished their work and proudly celebrated the adoption of their new constitution and by-laws during their first official meeting. A few hours after the inaugural meeting adjourned, the elected president of the newly formed chapter was unceremoniously arrested and jailed for being drunk and disorderly in public. Interest in the movement immediately plunged, then ceased all together. George Logan finally *wrote-off* the unpaid temperance group's legal bill as a bad debt. James hoped this would not be a continuing trend in the financial matters of his budding legal career.

Hon. Richard M. Young

James' memories turned to the figure of Attorney Logan proudly standing before Judge Richard Young[13], a friend to both of them, in an official meeting of the circuit court at Quincy's courthouse in October of 1830. Attorney Logan made the motion to approve the appointment of one James H. Ralston as an attorney and counsellor at law in and for the state of Illinois. The motion was granted and signed by Judge Young. The three men then adjourned the proceedings to Brown's tavern where they toasted each another on their success in adding a new and highly qualified attorney to the Illinois bar.

A short time after that joyful private celebration the townspeople of Quincy turned out in large numbers to mourn the untimely death of Judge George Logan. James wept as he and the other pallbearers carried their good friend and true to his final resting place. This memory brought more tears to James' eyes as he recalled the depth of the loss he felt, and how hard it was, in so many ways, to be without his mentor in the earliest years of his career. A smile returned to his face as he recounted the many number of letters exchanged and meetings held between James and Judge Young, his surrogate mentor and friend, who helped him through that troubling period.

The Big Snow in the winter of 1830 and 1831 in Illinois began to fall about the 3rd week in November. James recalled hearing discussions concerning the forecast by the locals as to the severity of the upcoming winter based solely on the thickness of the wooly worm's coat. The old-timers prediction was that it *warn't gonna be all that bad.* The accuracy of that consensus was worth just less than the price of that wooly worm coat by Christmas Eve when Quincy's snow depth reached about two feet. The snow was covered with a layer of ice nearly thick enough to hold an adult man's weight. Pure fear replaced the *ahh shucks* attitude of being able to make it through any *ole'* Illinois winter, when the temperature never reached above freezing for the first seven weeks of the new year. An additional two feet of snow accumulated and James watched the upward progress of a snowdrift that was fast approaching his second floor window. He had a fresh memory of neighbors helping neighbors keep from starving or freezing to death. Quincy townspeople risking life and limb to locate supplies from wherever they could be found, and Asher Anderson, and the other merchants meeting whatever price had to be paid to get them. When the calamity finally ended in early April, floodwaters from the mighty Mississippi inundated farms all along the river and crop planting did not start that year until late in June. New timers and old timers alike set a revised demarcation for historical events; before and after *the big snow*.

James knew his reverie of memories would abruptly end with the first light of day and he moved from his chair to the comfort of his goose down bed. He hoped to get a little sleep before facing the trepidation of what would usually be an expectedly joyous Christmas Day. A week earlier, James had momentarily let his guard down and accepted an invitation to enjoy Christmas dinner at the home of Colonel Samuel Alexander and family. The family was temporarily living four miles south of town while a home in town was being built for them. Col. Alexander had recently completed a survey of the proposed Illinois & Michigan Canal near the thriving little village of Chicago. He came to Quincy to oversee the planning, building, and be the first Register of the new U. S. Land Office. Not long after his arrival, Alexander's wife discovered James was unmarried. Since that time, she *had left no stone unturned* in an effort to introduce his *royally single majesty* to at least one of her daughters whom James assumed was at or beyond the age of marital consent. Other than flaunting his title of *colonel*, that he gained when he led a local volunteer state militia company, James respected Alexander. He knew he could certainly use the direct connection at the land office that this friendship with Alexander might secure. Nonetheless, he had no anticipation and even less hope that anything pleasant would come from any aspect of the imminent and dreaded visit.

On his way home from the Alexander cabin on Christmas evening, James was pleasantly surprised by the events of the day. He actually had a good time! In the middle of that thought James unexpectedly, and from *way out of the blue*, experienced what he believed was a flash of pure brilliance. The idea required that James write a letter before the luster wore off and, on arriving home, he immediately set his thoughts to paper with pen and ink.

25 December 1831

Dr. Joseph N. Ralston
Vanceburg, Kentucky

Dear Brother,

I realize with a most contrite apology that I have not frequently had the opportunity to correspond directly with you, relying instead on the goodness of our Father's actions to share posted news. I was saddened to read in father's latest epistle about the recent passing of your sainted wife Nancy. In spite of your grief, I know you must and will remain strong for your young son Virgil when he most needs his father's undivided love and attention. Your long-term well-being and happiness are of the utmost importance to me and, with that thought in mind, I have an idea I would like to share with you.

*I am presently well situated in Quincy. Though I am still living and working in rented quarters, it is my intention within the year to purchase land and build a home of my own. I am also in good standing and position with the prominent businessmen and general folk of the town. This situation is not in the least due to my social graces, as you will well understand, but primarily by means of my law practice. The success of this endeavor has presented me a great surprise and pleasure. Perhaps one day soon financial success can be added as an attribute. I **am** well-to-do with meat and skins of once live wild game, assorted fresh and preserved foods, and other payments in-kind for legal services rendered. I must not fail to mention the lifetime guarantee of shelter and hay for my horse. The lifetime, that is, of my horse.*

Quincy, Illinois ca 1839

Quincy is a fine town beautifully situated on limestone bluffs well above the Mississippi River. Its people are good-hearted, industrious, God-fearing folks who, with but few exceptions, are good neighbors to have. The town's population steadily grows, more fine structures are built, and there is diversity in occupations. All in all Quincy is a fine place to call home, save a single exception, its medical care!

During the three years I have been here, five doctors have come and gone. At present, Dr. Rogers, more qualified as a pharmacist than a medical doctor, is the only sober and reliable source of medical help. Mid-wives are able to birth only our healthy infants. Home remedies, including those of the local Indians, cure our ills or make them worse, and broken bones are left to their own crooked devices to heal.

*My idea, nay, **my plea**, dear Brother, is for you and your son to move at the earliest possible time to Quincy. It is in this place your son can grow to manhood. It is in this place where you can fulfill the oath of your profession to kind people, including my humble self, who are in great need of your advice, care, concern, and knowledge.*

If there can be anything more in my power to convince you of this action, please let me know of it. Otherwise, I, joined by many of the good townspeople, shall be anxious to warmly greet you and my nephew at Quincy's river landing and forthwith help you both settle in town.

Your loving brother,

[Signed] James

Chapter 4

Love and War

The Quincy rumor mill had not yet added the item to the town's unofficial social record. James reached a happy conclusion about his experience during the Christmas Day visit to the Alexander home and he had taken follow-up action. He just knew that until his action became more widely known, he had not heard the last about the yuletide visit from a third interested party. Just a week into the new year, James' office door swung open and the personage of Mrs. Colonel Samuel Alexander appeared. Knowing the question was rhetorical, but well mannered, he asked Mrs. Alexander how he could help her. She responded in her irritating high-pitched squeaky voice that always brought to James' mind the visage of a conversational mouse. She insisted he call her *Mary,* and asked if he had an enjoyable time at *her* home on Christmas day. Intentionally wasting no words, he said that he did and thanked *Mary* for asking. He patiently waited for the sure to follow return salvo. She told him her daughter Jane, as it turned out the only one of the three Alexander daughters old enough to marry, was overjoyed to make his acquaintance. She added that Jane cannot stop talking about how much she enjoyed your company. James was yet again amazed by the boldness of this woman and wondered if the lengths she would go to secure a husband for her daughter might even include some form of indentured servitude.

What *Madame* Alexander would not discover for several weeks was that James had arranged to *see* Miss Jane Alexander. Contrary to the genetic disposition of her mother, he found her to be every bit as witty, charming, and intelligent as she was lovely. In their first meeting, Jane had agreed to keep their decision to see one another a secret from her mother for reasons Jane completely understood. He was still unsure how the secret was so well kept, up to the moment Mrs. Alexander literally swooned at the news of their somewhat clandestine meetings. Although an offer of marriage had not yet been tendered or accepted, James and Jane both knew it would likely be the next step in their relationship.

About a month later, James received a reply letter from his brother Joseph. He read that Joseph, his son Virgil, their sister *Sarah* and her husband Thomas Stampler, had decided to move to Quincy. They all planned to arrive after Stampler had harvested his crops in the early fall.[14] James' reaction to the news? A loud *hurrah* shouted at the corner of Quincy's Hampshire and sixth streets, briefly spooking a horse drawing the carriage of pharmacist Hiram Rogers and startling several nearby citizens. When word spread that James had convinced his doctor brother to come to Quincy, his standing in the community immediately ascended a number of rungs on the social and business ladders.

At about noon on April 22, 1832, a courier arrived in Quincy from the state capital in Vandalia. He carried with him a proclamation from Illinois Governor Thomas Reynolds calling for the organization of a mounted militia from the northwestern counties of Illinois. They included the counties of St. Clair to the north, and Sangamon to the west, with instructions the militia rendezvous in Beardstown, Illinois. The proclamation confirmed the rumor circulating in town that the Sauk [or Sac] Indian brave, Black Hawk, along with an estimated five-hundred braves and eight hundred women and children, had crossed the Mississippi, west to east. He and his band crossed the river in early April from their current home in the eastern Missouri Territory [present day Iowa]. Although Black Hawk's intentions were unknown, it <u>was clear</u> that he returned to Illinois in direct violation of the terms of a treaty of the previous year. It was also clear the incursion was against the advice of other ruling Sauk tribal members, most notably Chief Keokuk, and U. S. Government Indian affairs officials. The aggressive warrior held little or no regard for white American settlers or their government, and, in the company of such a large number of braves, he was a real threat to the peace of the northwestern Illinois frontier.

The able-bodied men in Quincy viewed this *call to arms* as the opportunity for a real adventure. Never mind that very few of them owned a decent weapon or a horse strong and fast enough to use in a fight to the death with a force of battle hardened Indians. Even fewer of them had any form of disciplined military experience needed to make sure that orders were followed in the heat of battle. At least four and likely many more of the sixty to seventy males who filled the militia roster from Adams County belonged in the category of *gentleman soldiers*. These men primarily joined for the personal notoriety and the thrill of the hunt, yet completely oblivious to what the *hunt* would ask in return. About noon on the twenty-fifth of April, after many speeches and amid much pomp and circumstance, the Quincy and Adams County mounted militia members went off to war. Four of the *gentlemen soldiers* frivolously fancied themselves as the *four horseman of the apocalypse* destined as an elite group to eight handedly bring down the mighty Indian warrior, Black Hawk.

The four men, all attorneys, had become fast friends during the previous year bound by

William A. Richardson

Orville H. Browning

a common avocation, similarity in age, political party affiliation, and their common Kentucky roots. Their names were, Will Richardson[15], O. H. Browning[16], Archie Williams[17], and last but not the least, James Ralston. For the first few days of the adventure, Browning recorded the events in a daily journal. He detailed the deluge of rain encountered at the

Archibald Williams

outset of the trip just three miles east of Quincy causing a delay. The joining of all of the individual militia units into a single army at Beardstown and Rushville[18] and the arduously soggy trip to the Mississippi at Yellow Banks. After just eight days of the war, the silver-spooned man-child of the Browning family was tired of the inconveniences. He tired of the whole affair, disgusted with the leadership, sickened by the food or lack thereof, and just quit writing.

Blackhawk and his braves were spotted going northeast on the north bank of the Rock River near Dixon's Ferry. The militia, assembled at Yellow Banks, made a forced march of nearly 150 miles to the ferry in just under 4 days [*see map page 25*]. By the time the militia arrived, Blackhawk's *British band*[19] was nowhere to be seen and that added additional fuel to the already low morale of the now very tired and hungry troops. Two days later the camp was aroused by the arrival of exhausted, disoriented, and completely terrified troops who had been members of an advance detachment sent northeast from the ferry up the Rock River the day before to try to discover Black Hawk's location. As the troopers straggled into camp, they told the story of being attacked by a large number of Blackhawk's warriors near a place about 15 miles to the northeast near a rivulet called Old Man's Creek. They reported that many militiamen were brutally killed by the Indians in the surprise raid and the survivors literally ran for their lives.[20] The experienced regular army soldiers in camp well-understood how 275 ill-trained and undisciplined troops could be so badly routed by a band of Indians less than a fifth of its size.

Six days later about 60 miles south of Old Man's Creek at a spot called Indian Creek a small band of Indians were seen. They were thought to be from the Potawatomie tribe and not directly involved with Black Hawk. At Indiana Creek they massacred 15 white settlers including men, women, and children. This was the last straw for the leaders of the completely demoralized militia forces. These well-intentioned men finally recognized their error in assuming the volunteer militia could hold their own against the ruthless Indian warriors under Black Hawk's leadership. Less than a week later, the militia troops were disbanded, save for a small number who wished to continue the fight. The former proceeded to return to the comfort of home at the best possible speed including three of the four apocalyptic riders. James stayed the course.

Sauk warrior Black Hawk

James firmly believed that he should remain to complete the job he had agreed to undertake, he re-enlisted, and joined the company of Quincy's sheriff, Capt. Earl Pierce. As a private, he took part in the month long chase of Black Hawk's *British band* in what is today southern and western Wisconsin. He was present at the Battle of Bad Axe, a purposeful massacre of helpless Indian women and children accompanying the few remaining braves. It was an unforgiveable decision to show other Indian tribes the outcome if they did not peacefully keep their promises. The slaughter occurred at the site of what is today Victory, Wisconsin, at the confluence of the Mississippi and Bad Axe rivers in western Wisconsin. Black Hawk was conspicuously and predictably absent from the slaughter, surrendering two days later at Prairie du Chien, thus putting an end to the war.

James returned to Quincy near the end of August. He explained to Jane and his friends that he had literally run his horse to death trying to get home or he would have arrived sooner. In a private moment with Jane, he shared the details of his experiences and hardships of the last few months. He was glad he finished what he started though he was unkind to his three noted colleagues and comrades. James told her he expected the three of them to accept the accolades for their participation in a war that in reality they never actually fought.

1832 Black Hawk War Dates and Sites

1	04/06	Black Hawk across Mississippi at Iowa River
2	04/16	Sac camp at Rock River
3	04/25	at Prophetstown Winnebago, Fox, Sac camp
4	05/14	at temporary war camp [braves only]
5	05/17	at Lake Koshkonog camp
6	05/25	at Rock River rapids camp
7	07/21	Battle of Wisconsin River heights
8	08/02	Battle [massacre] at Bad Axe/Mississippi rivers
A	04/25	Quincy militia leaves for Beardstown
B	04/27	full forces at Beardstown
C	05/03	full forces at Yellow Banks
D	05/12	forced march from Prophetstown to Dixon Ferry
E	05/14	Battle at Old Man's Creek against Black Hawk
F	05/20	Indian Creek massacre
G	05/28	forces disbanded at mouth of Fox River
H	06/18	new forces at Fort Wilbourn
I	07/03	at Lake Koshkonong
J	07/09	at mouth of Whitewater River
K	07/12	at Fort Winnebago
L	07/21	Battle of Wisconsin River Heights
M	07/26	at Helena
N	08/01	at Kickapoo River
O	08/02	Battle [massacre] at Bad Axe/Mississippi rivers

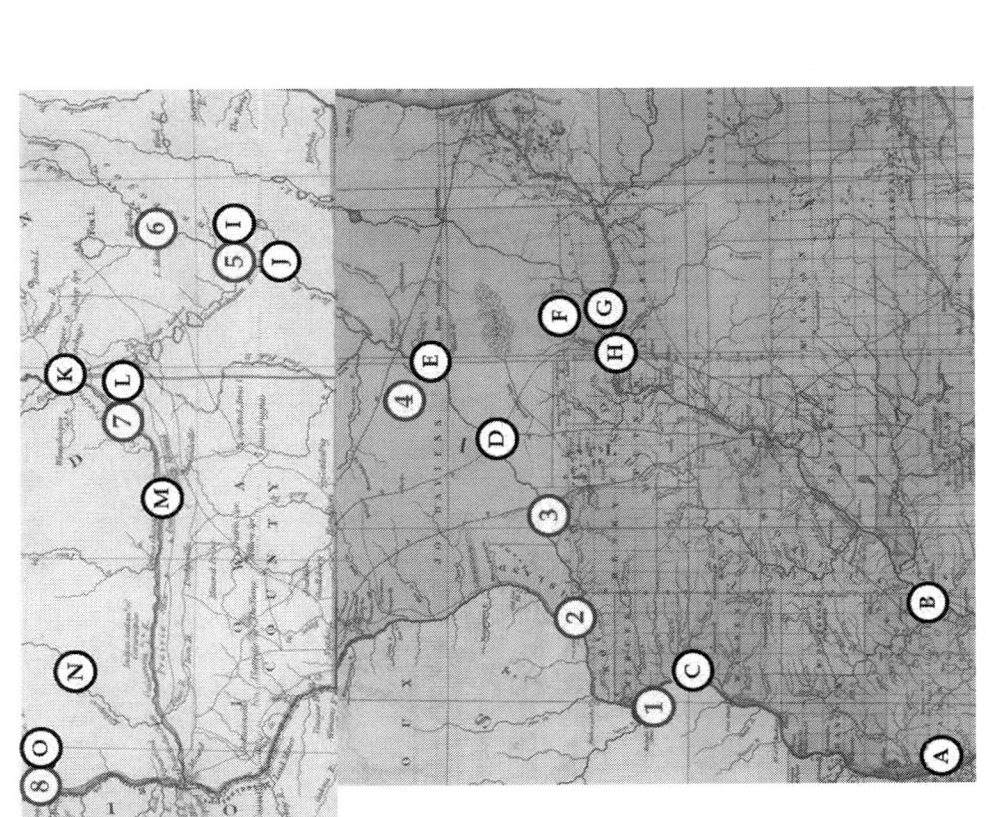

Illinois and Michigan Territory, 1832

In mid-October of 1832, Jane Alexander's face beamed as she lovingly looked into James eyes, tightly squeezed his hand, and repeating two simple yet powerful words, *I do.* The overflowing crowd at Quincy's small Congregational Church applauded and congratulated Mr. and Mrs. James H. Ralston, Esquire as they slowly walked down the aisle to the front door. They climbed in their waiting carriage that would take the honored couple in fine style all of two blocks to a reception at the courthouse.

Serving as James' best man was the tall and distinguished oldest brother of the groom, Dr. Joseph Neely Ralston. James and Jane had willingly postponed the wedding date three weeks so the newly arrived Kentucky members of James' family could be part of the happy event. Undoubtedly, the happiest member among the attendees witnessing the storybook affair had to be the tearfully joyous and relentless matchmaking mother of the bride, who reveled in what she believed was her single-handed accomplishment.

Joseph Neely Ralston

Chapter 5

Aiming Higher

During the previous five years in Quincy, James had solidified his position as one of the prominent attorneys in the county and he began to blossom in his successful career. He had served Quincy well for a time as Justice of the Peace and many of his friends now greeted and referred to him as *J. H.*, a term of familiarity and respect James proudly acknowledged.

Among James growing list of successes, there had been one profound personal setback. Just after the fourth of July in 1833, not a full year since her arrival, and despite the herculean efforts of Dr. Ralston, an outbreak of cholera quickly ended the young life of their sister Sarah Stamper. For weeks after her death James shouldered the burden of believing that had he not urged his family members to come to Quincy she would still be counted among the living. Jane was at last successful in convincing her grieving husband that only God knew why she had been taken from this earth at such a young age but she insisted it had nothing to do with her presence in Quincy. Her husband, Thomas Stamper, bereft with grief, left Quincy soon after his wife's death, and settled for a time in St. Louis, Missouri.

The clients James agreed to help provided him with challenging and wide ranging applications of the law. One of his cases required an administration of justice not unlike that of Solomon when the fate of a pet raccoon named Andrew Jackson hung in the balance for a couple seeking a divorce. The dilemma as to who would get the unusual pet was resolved when Andrew gave birth to a half-dozen healthy miniature look-alikes of the proud mother. James respectfully declined the couple's offer to have the pick-of-the-litter in lieu of payment for services rendered.

On the serious side of his work, James and O. H. Browning, the *Nero fiddler* of the Black Hawk War, took on the defense of one Thomas C. Bennett. Bennett was apparently a man of a somewhat lower economic order. He performed menial manual labor only during the short periods when he was not thoroughly drunk. One afternoon Bennett allegedly used a pistol and shot to death Mr. John Williams, a man of the same general social standing. The shooting ended a quarrel over the ownership of a jug of homemade corn whiskey. A passer-by discovered the body, having been drawn to scene of the crime by a number of hogs rooting over the remains. It did not take long for Sheriff Pierce to locate Bennett and confine him to jail. About two weeks later the entire case was presented at the courthouse in just a single day. The following day, in less than an hour, the jury handed down their verdict, finding Mr. Bennett guilty of the murder. The presiding judge sentenced the offender to death by hanging. The execution took place under the watchful eyes of most of the Quincy citizenry and the surrounding county. Children were excused from school to witness the special occasion of the gruesome event. The hanging was the first recorded legal execution in the short history of the town.

Sheriff Earl Pierce, more often called Captain Pierce, the rank he held in the Black Hawk War, was again in the public eye less than a year later. The popular, strikingly handsome, and trusted sheriff had a single flaw in his character. This *dark side* was known to only a few of the town's residents and nearly every one of the riverboat gamblers. He could not resist nor seldom won a game of *twenty-card poker*. *Cap'n* Pierce had accumulated a large sum of losses in the form of IOU's and he faced an ever-increasing demand to settle the debts. Had he *fessed up* to his problem, chances are he would have found many of his friends willing and able to help him overcome his evil habit. However, the sheriff apparently did not see that as an option. Rather than face the inevitable humiliation of his addiction, he and his wife slipped unseen from town during the dark of night. They carried with them a satchel containing the entirety of Quincy's recently collected tax revenue. His reputation now beyond repair, several mounted parties of local townspeople fanned out in all directions in a futile search for the now villainous sheriff. After the search was finally called off, rumors swirled for months that the couple had gone south to Texas where the sheriff's final card game ended as the result of a bullet from a local ruffian's colt revolver.[21]

James became even more sought after for his work with a new type of client. By an act of Congress in 1812, nearly 3.5 million acres of land were set aside in the present states of Illinois, Michigan[22], and Arkansas as bounty land for veterans of the War of 1812. The term *bounty* meant that soldiers received land as partial pay, or bounty, for their war service. In Illinois, Adams County was situated nearly in the middle of these lands called the *military tract*. Another bill enacted in 1820 made this public land even more attractive by selling it for $ 1.25 an acre to non-veterans as well.

The need to use the services of an attorney stemmed from greedy land speculators and state taxing authorities. These two entities were involved in a land title *tug of war*. The naïve war veterans or their widows were caught squarely in the middle of this chaos. A competent attorney was needed to determine who really owned the land. In Illinois, land ownership resolution was required by law to be provided by an attorney in the proximity of the land title in dispute. Hence, the attorneys in Quincy had hundreds of unsolicited clients knocking on their respective doors desperate for help. James had a distinct business advantage over his colleagues in this matter because his father-in-law, the register, was ***the man to see*** at the U. S. land office in Quincy.

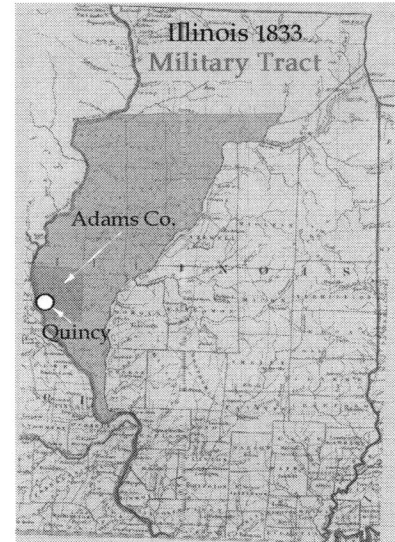

Our bright young lawyer was also personally involved in the acquisition of bounty land. James made most of his land purchases during the years 1833 through 1835, however, he bought a few tracts as late as 1844. He usually bought land that was in the proximity of small villages, hoping that if the village prospered the land value would increase. He understood the value of owning land and, many years later, when it came time to sell his acreage, he was not in the least disappointed with his profits.

James was happy with his position in the community, his improving economic state of affairs, and above all else, his marriage to his wonderful wife Jane. From his point of view he could want no more, a sentiment that was not shared by his brother and some of his closest friends. He received encouragement to consider using his recognized and widely known gift for finding solutions to difficult problems in the gladiatorial arena of politics. He viewed himself a *Jackson democrat*, he voted for party candidates, and followed the party's activities but never considered participating. The good Dr. Ralston was supportive of his brother's political notions. He was keenly aware when growing up James had always been painfully shy and hence awkward in social situations. This was a shortcoming directly opposed to any sort of successful political ambitions and Joseph set about to make some changes.

One evening in the privacy of James' home with only Jane looking on, Joseph filled James' mouth with an assortment of marbles and asked him, as distinctly as possible to read aloud several marked passages from Shakespeare's *Romeo and Juliet*. The purpose of this exercise was to take the reader's focus from what he was saying to overcoming a mouth full of marbles. About the time James' read the memorable line, *a rose by any other name*, he choked on a marble he swallowed. Jane was nearly in tears with laughter as James continued to read despite this bothersome setback. When a second and third marble joined the first in James' digestive tract, he could not contain his own laughter and about a dozen expelled marbles bounced a good distance in various directions on the wooden floor. Although the Doctor had remained stoic to this point, he could no longer contain himself and he too joined Mr. and Mrs. Ralston in sidesplitting laughter.

Calm again prevailed and Joseph had another somewhat peculiar exercise. Joseph retrieved a burlap sack he had brought with him to his brother's home. He pulled from the sack a pair of blinders. They were normally used to block the peripheral vision of a carriage horse proven to be skittish during trips amongst the commotion of a visit to town. Jane was again beside herself as Joseph tightened the somewhat oversized blinders on James' head. Shortly after Joseph affixed the blinders, James accurately imitated the sound of a horse whinnying and again Joseph and Jane could not contain their laughter. Joseph spent the next few minutes trying to convince his brother and sister-in-law that this was a serious undertaking to prepare James to gain a coveted political office. Before they quieted down, James could not resist asking his brother, who might be persuaded to vote for any political candidate standing on a soapbox wearing horse blinders. At last the exercise was underway with James' repeatedly reciting the only biblical psalm he knew by heart while Joseph, on one side, and Jane on the other, made as much of a diversionary ruckus as they could muster while trying to contain their laughter.

At Joseph's request, James became a member in good standing of Quincy's Bodley Lodge Number 94[23] of the ancient order of Free and Accepted Masons. Dr. Ralston and several other prominent men of Quincy were the charter members of the first such organization in Illinois. Socializing among the brothers of the lodge, most of whom James knew well, was not the learning experience Joseph had hoped. Despite Dr. Ralston's continuing efforts over time to improve his brother's ability to be relaxed in a political setting, James could not attain the level of composure or oratorical ability needed to carry him to a national stage. However, he did have some success in Illinois state politics just a few months

Vandalia, IL Courthouse
built 1836

after the country was shaken by the death of nearly two hundred brave soldiers and civilians at the Alamo mission in San Antonio.

In August of 1836, Squire Ralston was elected by a handsome margin to represent Adams County in the lower house[24] at the 10th session of the Illinois legislature. It was at the new courthouse building in then Illinois capital Vandalia[25] in December of 1836, that James first made the acquaintance of a two-term representative from Sangamon County, Abraham Lincoln, and a first term representative from Morgan County, the five-foot four-inch Stephen Douglas.

Chapter 6

A Legislator and A Judge

Since they first met at the opening meeting of the 10th session of Illinois legislature in 1836, the two democrats were inseparable. The sight of the short muscular Stephen Douglas, who would become respectfully known as *the little giant,* and the nearly foot-taller ribbon-thin figure of James Ralston walking side-by-side often elicited murmurs and quiet laughter on the streets of Vandalia. On one occasion a legislative group composed of state senators and representatives from Sangamon County called the *long nine* because they were all six-feet or taller, formed a friendly circle around Douglas and Ralston on the street. The long nine's apparent spokesman, Whig party congressman, Abraham Lincoln, offered to provide the diminutive Douglas with a foot stool on which he could stand above the shoulders of the taller men and *better see the light of day.* The unintimidated 23 year-old Douglas immediately replied to his would-be jokester that if he stood under a moonless night sky he could still hear an ill-conceived proposal from a Whig party member The crowd of men laughed and Lincoln complimented Douglas on his quick wit.

Stephen Arnold Douglas

Douglas and Ralston were fast friends for reasons beyond their shared political views and their Masonic membership. James envied the oratorical ability of his new friend who reminded him of how the short statured emperor, Napoleon, might have looked and sounded when he addressed his mighty armies. Douglas admired Ralston's straight-talking honesty and the man from the Kentucky backwoods who had gained success through hard work, gritty determination, and a razor-sharp legal mind. During their early years in politics and the legal profession in Illinois, they often sought out each other's counsel and guidance.

There were two important bills in this session of the legislature that required support from both the Democratic and Whig sides of the isle to be successful. The first was the ill-fated Illinois internal improvement act[26] and an act designating Springfield as the new capital of the state. As is often the circumstance in politics, bipartisan compromise is gained far from the public eye. In this particular case, Douglas said he would arrange a meeting with Lincoln at an out-of-the-way place where none of the participants would be recognized or even seen together. Although neither man was the lead spokesperson for their respective party, ever the strategist, Douglas knew Lincoln's gift for persuasion and his own talent for oratory far exceeded their current official political standing.

Douglas asked James to attend the meeting for a third, more personal, reason. Douglas

James H. Ralston

knew that James' long-time good friend, confidant, and mentor Judge Richard Young had been elected to the U. S. Senate. He would need to resign his judgeship of the Illinois' fifth judicial district prior to taking his seat in Washington. Douglas could imagine no one better qualified to recommend to the legislature to fill the position than his friend James and he wanted him to

Abraham Lincoln

be better acquainted and curry the favor of Lincoln to gain his vote. Douglas casually mentioned with a sly and telling smile that Ralston and Lincoln had in common their Kentucky roots and their service in the Black Hawk War, should his friend need any discussion points. A week later Douglas and James made their way to the back of a small wood-frame house on Thompson Street in Vandalia where the man they were meeting rented a room during the legislative session. They were greeted by Abraham, *please call me Abe*, Lincoln who cautioned James to duck his head at the door before entering his spartan but adequate room. James introduced himself to *Abe* as the tall *sidekick* of Mr. Douglas. Lincoln immediately recognized him from their meeting on the street and if he properly recalled the subject was sunlight and darkness. The 29 year-old Lincoln and the 31 year-old Ralston spent the next few minutes discussing the geography of their meager upbringing in the back wood hills and hollers of Kentucky. James laughed when Lincoln supposed that he had to walk a half-mile or so up a narrow dense forest trail just to *gaze upon the sun*. Lincoln then turned to Douglas remarking that he was sure he had never witnessed his *Democratic* friend remain quiet for such an extended period. Douglas responded that he was just becoming a student of what it was like to be poor; Abe and James laughed. Lincoln then said he understood from a well-placed source he believed was none other than Mr. Douglas himself that James had served in the fighting to defeat the renegade Indian brave Black Hawk. James confirmed Abe's observation and added that he had even enlisted for a longer term. Lincoln said he had done the same and they both laughed when Lincoln recalled the slackers who *scrambled home from the war at their earliest possible convenience.* Abe's brow furrowed when he recounted his war episode of the sadness and helplessness he felt as he stood over the grave of a soldier he had just buried at Kellogg's Grove[27], hoping never again to experience that grief.

When the evening was over, both Lincoln and Douglas had accomplished major objectives. With Lincoln's support, Douglas was sure the internal improvements act would pass and Lincoln was pleased to have Douglas' support in moving the state's capital to his hometown of Springfield. James was thoroughly delighted to have a new important Whig friend in the legislature when Abe agreed to support his appointment to the position vacated by Judge Young. On the walk back to their Vandalia hotel, Douglas was upbeat because of what had been accomplished in their meeting with Lincoln and he congratulated *to-be-judge* Ralston with a firm handshake and a slap on the back.

James liked the way *Judge James H. Ralston* sounded as it rolled from his tongue and the meaning of those words held an even greater interest. At the ripe old age of twenty-nine years, he may not have reached the pinnacle of his vocation but he had certainly come a long way since that morning he drove the third wagon out of Bath County. From an early age in Kentucky up to the time he left, his work never took him

> Vandalia, February 4th, 1837
> *To the Hon. the Speaker of the House of Representatives:*
> Sir:---
>
> Having been this day duly commissioned Judge of the fifth judicial circuit of this State, I do hereby resign my seat in the House of Representatives as the Representative from the county of Adams.
>
> Believing as I do, that a due deference to the opinions of the members of this General Assembly, in their voluntary election of me to fill a high judicial office, imperatively urges upon me its acceptance, and that a proper regard for the interest of the circuit and the administration of the laws within it, require me to enter upon the duties of the office without delay, I cannot doubt the propriety of my present course.
>
> Suffer me, Sir, to express, through you, to the members of this General Assembly my sincere gratitude for the many acts of kindness I have received from them during the two months we have convened together in a legislative capacity and to assure them of my ardent wishes for their individual health and prosperity. I separate from them, I hope without leaving one enemy among them, certain I am that I entertain no unkind feelings towards any.
>
> Believe me , Sir, sincerely
> Your most ob't Servant,
> JAMES H. RALSTON.

Letter to James Semple recognizing appointment to judgeship

farther away from home than Lexington or Cynthiana and the walk from the east side of Quincy to the west took less than 10 minutes. Now, he would find out what it was like to ply his trade by traveling nearly every road and trail in the state north and west of the Illinois River as judge of the fifth judicial circuit.

Jane was elated with the news of James' appointment and she was happy for him though she had not yet foreseen the loneliness she would face during her husband's extended absences. Instead, her giddy state brought back the memory of a story she remembered hearing as a child that she shared with her new circuit judge.

*The circus had just completed a successful stop in town and the roustabouts had no more than an hour before finished loading the tent and equipment on the wagons. All that remained of the circus' center ring was a large circle generously scattered with sawdust. Shortly after the circus wagons left, a man who earlier that evening had well met several glasses too many of whiskey, stumbled on to the circle and began to follow it around and around. Eventually two other men came along and witnessing the man repeatedly walking in circles, asked him what he was doing. The man replied that he was having a strange journey and that he kept repeatedly seeing a house like the one in front of him now. The two on-lookers just shook their heads and walked away where upon one of the men said to the other, **the man must be a judge learning the circuit.***

James was finally able to stop laughing long enough to suggest to Jane, that man may well be him within a year or two.

Despite the meager pay, the judgeship carried with it an inestimable reputation and influence. His position required a visitation at least three times each year to the courthouse towns on his circuit. Starting at Quincy, James traveled southeast to the town of Atlas, northeast to Lewistown, Peoria, Ottawa, and Chicago, then west to Galena, south to Knoxville, and Carthage, and back to Quincy; a trip of about 775 miles. One full circuit,

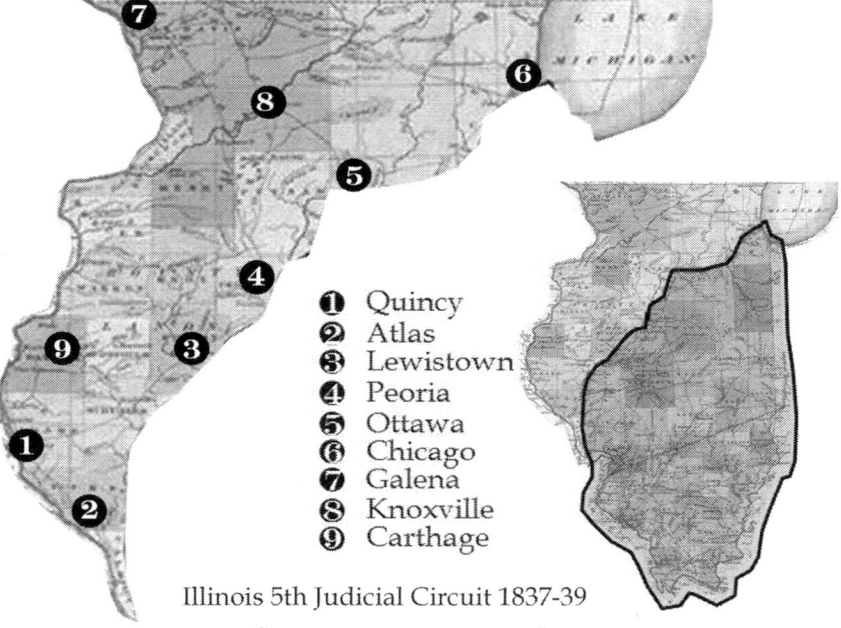

❶ Quincy
❷ Atlas
❸ Lewistown
❹ Peoria
❺ Ottawa
❻ Chicago
❼ Galena
❽ Knoxville
❾ Carthage

Illinois 5th Judicial Circuit 1837-39

traveling an average of 30 miles per day with up to 3 days to hear cases at each stop, took the judge and his small entourage about 55 days to complete which meant he was on the road about six months out of the year. Prior to completing a full year in his new position, James found the life of an itinerant judge not much to his liking, particularly during the winter months and periods of heavy rain. However, much to Jane's dismay, James stayed with the grueling routine for nearly another year and a half until the Illinois legislature once again proposed a change in the judicial circuits. In April of 1839, about four months before the end of his term, James presided over a case where, once again, he would cross paths with his fellow Kentuckian, now an Illinois attorney, and the leading Whig politician, Abraham Lincoln.

Lincoln stood in the defense of a young man named Fielding Fraim. Fraim was an Irish steamboat deck hand, who, in a drunken rage had pulled a butcher knife and ran it to the hilt in the chest of a fellow shipmate. The stabbing ended a melee between the two men that had started when the now deceased shipmate blew cigar smoke into Fraim's face at which he took murderous offense.

Hancock Co. Courthouse, Carthage, IL
completed for the Spring 1839 court session
The cupola was added in 1868.
Courtesy courthousehistory.com

The event transpired in a saloon in Frederick, Illinois, in Schuyler County a short distance from where the deckhand's boat was docked on the Illinois River. The murder so shocked and angered the local townspeople, Lincoln asked for and received a change of venue fearing his client could and would not get a fair trial. The case was moved to the courthouse in Carthage, the county seat of Hancock County, Illinois, where Judge Ralston would hear the case. This was one of the early trials in the recently completed structure. When the judge entered the courtroom he and Lincoln acknowledged each other with a nod and a friendly smile.

Lincoln had nothing with which to argue his case other than his subtle humor, and a demeanor with a pitched voice that exuded a sense of straightforward innocence and honesty. Apparently, in the jury's mind, these soothing traits did not come close to balancing the scales of *Lady Justice* in the favor of poor Fraim. At day's end, the jury returned with a guilty verdict. Lincoln could not convince Judge Ralston to set the verdict aside, and his client was sentenced to death by hanging on the 18th day of May 1839.[28] After court adjourned, Judge Ralston and attorney Lincoln reminisced for a few minutes, shook hands, and went their separate ways.

Chapter 7

The Mormon Affairs

*T**he Mormons must be treated as enemies and must be… driven from the state.* These were the inflammatory words proclaimed in Missouri Governor Lilburn W. Boggs' Executive Order 44 issued from the state capital in Jefferson City, on October 27, 1838. The order was issued as the result of several deadly confrontations occurring since the summer of 1838 between Mormon and non-Mormon factions in various counties of northwest Missouri. Four days later, General Samuel Lucas commander of the state militia located at Far West, Missouri, the Mormon seat of power in Caldwell County, arrested the Latter-day Saints founder and leader Joseph Smith, Jr., and several other ranking members of the church. The proposed action, resulting from a bogus court-martial held shortly after the men's arrest, concluded that the detainees should be executed for treason and other crimes against the state of Missouri. Lucas issued an order to General Alexander Doniphan, a commander of the Missouri State Guard, to take Smith and the other prisoners to the public square of Far West and shoot them at 9 o'clock the next morning. Doniphan flatly refused to carry out an order he knew amounted to murder. He told Lucas that if he tried to shoot Smith and the others he would personally see to it that the General would face a quite appropriate court martial himself. Lucas

Joseph Smith, Jr., ca 1840

relented and took the arrested men to a jail about 40 miles southwest in Liberty, Missouri. The effect of this event spelled the end of the Mormon's presence in Missouri and the fate of nearly 15,000 men, women, and children, faithful to the church, hung precariously in the balance.

Joseph Smith and the others were still jailed in Liberty in the early winter of 1839 when news reached the Mormons that a temporary safe haven had been found for them. The townspeople of Quincy, Illinois located just across the Mississippi River about 180 miles to the east of Far West in Illinois had offered the Latter-day Saints whatever help they could provide. Many of the Far West Mormons had passed through Quincy, six years earlier on their trip from Kirtland, Ohio to northwest Missouri. They remembered the

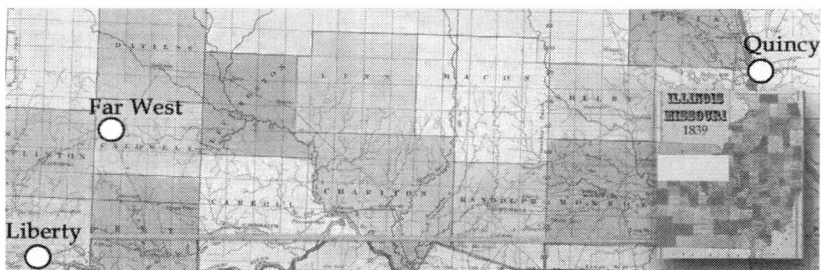

kindnesses shown them by the community. On Quincy's part, the motivation to extend an invitation to assist the Mormons was based on three reasons, not necessarily in the order presented. Compassion for a misunderstood and mistreated people, a needed economic boost to help offset the woes resulting from the panic of 1837, and, on the part of both Whigs and Democrats, wooing a very large bloc of voters sympathetic to their respective platforms.

On the advice of Judge Ralston and much to the dismay of the Quincy Whigs, the Democrats struck first by forming the Quincy Democratic Association. Excerpts from the minutes of a meeting of the association held on February 27, 1839 detail the intended sentiments and actions of the town's Democratic political leadership.

The members of the Democratic Association and the citizens of Quincy generally, assembled in the courthouse, to take into consideration the state and condition of the people called the "Latter-day Saints", and organized the meeting ... submitted the following:

The committee believes that our duties at this time, and on this occasion, are all included within the limits of an expanded benevolence and humanity, and which are guided and directed by that charity which never faileth.

Resolved, that the strangers recently arrived here from the state of Missouri, known by the name of the "Latter-day Saints", are entitled to our sympathy and kindest regard, and that we recommend to the citizens of Quincy to extend all the kindness in their power to bestow on the persons who are in affliction.

Resolved, that a numerous committee be raised, composed of some individuals in every quarter of the town and its vicinity, whose duty it shall be to explain to our misguided fellow citizens, if any such there be, who are disposed to excite prejudices and circulate unfounded rumors; and particularly to explain to them that these people have no design to lower the wages of the laboring class, but to procure something to save them from starving.

Resolved, that a standing committee be raised and be composed of individuals who shall immediately inform Mr. Rigdon[29] and others, as many as they may think proper ... that any individuals, either from destitution or sickness, or if they find them houseless, that they appeal directly and promptly to the citizens of Quincy to furnish them with the means to relieve all such cases.

Resolved, that we recommend to all the citizens of Quincy, that in all their intercourse with the strangers, they use and observe a becoming decorum and delicacy, and be particularly careful not to indulge in any conversation or expressions calculated to wound their feelings, or in any way to reflect upon those, who by every law of humanity, are entitled to our sympathy and commiseration.

J. W. Whitney[30], [elected] Chairman.
Quincy, February 27, 1839

James took his personal interest in the Mormons a step further. He made a point to be one of the first attorneys to meet with Joseph Smith, Jr. in Quincy in April 1839. This was after Joseph and his Mormon followers were aided in an escape from their Missouri captors at Liberty. This early acquaintance and his sound counsel gained James an ongoing association as a key attorney specifically for Joseph Smith and generally for the Latter-day Saints, a connection that would last for over five years.

In the spring and summer of 1839, Judge Ralston was also instrumental in assisting the Mormons in acquiring a significant amount of land in Hancock County, Illinois in and around the small village originally named Venus, at the time named Commerce. Joseph Smith, Jr. had personally chosen this land on the Mississippi River about 17 miles north of Warsaw and 47 miles north of Quincy as the new Zion[31] of the Church of Jesus Christ

Idyllic sketch of Nauvoo ca 1843
Mississippi River foreground
Mormon temple upper right

Nauvoo ca 1846
Temple upper center

of Latter-day Saints; it would be renamed Nauvoo, a Hebrew word meaning *to be beautiful.*

In the later part of the year, James' workload had become more than he could manage. He decided to try to seek out a fellow attorney who shared his political affiliation and who had some knowledge of and experience with the Latter-day Saints. He shared his intended action with several of his Quincy colleagues and the name of an attorney, Calvin A. Warren[32], currently residing in Warsaw, came to his attention. The firm of Ralston and Warren was formed and within a month another partner, Almeron Wheat[33] was added. For a period of about two years, the firm of Ralston, Warren, and Wheat took center stage in the legal profession in Adams and Mormon controlled Hancock County.

In August of 1840, James campaigned for and was re-elected to the Illinois state legislature this time in the upper house as a senator. His decision to run was made at the last minute largely due to the requests and support of the Latter-day Saints. The church anticipated that several issues on their behalf, foremost of which was approving a state charter for Nauvoo, would be introduced to the legislature during the upcoming winter and spring sessions. The presence of Judge Ralston in the legislature could facilitate a positive outcome, which indeed turned out to be true.

A month following his election to the legislature, James was once again on the business of the Mormons making his way to the Quincy riverfront. He planned to attend an auction sponsored by the U. S. Government consisting of equipment recently used by the Army's Corps of Engineers in their work on the Mississippi River at and north of St. Louis. In addition to deepening and clearing the St. Louis harbor of debris, the engineers also surveyed and blasted out the Des Moines limestone rapids near Keokuk, in the Iowa Territory. The work deepened the draft at the rapids allowing larger steamboat travel north of that point on the Mississippi. Although the engineer troops had not finished their work, federal financial contingencies forced the cancellation of the project and necessitated the sale of the equipment.

Lt. Robert E. Lee, 1838

Of particular interest to the Mormons was the small side-wheeled steamboat, the *Des Moines*, and two shallow draft keelboats used in the work. The steamboat was intended to transport newly arriving European church members up the Mississippi from the port of New Orleans to Nauvoo. The keelboats were to ferry church members back and forth across the river. Squire Ralston introduced himself and shook hands with the young army captain who commanded the engineering troops and was the agent in charge of the auction, Capt. Robert E. Lee.[34]

In answer to Judge Ralston's questions about the condition of the steamer and the keelboats, Lee responded that the steamer was in good mechanical order and he smiled as he related it had served him well as a suitable river home while away from his Virginia home. He added that the keelboats had seen heavy work but were quite water worthy. James was impressed with the genteel demeanor of the handsome well-spoken captain and believed the accomplished officer was likely a first-rate military man. Judge Ralston was successful in completing the purchase of the three boats for a price of $4,868. A note was issued for the purchase of the boats secured by Mormon land holdings and multiple signatories, including Joseph Smith, Jr. The note was to be paid within 8 months' time.[35]

The presidential election of 1840 took place between October 30 and December 2, 1840. Although of very little consequence at the time, the Illinois presidential election process included an event involving the two sometimes friends and sometimes foes, Democrat Judge James Ralston of Quincy and Illinois Whig Party leader Abraham Lincoln. Ralston and Lincoln were but two of the Illinois Electoral College members for their respective parties and in that role they garnered votes for their party's candidates for president, Democrat Martin Van Buren and Whig, William Henry Harrison. When the voting was complete, elector Ralston bested elector Lincoln by a mere 200 votes, adding one electoral vote for Van Buren from Illinois. Ralston's win came as the direct result of a Mormon voting mandate issued by Joseph Smith instructing each Latter-day Saint voter to cross through Lincoln's name on the ballot and write in Ralston's name. Smith held no personal ill feelings for *Honest Abe* but his name happened to appear at the bottom of the ballot directly above the blank write-in area. Smith's directive was a show of Mormon appreciation for Judge Ralston's on-going support. The effect of the single electoral vote swing proved insignificant at the national level since Harrison handily won the electoral vote 234 to 60. This act did however make it clear that the political influence of the Mormons in Illinois politics was no trifling matter.

The anti-Mormons in the state of Missouri were not yet finished tormenting the Latter-day Saint prophet, Joseph Smith, Jr. and his many thousands of followers. Rumors were rampant that there was a growing dissatisfaction among some Illinoisans with the presence of the Latter-day Saints in their state. Missouri Governor Lilburn Boggs took advantage of the rumor and issued a requisition to Illinois Governor Thomas Carlin to extradite Joseph Smith back to Missouri to face treason and other charges that arose from the bogus court martial in 1838. Carlin signed the requisition in September of 1840 but no arrest attempt was made until early June of 1841. It had been over two years after Smith and the others had escaped captivity and crossed the Mississippi into Illinois. Judge Ralston was once again at work defending his Mormon client despite an ever-increasing risk to his own popularity. James arranged for the legality of the extradition to be heard before his good friend and now Circuit Court Judge Stephen Douglas in Monmouth, Illinois on June 10, 1841. In Smith's defense was another good friend of James, O. H. Browning. The case was quickly dismissed and the prophet returned to Nauvoo a free man.

The next month James was once again convinced to make another run at being elected to political office. This time the grand prize was a seat in the U. S. House of Representatives in Washington D. C., the big political stage. Though the Whig Party power in the election district was strong, all but one of Judge Ralston's Democrat supporters suggested his chances would improve if he would identify with a more liberal faction of the Democratic Party, the *Locofocos*.[36] The one dissenting opinion was voiced by James' brother Joseph who still believed his brother's oratorical ability and *strictly business* demeanor would be wholly inadequate to persuade voters to join his cause.[37] Noted essayist and lecturer of the time, Ralph Waldo Emerson, wrote about the Locofocos, *the new race is stiff, heady, and rebellious; they are fanatics in freedom; they hate tolls, taxes, turnpikes, banks, hierarchies, governors, yea, almost laws.*

Judge Ralston's unsuccessful run for the House of Representatives put a significant stress on his current cash flow. After mulling the situation over and discussing it in depth with his best friend and wife Jane, they decided that there was nothing wrong with asking his client Joseph Smith, Jr. for a loan of $500; which he got at the rate of 12% per annum to be repaid the following spring.

Judge Ralston recognized from the time of his early meetings with Joseph Smith, that the handsome, intelligent, and well-spoken young man exuded a sort of magnetism. He had a natural leadership ability that mesmerized a large following of people who reveled at being in his presence. He also witnessed in the *prophet's* decision making a regular disregard for attention to the details of a matter in favor of achieving a broader goal. This disregard occasionally included ignoring the advice of his well-meaning advisors. In many ways, Smith reminded James of a spoiled child who happily basked in the adoration of success and cried in failure, with no inkling as to what it took to gain the former and to avoid the latter. James knew that controversy would follow his client in whatever he did and wherever he went. Under normal circumstances a client such as Smith would be an attorney's dream, though there would prove to be nothing normal about the Mormon prophet.

The self-proclaimed prophet's latest endeavor was the ownership of a mercantile business in Nauvoo that was housed in a handsome red brick building, called the *Red Brick Store*. It opened its doors for business in January of 1842. Though Nauvoo currently had a large number of such businesses, Joseph's vision was that a first rate general store operated by the prophet himself could and would not fail. He planned to provide the church faithful with quality merchandise while making a

Red Brick Store before and after restoration

solid profit. Several suppliers provided thousands of dollars' worth of goods backed by Joseph Smith's signature alone. The detail that Joseph neglected to address in this venture was how to handle the rejection of the faithful if the prophet and *sainted one* refused to sell them an item they could clearly not afford. He avoided the rejection by selling the item knowing the cost would not be paid. The financial losses suffered by the store coupled with amounts owed on land purchases and for the government boats, created a mounting personal debt for Joseph. It would take a miracle of biblical proportions to pay the debt down. The only upside to the store was that the second floor of the building hosted a diverse array of gatherings ranging from Masonic lodge to Ladies Relief Society meetings.

Serendipitous to Joseph's debt problem was the February 1, 1842 effective date of the new Bankruptcy Act passed by congress in August of the previous year. Under this act, any person capable of proving their inability to repay their accumulated debt could have that debt forgiven by a judge in a court of law. Calvin Warren, James' junior law partner, became expertly familiar with the act and in April counseled Joseph Smith, his brother Hyrum, and Sidney Rigdon about its terms. Shortly thereafter the three of them declared themselves bankrupt much to the chagrin of their numerous debtors. In the final result, Rigdon and Hiram Smith were successful in being relieved from their debt but Joseph was not.[38]

On an early May evening in 1842, Lilburn Boggs, the ex-governor of Missouri who had so tirelessly and maliciously attempted to eradicate the Latter-day Saints from the face of the earth, was shot through a window of his office at his home in Independence, Missouri. Though his injuries were severe enough to have killed him, the governor somehow survived the ordeal albeit it took quite some time for him to heal. The finger of suspicion from loyal anti-Mormon activists immediately pointed directly at either Joseph Smith or an accomplice working at the behest of the despised *prophet.*

Two months after the attempt on Boggs life and to the surprise of no one who followed the unfolding events closely, the current Governor of Missouri, Thomas Reynolds, backed by an affidavit from Boggs, issued another requisition to Illinois Governor Thomas Carlin. This time the request called for the immediate arrest and extradition to Missouri of Joseph Smith and one Orrin Porter Rockwell. It was claimed Rockwell was the Mormon who allegedly pulled the trigger in the attempted murder of Boggs. Both would stand trial for the crime. This was the second time in as many years the Missourians had requested the extradition of the *prophet* back to the borders of their state. Illinois Governor Carlin, once again, acquiesced and ordered the sheriff of Quincy to arrest Smith.

From his location in Quincy, Judge Ralston knew every detail of the plan to find Smith and bring him to custody. James secretly kept his client informed of the proceedings and when it became obvious that the sheriff would accomplish his assigned task, Judge Ralston made a suggestion to Joseph. It was now the opportune time to become unavailable at some unknown location. Smith and Mr. Rockwell promptly accomplished their assignment. James had begun the second year of his term in the 13th Illinois legislative session, and while the sheriff continued his futile search for the fugitives, the senator cleverly arranged for the very eloquent and accomplished trial attorney, Justin Butterfield[39], to represent Joseph in his latest extradition proceeding.

Smith remained *incommunicado* while Squire Butterfield spent the next three months researching the extradition request and determining the proper defense. In December, Butterfield directed Smith to give himself up in the safe confines of Nauvoo and then be brought to Springfield where his case would be heard before Judge Nathaniel Pope. At the beginning of the hearing in early January of 1843, the court was called to order. Butterfield noticed that a number of ladies were in attendance seated on both sides of the courtroom. He slowly rose from his chair and bowed toward the judge saying, *may it please your honor that I appear before the Pope,* then bowing to the ladies, *in the presence of angels,* and looking at his client, *to defend a prophet of the Lord.* He then rhetorically asked *can there be but any higher calling for a humble servant of the bar?* It took several minutes on his gavel for a smiling Judge Pope to restore order in the court.

Butterfield's defense was two pronged. Firstly, he presented an affidavit signed by Stephen Douglas, Almeron Wheat, and James Ralston, among others. It affirmed that Joseph Smith was in Nauvoo reviewing the Mormon Legion[40] the day following the shooting of Boggs. Therefore, Smith could not have directly been in any way involved in the shooting in Independence, Missouri. Secondly, he provided evidence that proved Governor Carlin's arrest warrant was invalid. Judge Pope agreed with Butterfield on both counts, the Missouri extradition request was denied, and Governor Carlin's arrest warrant was voided. Once again, Joseph Smith returned to Nauvoo a free man.

In the midst of the latest in the series of efforts undertaken by James on the part of his Mormon clients, another Ralston family member joined his two brothers in Quincy. William H. H. Ralston[41], the youngest of the four surviving Ralston males moved from Lexington, Kentucky where he was living with the second oldest Ralston brother, preacher Thomas. William was a recent graduate of law from Transylvania College, thanks to the generosity of brother James, and he ably stood ready to practice his profession in Illinois. William was treated to a glorious *welcome to Quincy* celebration that included the families of Dr. Joseph and James.

Sentiment against the Mormon presence in Adams and Hancock counties grew during the year 1843. Joseph Smith's latest actions made it clear that the prophet had *turned the other cheek* more often during the previous two years than he would have liked. As a result, the pressure from the anti-Mormons again ratcheted up in Missouri and now in Illinois, and the prophet reached his breaking point. Ironically, Smith's final straw came from an action he perpetrated within the limits of *his* city, Nauvoo.

In May of 1844, William Law, a well-respected member of Joseph's inner circle, broke ranks with the Mormon leader based primarily on Law's opposition to plural marriage. Though as late as the 26th of May, the prophet stood in front of the unfinished Nauvoo temple and once again denied having more than one wife. Three indictments were issued in Carthage, the county seat of Hancock County, against Smith, one of which accused him of polygamy. William Law bought a printing press and, from a small office in Nauvoo, printed the first, and only, edition of the Nauvoo Expositor on June 7, 1844. The paper railed against the Mormon leader. It quoted signed affidavits of fellow church faithful that disagreed on a multitude of subjects including Smith's newest revelation of giving every man the privilege of marrying ten virgins.

Smith declared Law's newspaper a nuisance. On June 10 the Nauvoo city council gave their leader, the residing mayor, the right to order the town marshal to completely destroy the paper's type, all remaining issues of the Expositor, and the printing press in full public view; literally, a fatal mistake. When word of this action reached Thomas Sharp, a long-time Smith adversary and owner of the Warsaw Signal newspaper, bold headlines screamed for action. The action could include, if necessary, the use of *powder and ball* to stop this robbery of man's property and rights. Fearing reprisals from non-Mormons, Smith called out the Nauvoo Legion and declared martial law in Nauvoo on June 18. Illinois Governor Thomas Ford fueled the escalation of the whole affair, perhaps purposely, when he called out the state militia. Ford got word to Smith via a letter that to avoid an all-out civil war in Nauvoo he would guarantee the prophet's safety if the leader agreed to stand trial in Carthage for the destruction of the newspaper.

Smith ordered the Legion to stand down but, not believing Governor Ford's promise, he made a successful secretive Mississippi River crossing from Illinois to Iowa to avoid prosecution. Joseph's only official wife, Emma Hale Smith, sent a warning message to her husband. His action would be viewed as an act of cowardice by the church faithful and could cause additional irreparable unrest in Nauvoo; Smith returned. The next morning, June 25, 1844, no escorts promised by the Governor could be found. Joseph and Hyrum Smith accompanied by ranking Mormons, Englishman John Taylor and

Willard Richards, rode to Carthage to turn themselves in. The foursome had planned to spend the night at a local hotel but they were arrested and brought to the jail not for incarceration but supposedly for their own safety. Sometime in the afternoon of the 27th, a Mormon visitor, Cyrus

Carthage Jail before and after restoration

Wheelock came to the jail and offered weapons that were taken by Joseph and Hyrum for self-defense in the event of any trouble. That evening, a mob of armed men easily numbering over one-hundred many of whom were likely from the nearby state militia authorized by Governor Ford stormed the jail. When the chaos ended, the Smith brothers lay dead, Taylor was wounded, and Richards unharmed.

The following day, Judge Ralston visited the jail, met briefly with and consoled Taylor, and assured him that all that could be done for the two surviving faithful was being done. Mormons and non-Mormons alike in Hancock County braced for what they believed would be a massive attack by the Nauvoo legion at Carthage in retaliation for the prophet and his brother's cold-blooded murder; it never came. There was little doubt in the mind of any of the key players surrounding the events that took place at Carthage, including the prophet himself. The inevitable outcome would be, at a minimum, the death of Joseph Smith. Smith had said that he would act the martyr to save the future of the church although he took the offered weapons and emptied every chamber at the attackers in a futile attempt to save his life. At the end of the affair, Governor Ford offered little more than a hollow promise that the killers would be brought to a fair and timely justice. For Brigham Young, the fact that he ordered the Mormon legion to stay in Nauvoo could be interpreted that it was time for a change in the leadership of the Latter-day Saints. Since Brother Young would be an obvious contender for that

Brigham Young ca 1850

coveted position, he saw no need for any useless loss of life among the church faithful.

Chapter 8

An Ill Wind Blows

The bodies of Joseph and Hiram Smith were moved from Carthage to Nauvoo accompanied by a large number of the faithful. They somberly placed each mournful step in front of the other the entire route of the cortege. The funeral in Nauvoo may have been the largest single assembly of Mormons ever held. Words of praise for the sainted lives of the dead martyrs were at times difficult to hear above the sound of weeping. Workers at the river nearly a mile distant could hear the mournful sounds of sadness. The speakers ended with Brigham Young admonishing the faithful *not to let their faith diminish or lessen their fervor for life, for they and the spirits of Joseph and Hiram would once again be lifted up to the glory of God in a revitalized Zion.* Unknown to all but a few of the Mormon *inner circle,* the coffins lowered into the rich earth near the still unfinished temple at Nauvoo after the last *amen* merely contained weighted burlap sacks and not the remains of the brother's Smith. This action was taken to eliminate any possibility of sacrilegious activities. Meanwhile, the bodies had been deeply buried near the foundation of Nauvoo House[42] that was at the time under construction.

Emma Hale Smith Bidamon

Not two months following the *prophet's* death and burial, Joseph's wife Emma Hale Smith made a trip from her home in Nauvoo to Quincy to see James. In recent years, Emma had been the lead decision maker in the Smith family for all things of a business nature. The death of her husband would in no way diminish that role. The purpose of her visit was to gain Judge Ralston's opinion about the ownership of the property Joseph and Emma owned near Quincy called the Cleveland farm. The judge told his good friend how sad he was with the death of her husband. He then told her that despite the massive amount of debt her husband had accumulated there was little doubt the property now belonged to her and would most likely remain that way as long as she wished to be its owner.[43]

While the gears of justice slowly ground toward a trial of the alleged murderers of Joseph and Hyrum Smith, James could temporarily put aside his duties on behalf of the Mormons. He had allowed himself to be cautiously optimistic that his wife Jane, with the able help of his doctor brother, would bring her latest pregnancy to a successful completion. This very important moment had presented itself on four earlier occasions sadly resulting in a miscarriage, a stillbirth, or an infant death. Each sad event caused Jane to suffer lengthy periods of deep depression brought on by the loss of her child and her feelings of maternal inadequacy. She had always eventually rebounded from each event more determined than ever to bring a new life into the world that would nurture a newfound happiness for James and her.

The loud crying James heard from the second floor bedroom of the substantial Ralston home in the middle of Quincy brought tears of joy to the judge's eyes. He glanced at the calendar then at his pocket watch and knew that 7 o'clock in the morning on the 19th of January 1845, would be a time and date forever etched in his memory. The good Dr. Ralston descended the stairs with a broad smile on his face and shook his brother's hand. He told James to wait a moment while the nurse wrapped the newborn then he could go to Jane's side and they could share the wonder and joy of their new daughter.

The radiant smile he saw on Jane's face as he entered the bedroom matched nothing he had ever seen before. He moved closer and Jane gently removed the blanket from their daughter's head and told her husband to say hello to their new daughter *Elizabeth Jane*. The utter joy of that moment contrasted with the earlier times of profound sadness caused James to weep uncontrollably. When he regained his composure, he tenderly kissed Jane then his daughter and whispered how much he truly loved them both. Jane gently put her hand on her husband's face and slowly stroking it, quietly told him that this moment more than made up for the others and she had never been happier in her life. Father, Mother, and child tightly held on to each other for the longest time fearing that letting go might reveal this moment as a dream rather than reality. James was not in the least ashamed of knowing that he would spoil his new daughter in every way possible and through it all he would love the miniature image of her mother more than life itself.

Contrary to the promises made by Illinois Governor Ford, the trial of the alleged murderers of the founder of Mormonism was neither timely nor fair. The trial, held at the Carthage courthouse, did not commence in earnest until the 24th of May 1845, nearly 11 months after the murders were committed. The names of the trial's legal professionals read like a who's who list of Judge Ralston's' career acquaintances in Quincy. The presiding judge was none other than the Honorable Richard M. Young, now a member of the Illinois Supreme Court. He was James's early benefactor and mentor, and the man primarily responsible for the word *esquire* appearing after his own name. For the defense were William Richardson, O. H. Browning, and Archibald Williams, who, along with James, were Quincy's self-appointed four apocalyptic horsemen of the Black Hawk War. Lastly was Calvin Warren, also for the defense, James' former law partner, who had personally taken unfair advantage of the bankruptcy laws. For the prosecution was one time Illinois State Attorney General Josiah Lamborn, appointed by Governor Ford. At his side was *pro tem* states' attorney, James H. Ralston, appointed at the request of Judge Young. James returned to the site where, among other legal events, he was the presiding judge six years earlier in the murder trial of one Fielding Fraim unsuccessfully defended for murder by Abraham Lincoln. Now, James knew his participation in this trial was moot in that there was no earthly way anyone would ever be convicted of the Smith murders.

The overflowing crowd that spilled into the Carthage square surrounding the courthouse in the third week of May was not there to wonder about the trial's outcome, it was long before decided. They were there to view the dignitaries who came and went during the brief affair. Six short days later, on the 30th of May, it took the jury just two hours to find all of the defendants innocent of the murder of Joseph Smith. One month later, the presiding trial judge for the murder of Hiram Smith involving the same defendants dismissed the proceedings. No attorney for the prosecution had been appointed and thus, one was not present.

After the death of the Smiths and even more so following the trials of the alleged murderers, the partisan political sentiments in Hancock and Adams counties were no longer defined by traditional political party lines. Instead it was based on the Mormons and those who helped them versus the much larger group of anti-Mormons. Judge Ralston, viewed as a member of the former, had seen his popularity diminish and his reputation sullied by the members of the latter. In fact, some believed, and perhaps rightfully so, that had it not been for Judge Ralston's shrewd counsel and actions, the saints might never have come to this part of Illinois. Or, if they had, they would have been long gone by now. At any rate, the anti-Mormon group requested a meeting with Brigham Young and other Mormon leaders, on the 1st of October 1845, to discuss the intentions of the faithful with regard to their remaining at Nauvoo. Since a time shortly after the trial, the Mormons had already made an unpublished decision to leave

Nauvoo and travel to the west, perhaps as far as the Pacific Ocean and Vancouver Island. At that meeting, Young made that decision a formal commitment to the anti-Mormons and pledged to begin the migration by May of the following year.[44]

On the 25th of October 1845, Brigham Young sent a message to Judge Ralston, who was staying with his brother William and his new bride in Warsaw, Illinois. Young requested a meeting with the judge on a matter of some urgency. James made the trip to Nauvoo the next day and met with Young who wanted James' advice about trying to sell the temple and other Mormon property in Nauvoo. James suggested that one path to consider might be to contact the officials of the Roman Catholic diocese to see if there may be any interest. Young had a shallow smile when he commented that he believed the significant differences between his faith and that of the Catholics could be set aside long enough for the two to reach an agreement beneficial to both. Young asked Judge Ralston if he would make an initial contact with the diocese and James agreed he would.

Near the end of December, two Catholic priests arrived in Nauvoo and toured many of the public buildings including every floor of the temple. Judge Ralston was told in early January that the Catholics could not raise the funds necessary to buy any of the buildings but that they would be interested in a lease for a single building. A lease could be negotiated provided Young's requirement that it be insured against *fire and mob* be stricken. The judge sent a messenger to Young with this information. When the messenger returned, James asked about Brigham's response to the Catholics and the lad replied Mr. Young refused the Catholic offer. Another source eventually told James that Young's reply had something to do with the Catholics traveling to hell in their own way. Based on speculation by some historians, Young had included the insurance clause to pay the Mormons for loss from fire regardless of how the flames originated.[45]

By the time Brigham Young led the first of what would be several waves of Latter-day Saints from Nauvoo to the West in mid-February of 1846, James and Jane had also made a decision. They agreed that they too had overstayed their welcome and it was time to look for new opportunities beyond Quincy. Though James did not show it, Jane knew her husband was deeply hurt and offended with the treatment he received from the once friendly Quincy townsfolk. They both knew they would miss their home and their close friends of nearly 15 years.

Chapter 9

In the Army Now

On February 14th, 1846, after nearly a full year of political maneuvering, the citizens of the Republic of Texas ratified a treaty that annexed them into the United States as the country's 28th state. This action was the culmination of a hard-earned and bloody struggle that all began a quarter of a century earlier. The arrival of the first American homesteaders, called *Texians*[46], were invited by the Mexican government to populate its poorest state, *Coahuila y Tejas*. In 1836, these heroic Americans fought bravely for and won their independence from Mexico. The rag-tag army of General Sam Houston finally defeated the Mexican army led by General Antonio Lopez de Santa Anna at the Battle of San Jacinto. The treaty Santa Anna was forced to sign in May of 1836 making *Tejas* an independent republic was never officially ratified by the Mexican government. Mexico still viewed Texas as its most northern trouble-making state. There was no doubt that this latest statehood action by the United States would force the hand of the Mexican government. They would either withdraw their troops from the contested border along the Rio Grande River region and not challenge the United States government. Or, they would go to war with their northern neighbor. No reputable bookmaker of the day would have taken a bet that the Mexicans would tuck their collective tails and whimper away to Mexico City. In fact, when the Republic of Texas sent an envoy to Washington D. C. a year earlier to discuss annexation and statehood, the United States had quietly begun preparations for war.

Now, President James K., *Manifest Destiny*, Polk, and General, *I want to be President*, Zachary Taylor patiently bided their time. They waited for the Mexican troops under the command of General Mariano Arista to take some action that would be the excuse needed for declaring war against Mexico. Taylor, tiring in patience, baited Arista by sending 70 U. S. troops on a patrol under Capt. Seth Thornton into the contested territory between the Nueces river on the north and the Rio Grande river south on the border of Texas and Mexico. Arista, took the bait, *hook, line and sinker*, ordering his 2,000 Mexican cavalry troops to attack Thornton's suicide mission patrol. The skirmish resulted in 16 American casualties including Captain Thornton. Eighteen days later, May13, 1846, congress approved a declaration of war against Mexico.

When news of the war reached Quincy and a call for volunteers was issued, little time was lost in filling the quota with men seeking adventure and unquestioned proof of their patriotism and manhood. After a lengthy, earnest, and tear-filled discussion between James and Jane, Mrs. Judge James H. Ralston reluctantly agreed to let her husband volunteer his services to his country. Given his current circumstances in Quincy, his involvement in the war somewhere other than Quincy was eerily serendipitous. In exchange for her approval, James swore that he would make himself available only in a supporting role located some distance from any real fighting near any front line. Despite his successfully negotiated compromise with Jane, James clearly understood and was sympathetic to his wife's feelings; *at long last we now have a child to love, I will not in the least be happy in your extended absence, and, above all else, I love you dearly just as I know you love our daughter and me.* True to his word, James wrote a letter to President Tyler offering to serve the country in a non-combatant role. His letter found its way to the office of Brigadier General Thomas S. Jesup, the current quartermaster general[47] of the U. S. Army. Within three weeks James received a response offering him a position as assistant quartermaster with a rank of captain. With a forced smile, Jane kissed her husband on the cheek after he was sworn in as a Captain in the Quartermaster Corps in the Quincy courthouse, June 26, 1846.

James began the trek to his assigned duty in southern Texas in early September taking a side-wheeled steamboat south nearly the entire length of the navigable Mississippi to New Orleans. From New Orleans he went by a steam packet ship to Port Lavaca, a normally sleepy port on the Gulf of Mexico a short distance north and east of Corpus Christi, Texas. Now, Port Lavaca was a bustling hub of activity for the transport of men, mules, and materials to the front near Monterrey Mexico. Prior to James' arrival in Texas, United States army troops had, to no one's real surprise, already had some successes against their out-gunned and out-commanded enemy in Mexico at Palo Alto in early May and Monterrey in July. The Mexican army had begun a counterattack against the American occupation forces in Monterrey. The counterattack occurred nearly to the day that Captain Ralston joined an Army wagon train for the 250-mile trip south to the staging area near the front at Port Isabel, Texas. When word of Generals Wool and Taylor's battlefield victories was received on the 26th of September, James was ordered to return to Port Lavaca. From there he continued to San Antonio where he would be the assistant regimental quartermaster for General Wool's Center Army.

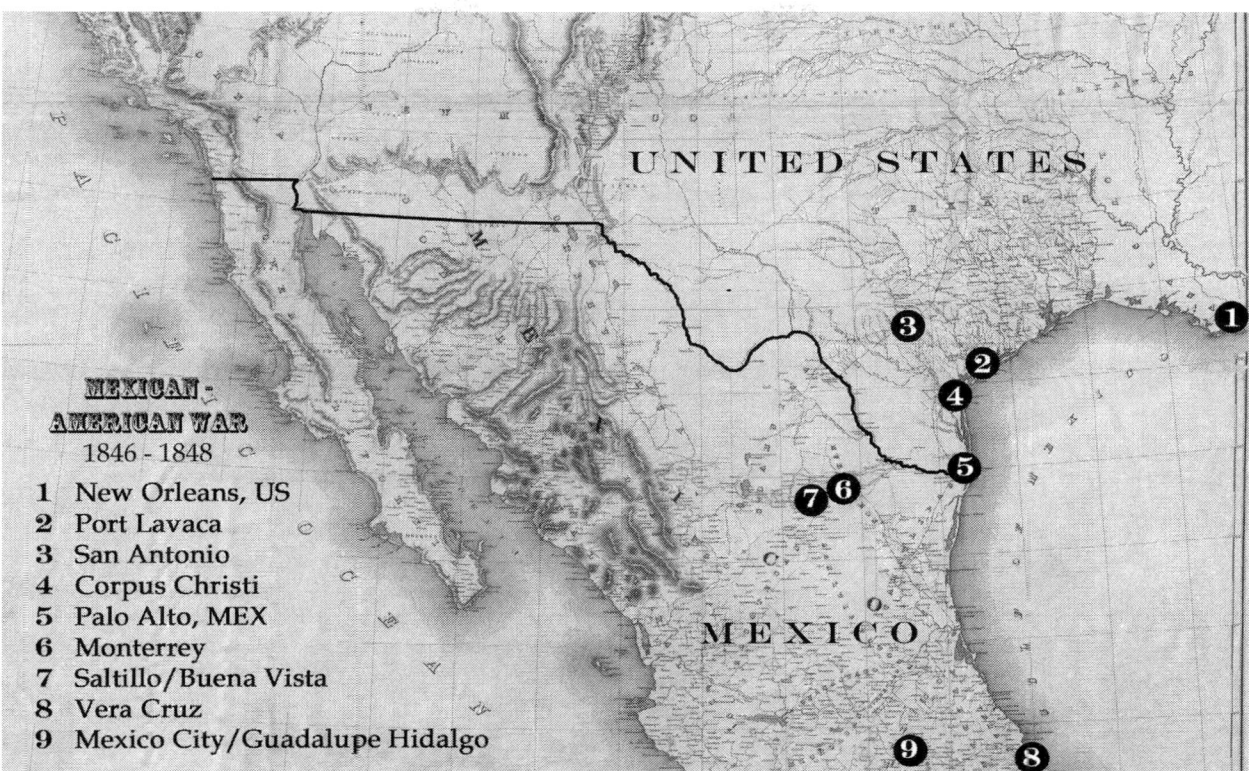

MEXICAN-
AMERICAN WAR
1846 - 1848

1 New Orleans, US
2 Port Lavaca
3 San Antonio
4 Corpus Christi
5 Palo Alto, MEX
6 Monterrey
7 Saltillo/Buena Vista
8 Vera Cruz
9 Mexico City/Guadalupe Hidalgo

To this point in early October, James had successfully dealt with the trials, and tribulations that he faced on his circuitous journey from Quincy by foot, horseback, steamboat, stagecoach, and wagon to San Antonio. Captain Ralston was not used to the stifling heat and humidity encountered on all of the legs of his trip. He had thus far been unable to rest comfortably for the better part of the nearly six-weeks of travel and he was thankful his body had staved off any ill effects from the fatigue. He missed Jane so much that he had made a point of sending her several letters. He wrote how happy he would be if he could just turn around and come home, jokingly adding despite the possibility of being court-martialed and facing a firing squad for desertion. James arrived at San Antonio and discovered that the place where he would be working was the very spot just over ten years earlier where brave Texans had fought and died for Texas independence. He tried to recall everything he knew about the event and the setting at the Alamo.

Early Texas was a vast lawless frontier where only the strong could and would survive. When the Mexicans realized they were losing control of these *Tejas* settlers with *fire in their bellies* they sent armed troops to the populated areas to abolish their established self-government. The Texans fought back.

The most remembered of those battles took place at the Valero Mission, *El Alamo,* in San Antonio. For twelve days, about 250 Americans withstood a siege of over 2,400 Mexican soldiers under the command of Santa Anna. When the smoke cleared on March 6, 1836, all but a few native Mexicans at the mission were dead including the famous names of Travis, Bowie, Crockett, Bonham, and the lesser-known names of Fauntleroy, Kent, and a Dr. Pollard. To the best of James' memory he also knew that additionally several unnamed Alamo defenders had died along with about 600 Mexican soldiers. At the hour of their death at the Alamo, the brave Texans were unaware that a formal Texan declaration of independence from Mexico was made four days earlier. Fifty days after the Alamo, Texan forces under the command of General Sam Houston executed a surprise attack against the enemy using the rallying cry, *remember the Alamo,* and thrashed Santa Anna at the Battle of San Jacinto.

On October 13th, 1846, James first saw the ruins of the Alamo that appeared much as it had at the end of that mercilessly bloody day ten years earlier. He knew at that moment he was personally destined to undertake an assignment that exceeded the purchase, temporary storage, and distribution of supplies and material for General Wool's army. He felt drawn, to the best of his means and ability, to restore this shrine of sacrifice and patriotism to a condition befitting its hallowed place in American history. Captain Ralston knew the first step would be to put in place a team of fellow soldiers to help him accomplish all of the tasks.

The Quincy Rifles was originally a unit of the state militia who, at the request of Illinois Governor Ford, had been activated immediately before the death of the Mormon Smith brothers. The unit remained active for the period until well after the pointless trial of the accused murderers. Although composed of men primarily from Quincy, they had been stationed for a majority of the period of their service in and around Nauvoo in Hancock County. When war was declared against Mexico, many of the original members of the *Rifles* had volunteered for federal service. Like Captain Ralston, the unit was assigned to General Wool's army and sent to San Antonio in anticipation of their movement to the front at Monterrey.

One particular member of that unit, a well-respected sergeant by the name of Edward Everett[48], had recently come to Captain Ralston's attention. Sergeant Everett had been sent to apprehend a roughneck Texan causing a problem for soldiers in a local saloon. The result of that assignment was a bullet fired by the miscreant that badly wounded the sergeant's right knee requiring immediate medical attention. When James went to interview the wounded man for a position in his office, he saw first-hand the tent covered hospital and the lack of attention being given the man. He immediately ordered

Everett be sent to his quarters where he could personally see to the sergeant's healing process. Even after his knee healed, Everett was declared unfit for duty at the front and Captain Ralston requested he be assigned as his lead quartermaster clerk. Thus began a mutually beneficial friendship that would last the entire length of their service. The Captain and the Sergeant began the duty of selecting staff and the assembled group worked well as a team despite the good-hearted yet accurate observation that Captain Ralston *could use a fellow up in very few words.*

Edward Everett ca 1900

The work of the quartermaster unit in San Antonio was substantial in that they were always kept busy with the repair of returned materials such as muskets and wagons, the care of a large number of horses and mules, and supplying food and pay to General Wool's fighting army.

In the middle of November, Saltillo Mexico was occupied and on February 23rd and 24th of 1847 the indecisive battle of nearby Buena Vista was waged [*see map on page 55*].

During all of his official quartermaster duties, James maintained a vision of the use of the Alamo as a storage depot for supplies and just as importantly restoring the damage to the fabled mission chapel done ten years before. In early spring of 1847, James was finally successful in convincing his superiors about the value of his project and with a great deal of anticipation and attention to detail, the work began. Sergeant Everett was able to find a crude drawing of the Alamo's appearance before the battle in 1836. He used his superb artistic skills to produce a rendering of the current general mission's appearance and more specifically the historic

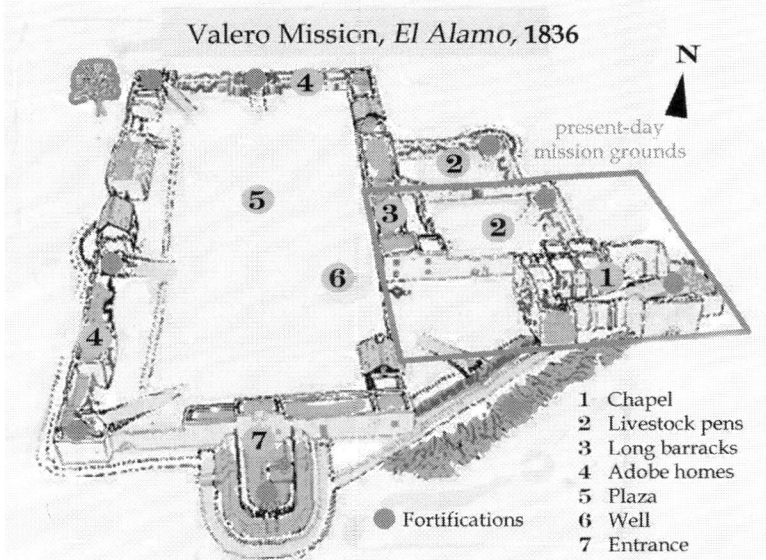

Valero Mission, *El Alamo*, 1836

present-day mission grounds

1 Chapel
2 Livestock pens
3 Long barracks
4 Adobe homes
5 Plaza
6 Well
7 Entrance

● Fortifications

mission's chapel. These drawings were used by Captain Ralston and Sergeant Everett during the construction project to assure the work would not detract from or destroy the cherished site in any way.

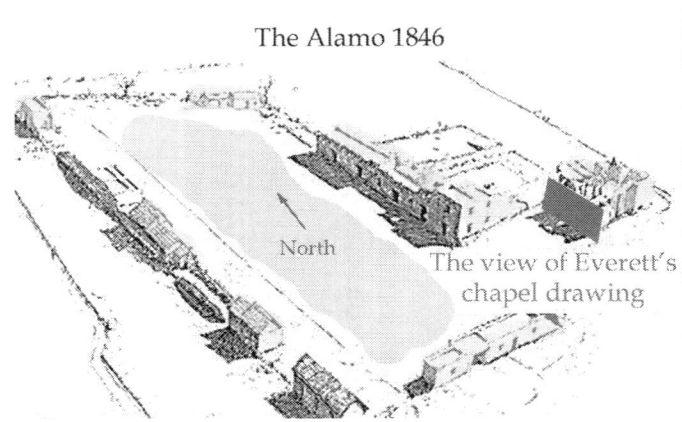

The Alamo 1846

North

The view of Everett's chapel drawing

Edward Everett sketch
before reconstruction of the chapel, 1846

In late February of 1847, Captain Ralston responded in a letter to one of the two-army inspector generals, Colonel George Croghan, concerning Indians in the State of Texas. The federal government had the responsibility in Texas for Indian affairs but unlike the other states it did not control the public lands. The issue that arose was that federal Indian agents in Texas had no power to promise any Indian tribe reservation land in exchange for signing treaties that gave their word they would behave themselves. James was asked to assess the situation and provide Colonel Croghan with his written legal opinion. James responded to Croghan writing that during his time on the frontier he had been actively involved with Indians and had never had a bad account with any of them with the notable exception of Black Hawk. He further stated that Texas could not stand by its position of not allowing Indians to own land in the state and that such a position would eventually drive them away. Texas did not change their law and in hindsight, the state did not become a haven for Indian reservations, and with the exception of the Comanche Tribe, it had few Indian problems.

Since early November of 1846, Jane had repeatedly written letters insisting that James find a way for her and Elizabeth to join him at his post. James replied explaining that the present San Antonio was nothing short of a wild and wooly village full of Texans ready for a fight at the drop of a hat in any one of the large number of saloons. That, he wrote to her, combined with the sun's oppressive heat, nearly intolerable humidity, and the dust drawn up by the army's activities in the town left the appearance of a hell on earth. Despite her husband's written descriptions of San Antonio, she summarized as *that hellhole*, she was adamant and not in the least concerned how Captain Ralston was to go about making her wish come true or what the consequences might be. She just knew that she and their new daughter needed to be by his side in Texas. When James made a request to his superiors about the possibility of bringing his family to San Antonio, the official position of the army was that they wanted nothing to do with the request. Their collective response was that they had enough worries about keeping the soldiers in San Antonio safe. They would not add to their concerns with what they viewed as a *defenseless female* and *infant child* in the middle of the fray. It was clear that if James decided to bring his family to Texas their safety would be his responsibility. In March of 1847 he assumed that responsibility.

The Ralston's were a family once again. James found an adobe home not far from the bustle of his workplace at the mission and he was revitalized by Jane and Elizabeth's presence. He took every care in making sure their needs were met including stationing one of several of his most trusted soldiers at his home when he was not present. Jane also flourished for a time quickly learning some Spanish that allowed her to make good friends among many of the local women. She made a point of taking Lizzie along on her frequent trips to the market. When James was able to join them, the three Ralstons enjoyed visiting the Texas countryside reveling in each other's company. James and Jane were happier in their temporary home in south Texas than they had been for some time in Quincy and they were living Jane's dream for her family, together again.

Then, slowly but ever so steadily Jane's health began to falter. The first sign of a problem was a persistent shallow dry cough that was not accompanied by a fever or any symptoms of a cold. When Jane's energy seem to flag on most days by late afternoon, James took her to see the Army's second-in-command physician at San Antonio, Dr. Thomas Foster. Foster gave her a thorough examination, prescribed a remedy for her cough, and declared her, in his experienced medical opinion, illness free. With her cough under control, Jane seemed to be returning to a picture of health until the fainting spells began. Jane was immediately taken again to Foster for another examination. The doctor confided in James that after listening for an extended time to her heart and lungs he feared a weakening in her heart. When James' questioned what he should do for his wife, the doctor suggested that extended bed rest may help but only time would confirm or deny his prognosis. A month later, thirty-six year-old Jane died quietly in her sleep.

Captain Ralston stoically endured the saddest days of his life that to him seemed to last an eternity. San Antonio's army chaplain presided over the memorial service that was held in the shadow of the ruins of the Alamo chapel. The canvas cover was removed from an army freight wagon allowing full view of the flag draped coffin containing his beloved wife. It was slowly driven on dusty *Houston* street a little over a half-mile to the city's cemetery[49] west of the Alamo. Captain Ralston walked immediately behind the wagon in his full dress blues, including a sheathed saber and black armband, with Lizzie securely in his arms. The tall sad soldier was followed by his uniformed quartermaster staff, other mission troops in parade formation, and about a dozen Mexican friends. The Mexicans included the Ralston's housemaid and Lizzie's part-time nanny with a mourning serape draped over her right shoulder. At the cemetery, the members of the cortege surrounded Jane's grave, the chaplain concluded his remarks with the timeless burial phrase *ashes to ashes, dust to dust.* Save for the muted sounds of grief, Jane was silently lowered to her final resting place, gone from this earth but never forgotten.

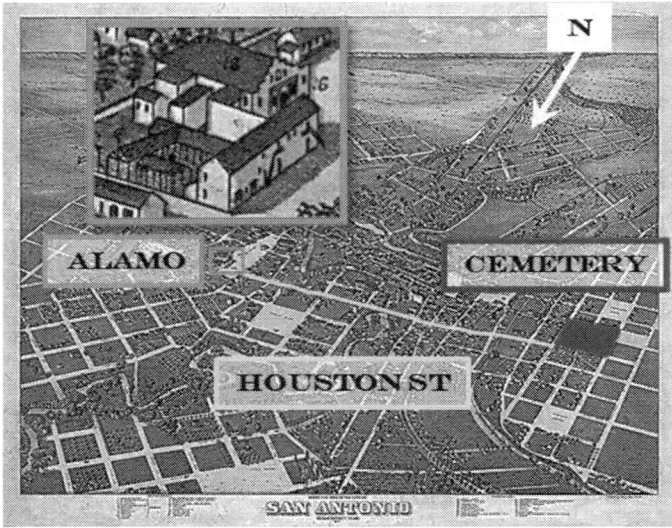

San Antonio, TX, 1873

It took some time for James to accept a future that did not include Jane by his side. Nor could he deal with the belief, despite Dr. Foster's insistent protests, that his decision to move Jane to the heat and dust of south Texas caused her premature death. In the absence of her mother, James made a point of spending as much time as possible with Elizabeth. It soon became clear that even with the help of friends and Lizzie's Mexican nanny, the frontier nature of San Antonio was not a suitable place for his infant daughter. Another member added to Captain Ralston's staff in the months before Jane's death was none other than Jane's brother, Perry Alexander. Alexander had literally been recruited to come to San Antonio by James when he understood the seriousness of her condition. Perry responded to his request to have an Alexander family member close by. Perry proved to be not only helpful in his quartermaster duties but, after Jane's death, he accompanied Lizzie back to Quincy in October of 1847. His trip was *coincidentally* in conjunction with acquiring additional wagons for the San Antonio based Center Army.

By the end of the summer of 1847, American army forces had laid siege to the Mexican gulf port of Vera Cruz and General Winfield Scott's troops had steadily moved inland toward the Mexican capital [*see map on page 55*]. After one last major push on September 13th and 14th, General Scott was triumphantly paraded in his immaculate dress uniform through the heart of Mexico City to the presidential palace. Though there would be a number of additional skirmishes continuing in early 1848, for all intents and purposes the war had ended. Now, the political maneuvering began in earnest to make sure the United States got what it always wanted from the whole bloody affair; land! In San Antonio, word of the war's progress was slow to arrive. The only reliable source of information came from horseback messengers who were often weeks in arriving as far as San Antonio. Word of General Scott's entry into Mexico City arrived in mid-October at about the same time as Captain Ralston's construction project on the *Long Barracks* was completed.

This work restored the building to its original look though modernization of the inside spaces allowed for the building's use as efficient warehousing and office space. It was reported that during the project *a fair number of bats were displaced, though there was little regard for this event or for the final disposition of their whereabouts.* Sergeant Everett once again put his artistic and architectural skill to work and provided a scaled rendering of the completed building. There was some speculation by both Captain Ralston and Sergeant Everett that perhaps they should lay out a plan for

Everett's drawing of the restored Long Barracks
adjacent to the mission chapel [right]

improvements to the chapel.[50] They jointly decided to draw the plans for the restoration of the shrine and began the tedious and painstaking removal of stone debris. They took archeological care in removing and identifying human skeletal remains discovered during the process. The chapel project was not fully completed until shortly after the Captain and his multi-talented sergeant left San Antonio.[51]

The war finally began to visibly *wind down* as the call for materials and supplies slowed to a trickle. Captain Ralston saw some time in his schedule, heretofore unavailable, for the rare activity of socializing. In December of 1847, James was instrumental in organizing a Masonic lodge almost exclusively composed of fellow army members in San Antonio. The lodge that was granted a state charter as Alamo Lodge number 44 on January 15, 1848. James enjoyed the renewed comradery of the Masons that met for a time at the south end of the second floor of the newly constructed Long Barracks.

The Mexican-American War formally ended with the signing of the Treaty of Guadalupe Hidalgo in the town just north of Mexico City on the 2nd of February 1848. Changes made to the original treaty by both sides and ratification of the United States and Mexican governments was finalized July 4th, of the same year. Perhaps the biggest single victory for the *eminent domainists* was that for $15 million dollars the U. S. gained ownership of a large amount land. The purchased area would eventually become the states of California, Arizona, New Mexico, Nevada, Utah, and parts of Wyoming and Colorado. A grand total of 522,468 square miles or 334.44 million acres for a cost of about $.04 ½ cents per acre. The land area acquired represented about a 22% increase in the total area under the American flag at the time of the treaty.

Before James left his assignment in San Antonio he received a touching letter from his brother, Reverend Thomas, asking for permission to bring Lizzie from Quincy to his home in Lexington.

Dear Brother,

…As you are aware, God did not bestow for our life's plan the blessed treasure of children. My wife Josephine and I would like nothing more than to undertake, for whatever period you deem possible, the love and nurturing of our niece and your daughter Elizabeth Jane. It is with some humor I remind you that Josephine can in short order be replete with references avowing to her childcare knowledge and skills. I, on the other hand, would fall short in every aspect of that responsibility except for the love I have for you, your beautiful child and the memory of your remarkable and beloved Jane….

Uncertain as to when he could return to Quincy, James was pleased to accept his brother's heart-felt request.

In October of 1848, Captain Ralston received a letter from the office of the army's quartermaster general stating that he and his lead sergeant would be relieved of their duties in December. James now knew he would be leaving the Alamo by the end of the year having no notion of what he would be doing next or where it would be done.

Chapter 10

Home from the War

Captain Ralston and Sergeant Everett had done well in their service at the Alamo and their fellow soldiers were sad to see them go. There was a rowdy observance of their departure at a local San Antonio saloon that was held in good fun. It gave those left behind a chance to show their appreciation for their leader and his able assistant. It also provided the opportunity for the troops to get to better know their new leader, academy graduate Captain Morris Smith Miller. James left his post of nearly three years with bittersweet memories and he made one last visit to the resting place of his beloved wife. He made a promise to Jane that he would make sure their daughter was safe, happy, and above all else deeply loved.

Three weeks after they left San Antonio, the weary travelers arrived in Washington. The purpose of the mid-January 1849 visit was to complete the rather tedious process required by quartermasters for discharge from the army. During the journey, they had taken nearly every conceivable means of transportation available at the time. A wagon and horseback from San Antonio to Port Lavaca. An ocean steamer from Port Lavaca to New Orleans. River steamers from New Orleans up the Mississippi and Ohio rivers to Wheeling, Virginia [now West Virginia]. A stagecoach across the Alleghany Mountains to Philadelphia. A steam railroad train from Philadelphia to Washington D. C. and by foot from their hotel to the war office at 17th and Pennsylvania Avenue.

The two men laid out the paperwork from their quartermaster activities at San Antonio for the auditors, then waited nearly six weeks before the favorable review of their records was completed. While they waited, the Captain and the Sergeant took good advantage of their time by touring the capital, observing congress in action, and meeting with a number of distinguished politicians. These men had expressed an interest in hearing about the construction work the two oversaw at the Alamo shrine and in paying their respects to Sergeant Everett, the cousin of their long-time colleague. Included in the group well met was Kentucky's Henry Clay, Massachusetts' Daniel Webster, South Carolinian John C. Calhoun, and Missouri senator Thomas Hart Benton. James had a lengthy reunion with his good friend and current Illinois senator, Stephen A. Douglas. He also spent nearly two full days with his very close aging tutor and friend, Judge Richard M. Young. Young, after a long and distinguished judicial and political career in Illinois and the nation's capital, was serving in his twilight years as the commissioner of the General Land office in Washington. Captain Ralston and his faithful assistant and friend, Sergeant Everett, exchanged a final salute and went their separate ways.

James was honorably discharged from the army, March 3, 1849. Two days later, he spent his last day in Washington during a light snowfall as a distant observer of the inauguration of America's 12th president and the hero of the recently concluded war with Mexico, Zachary Taylor. James had never had the opportunity to officially meet the new president though he had seen him on several occasions in San Antonio. A suspected case of cholera that claimed Taylor's life fifteen months later would not allow historians an adequate amount of time to compare his political versus his well-documented military savvy. After the inauguration, James returned to his hotel still without a specific plan other than to see Lizzie as soon as possible and give her the biggest hug and kiss of her young life. Two weeks later, at his brother's home in Lexington, Kentucky, he had a happy reunion with his daughter. During his brief stay, the two brothers talked for hours about what James' future might hold and they both concluded that a trip to Quincy would determine if he could once again settle there and be content with only his young daughter by his side.

The rumbling wheels and jostling of the stagecoach brought back memories of James' first trip to Illinois made over 20 years earlier with his uncle William and his family. He remembered how excited yet nervous he was to face the challenges of forging an unknown future on the Illinois frontier. Although the scenery that now passed by his small window looked familiar to him, his current circumstances were not at all the same. When James whispered aloud to himself asking if given the opportunity would he do the same thing all over again, Lizzie tugged at his coat sleeve and asked *Daddy* if everything was all right. He assured her everything was better than fine now that she was by his side. He leaned over and kissed her on the forehead, gave her a reassuring hug, and resumed his thought about the whispered question. Would he be a friend and resource through thick and thin to the often misunderstood and maligned Mormon faithful? Would he do the same thing he had done knowing full well this work would lead to a deliberate *shunning* by many of the non-Mormons he had counted among his friends and supporters. James firmly believed there was no doubt that he would. Now, with a majority of the Latter-day saints long gone to the Utah Territory, could he and his one-time acquaintances let bygones be bygones. Could he again live among them as a trusted friend and advisor? Without his companion and the woman he so dearly loved and depended on by his side could he again be a respected leader in the community? Would he be able to assure Lizzie's happiness in the place she was born though much too young to remember? He knew the not-to-distant future would hold the answers to all of his questions.

The stagecoach entered Quincy though for some strange reason it did not seem as though it had been three years since James had left. He waved out the window when he saw a number of recognizable faces. The first to greet the travelers was the smiling Dr. Joseph Ralston slapping his brother on the back. He jokingly referred to his brother as *the Mexican conqueror* and his niece, Lizzie, in the comfort of her father's arms, *the queen of the Rio Grande*. In addition to the Dr. Ralston family, the small entourage gathering around included the *properly* friendly O. H. Browning and his wife, Eliza. James' younger brother and attorney William and his family who now lived a short distance

John Neely Johnson

north in Warsaw, Illinois. He was pleasantly surprised to see another greeter from the small Mississippi riverfront community of Keokuk, Iowa. Another relative, eligible bachelor, budding attorney, and first cousin John Neely Johnson. The handsome, intelligent, and gregarious *J. Neely*, as he preferred to be called, was the son of his mother's youngest sister, Juliette and her husband George Johnson. He had come to Quincy shortly before James left for the Army arriving in Illinois late in 1845. He had come from his parent's home on the banks of the Ohio River at Evansville, Indiana where his father kept a tavern. Like James had done a number of years earlier, J. Neely was looking for a future on the frontier and he had knocked on his respected older cousin's door for help and advice. James was instrumental in finding legal work for his cousin in Keokuk and he was eager to find out how he was doing. The small crowd left the stagecoach station, Lizzie still in the security of her father's arms, and they all walked the short distance to Dr. Ralston's home for more of the happy reunion that would last well after a late evening dinner meal.

Near the end of his long homecoming day, James had excused himself from the affair and was enjoying tobacco and the cool breezes of the clear late March evening. He stood on the large front porch of his brother's comfortable wood-framed combination home and office. After being assured he was not intruding, James was joined by J. Neely who wanted to make a special point of thanking his older cousin for procuring his junior partner position in the Keokuk law firm. He also knew of the circumstances of James' departure from Quincy and he was hopeful that the judge would be able to re-acclimate to Quincy's professional and social circles. James thanked J. Neely for both of his comments and was about to return inside for what remained of the welcome home celebration when his cousin made an additional *by the way* comment. He told James that he had been following the gold discovery in the northern part of the new California territory near a once sleepy village called Sacramento. He was sure that in the least there would be a need for attorneys in the area. At best perhaps a man could add to his wealth with a gold nugget or two. James all but ignored the observation of his young and impetuous cousin momentarily putting aside his own still burning spirit of adventure. Three weeks later James received a message from J. Neely telling him that he and his brother, William, were leaving Keokuk for the *wild-west* California coast. He added that if he arrived safely, James would have a good friend who owed him a great debt if he ever decided to cross the continental divide. A part of Judge Ralston wanted very much to join the next wagon train west.

James made a special point of spending the next few months circulating through every nook and cranny of Quincy shaking as many hands as he could find and trying to reestablish acquaintences and friendships. To everyone's surprise who was sure James was a *heathen*, he could now be regularly seen on Sunday attending services with his daughter at the Quincy Baptist church where he had been befriended by the church's pastor, Reverend Aaron Jackson. The outgoing reverend had arrived in Quincy the year before and the recent passing of Jackson's wife was a common thread between the two men. The Judge had a standing invitation to attend a mid-afternoon Sunday meal at Reverend Jackson's home that the reverend referred to as *an enjoyable meeting of two like minds and two sinful souls*. The event was eagerly hosted by Jackson's attractive and well-educated daughters, 21-year-old Harriet and 15-year-old Mary Amelia. James was thankfully able to make arrangements with the Jackson daughters to occasionally watch over Elizabeth when his work kept him away from home for extended periods. Otherwise, Lizzie could often be seen playing near her father's desk in the library of the home he rented, conveniently situated near the courthouse, the Reverend Jackson's, and Dr. Ralston's house.

With the exception of his new friends, the Jacksons, and a few stalwart friends, mostly members of the bar who clearly understood the attorney relationship James had with his well-paying Mormon clients, Judge Ralston was avoided. He found that the indelible memory of a majority of the good citizens of Quincy, including many of his brother Masons, had not, and likely would not choose to forget his Mormon affiliation. It was clear that James was doing his level best to fashion a new life in Quincy but the painfully polite and restrained citizenry would just as clearly have none of it. The only redeeming fact in the whole affair was that, thankfully, the daughter was not held accountable for the perceived *sins* of the father.

Mary Amelia and Harriet Newell Jackson

Lizzie continued to flourish and formed a close attachment with the older Jackson daughter, Harriet, as a surrogate for a deceased mother she never really knew. Harriet loved Lizzie in return. It was becoming obvious, seemingly only to James, that the attractive woman half his age sought a relationship with Judge Ralston that was more than just being a nanny for his daughter and good friends. James longed for female companionship that would ideally include being a mother to his daughter but, of all things, a preacher's daughter, half his age, in a town that would just as soon he was not there. It was not likely!

James and Lizzie spent Christmas day of 1849 at the Jacksons. The Jackson daughters had boldly implemented an idea, called a *Christmas Tree*, they saw and read about in a noted ladies journal of the day. They had cut a young pine tree from down by the river and dragged it all the way to their house where they had carefully decorated it with fruit and paper figures and placed the tree squarely in the middle of their living room. Beneath the tree were several boxes wrapped in colorful swaths of cloth that contained handmade gifts for family and their guests. The good reverend was sure this *pagan ritual* would never be widely accepted while James, and, of course, Lizzie, were fascinated with the whole idea. James was particularly pleased with Harriet's gift, a hand-knitted neck scarf, that she proudly told him was patterned after the very tartan used by the Scottish *Ralston* clan. After Christmas dinner, Squire Ralston and Reverend Jackson went to the front porch to partake in the enjoyment of tobacco and James asked his friend what he should do about the situation in Quincy. Aaron told him that as a man of the cloth he should encourage James to *turn the other cheek* and carry on. However, as a friend, he would recommend moving to a place where he and his daughter could put down new roots and where both of them would be happy.

Chapter 11

The California Frontier

The wheels of change were set in motion. In January 1850, James wrote his brother Thomas in Kentucky asking if he and Josephine would once again be kind enough to care for Lizzie because he was planning to travel to the California Territory, leaving sometime in April. He also confided his news of the planned journey to his brother Dr. Joseph and the Reverend Aaron Jackson. Reverend Jackson's response in finding out about the trip was a smile and a congratulatory pat on the back. James was completely taken aback when the reverend confided that when the news came out, he would have one upset and distraught daughter that would require an extra dose of love and counsel until the pain of his absence faded. James thought he was the only one who noticed Harriet's feelings and Aaron laughed and admitted that the Jackson family withheld few secrets. The reverend's closing wistful comment, *perhaps one day,* were the last words spoken between the two men on that subject, for the present time.

By early April James returned to Quincy after delivering his daughter to the Kentucky home of his brother, Pastor Thomas. He told Thomas that he would be around to gather his daughter sooner rather than later. James left a smiling and laughing Lizzie already in the middle of a make believe *tea time* with Aunt Josephine. She did stop long enough to give her departing father a big hug and a kiss. James preparation for the journey amounted to filling a steamer trunk to just barely full with all of his earthly possessions. Filling a waist wallet with all of the cash he had on hand and most of what he had on deposit at the Quincy bank. He finished hand written notes of instruction for each of his small number of clients. His still long-time friend O. H. Browning had agreed to make contact and to assume responsibility for his clients after he left.

There was little fanfare at Judge Ralston's departure. It had become routine for little recognition of a passing or departing wagon train heading for the gold fields or Oregon's forests by way of Quincy's busy ferrymen. Hand waving and a few words of encouragement directed at the travelers had replaced the celebration that in the beginning of the *rush west* included a large community turn out. Always accompanied by the music of the town's brass band. Reverend Jackson and his oldest daughter decided it was best for her to cry on her father's shoulder in the privacy of the Jackson living room and not in full public view. Her sister Amelia was sent as an emissary to provide a full report. The judge spotted Amelia before he mounted his horse to leave and he asked Amelia to be sure to tell her father and sister that he would send contact information when he arrived and that he full well expected regular letters. He then shook her hand telling her it was for her father and he kissed her twice on the forehead saying that one of them was for her and the other was for her sister. When James gallantly rode away, Amelia considered her assignment completed and in as good a form as any male her age, she grabbed hold of her skirts and ran home at top speed to report the latest Judge Ralston news.

It is impossible to use the word uneventful to describe a journey of nearly 2,100 miles. The trail crossed a seemingly endless expanse of waving prairie grass, fording torrent rivers, and climbing then descending the many passes of the majestic snow-covered Rocky Mountains. Suffering the stifling heat of the mountainous, sandy, rock strewn, and *bone dry* high desert. Then, viewing the expanse of welcoming lush green valley forests while descending from the glacial chill of the high Sierras. The marked and unmarked graves and the bleached bones of domestic animals spotted along the trail served as a constant reminder. With each and every step, a clear and ever present danger could bring with it starvation, disease, or injury that could result in agonizing or instant death. Simply understated, James and the nearly two-hundred other souls in his wagon train safely reached Sacramento, California in mid-July of 1850, slightly over 100 days after leaving Quincy. What happened in Sacramento shortly after James' arrival was nothing short of political intrigue.

Judge Ralston's reasons for joining the emigrants on the trail to *El Dorado* had nothing whatsoever in common with the gold fever that consumed every thought of a majority of the other travelers. The vision of a gold strike emancipating them and their loved ones from a life where hard work with little financial reward was a constant. Gold, and the wealth that accompanied it, was the answer to their every earnest prayer. Indeed, James sought the same happiness and contentment, however, his means to that end, as it had before, would come about through the use of his legal and political savvy on another new frontier, California. Consequently, rather than heading for the gold fields with the thousands of others, James immediately sought out his cousin. J. Neely Johnson, he discovered, could be found in the office of the city attorney in Sacramento, a position he had been elected to a few months earlier.

The reunion was a happy one. James and J. Neely talked for hours about their experiences crossing the country. His cousin told James about what he had done since arriving in the territory. Neely had started by heading to the foothills of the Sierras where he was the only practicing attorney in the boomtown of Mormon Island near where the first gold strike was made in 1848. He quickly left the area after discovering his chance of succeeding in the lawless gold fields was on a par with a snowball in hell. For a time he drove a wagon carrying freight between Sacramento and Stockton until he met attorney James C. Zabriskie who introduced him to some of the more prominent men in Sacramento. J. Neely was sure Judge Ralston and Zabriskie, a *flaming democrat*, could become fast friends. Over dinner at the Columbia Hotel the men discussed James' future in Sacramento. J. Neely shared an upcoming event that might be just what James' needed to get his foot in the judicial, political, and social doors of the booming frontier town.

He told James that within a week or so a meeting would be called. The subject, to discuss what the town and the surrounding area might be able to do to provide assistance for some of the emigrants in dire need of help on the high desert just east of the Sierras. James immediately added that he had just seen first-hand the problems many of them had in getting enough food for their animals and themselves.[52] J. Neely said that many of the prominent men of the town, including his friend, Zabriskie, were involved in an effort to raise money and to use that money to buy and then and distribute supplies to those most in need. His cousin promised to keep James apprised of the events.

The Committee for the Relief of Overland Emigrants was formed in late July of 1850 and included the names of many of the leading men who held important positions in the territory. For instance in Sacramento; a territorial chief justice of the supreme court, territorial attorney general, former city attorney, town mayor, county judge, town treasurer, two newspaper owner/editors, and four state legislators, one of whom would become the third California governor. In other words, people that *needed to be known* in Sacramento. J. Neely was given $3,000 and appointed by the committee to be the first on-site responder.

J. Neely asked James to travel with him to the Carson River valley, about 200 miles from Sacramento just east of the Sierras, to help him assess the emigrant needs, purchase needed food supplies, and distribute them to the families closest to starvation. The two men arrived in the valley on the 5th of August and began to complete the assigned task. The pressing needs of his job forced J. Neely to return to Sacramento on August 13th and James stayed on to continue the work and to wait for a wagon train with more supplies due to arrive from Sacramento before the end of August. Neither J. Neely nor James planned to let their *pro bono* humanitarian deeds go unnoticed by the prestigious relief committee or the good citizens of Sacramento.

J. Neely arrived back in Sacramento on August 18th and that evening he provided to the relief committee a personally delivered detailed written report of his actions that in turn was published in the local newspapers two days later. Near the end of the report, City Attorney Neely made an intriguing observation that purposely provided an introduction for his cousin to the elite and general citizenry of Sacramento.

Too much praise cannot be awarded to Judge James H. Ralston, who recently crossed the Plains, from Quincy Ill., for his devotion to this cause. He kindly assisted me several days previous to my departure, and then consented to take charge of the station, without compensation, until relieved.

J. Neely made no mention that Judge Ralston was even a friend let alone his cousin, intimating instead that he happened upon this fine humanitarian in the remote lush green of the Carson River Valley and without his help the mission would not have been nearly as successful as it was. No doubt interest abounded to find out more about this unknown *Good Samaritan*; it was not long in coming.

On the 13th of September, under the heading, *Report of Col. Ralston*, the San Francisco Daily Alta newspaper published a copy of a letter dated September 6, 1850, written by Judge James H. Ralston. *To the Committee for the Relief of destitute Immigrants appointed by the Citizens of Sacramento.*[53] Excerpts from this heart-wrenching account of the instantly and mistakenly promoted *Captain, now Colonel,* Ralston follows.

Gentlemen – On my way hither, I met, on the 27th July last, at the west end of the Great Desert, terminating on the Carson river, my friend J. Neeley Johnson, Esq., charged with the distribution of the funds and provisions furnished by the benevolence of the citizens of this and other cities to relieve the destitute and suffering emigrants on their way across the Plains. Having passed many thousands of the emigrants en route, I was enabled to impart to Mr. Johnson much information touching their distressed condition. I also at once gave him all the aid in my power in relieving the sick, destitute, and starving among the crowds who thronged the trail.

Judge Ralston wrote that J. Neely was a *friend* but not a close relative and he misspelled the middle name of his *friend*. The implication is clear that James coincidentally met Mr. Johnson on July 27th on his way to Sacramento though James knew first-hand his *friend* did not arrive in the Carson River valley until August 5th.[54]

On the 7th of August[55], Mr. J. [Johnson] left the station on Carson River on his return to this city; and I then took exclusive charge of the remnant of your supplies, and continued to issue them until the 27th August, when they were wholly exhausted. During this time about one thousand emigrants, all destitute of the means of subsistence, were supplied by me. The amount furnished each was necessarily small, but still of great value to the suffering, enabling them to pursue their journey to places of greater abundance, so that none perished of absolute starvation this side of that station, though I have good reason for believing that several perished east of that station from the want of the necessities of life, and still greater numbers from diseases caused by suffering and hardship incident to the trip, and from the use of unwholesome meat stripped from the carcases of dead animals lying by the way-side.

During the same time, 24 families all that applied for assistance — received such aid as they required and I was enabled to bestow; but I had to regret my total inability to supply many of their most pressing wants. In many cases, they were not only destitute of subsistence, but all their animals had died or been stolen by the Indians... As the provisions in my hands grew scarce, I could no longer pursue this course; and as I had no part of the Charity Fund in my possession, and my private means, available, were soon exhausted, I could do but little to aid them. In several instances I was compelled to behold, without power to aid, aged men and women, "Whose tottering limbs proclaim their Lengthened years"[56], pursue their toilsome journey on foot, carrying their little bundles of clothes and provisions... Several men had remained at the station for weeks, unable to pursue their journey on foot, and without ability to procure a conveyance of any kind... Unable myself to furnish or procure them a conveyance, I left one family at the station, supplied with several days' subsistence, but without any means whatever to convey themselves further. If individual charity has not supplied their wants ere this, I hope your agent may speedily furnish the requisite aid...

At the time of my departure from Johnson's Station, provisions were exceedingly scarce among both emigrants and traders, but I met on the road large supplies in the hands of enterprising traders. I think, therefore, the amount of provisions en route to the Desert in the hands of traders, and the amount lately sent forward by the active benevolence of the citizens of California may be sufficient to supply the emigrants. But a larger amount of money should be in the hands of your agent, to enable him to purchase teams or hire conveyances for the destitute families, the sick and the decrepid who are unable to walk. This would enable him to effectually aid them across the mountains. Otherwise, many of them will be left to perish. The Carson River Road seems to be the only road travelled by emigrants in great numbers, the Truckee route having been abandoned on account of high water and other causes.

All of which I most respectfully submit to your consideration. I have the honor to be, gent., Your ob't serv't, J. A, RALSTON[57]

Messrs. Henley, Bigler, and others of the Committee

James arrived early at his second floor office above the courtroom on 4th street near J street with the daily edition of the Sacramento Transcript under his arm. The satisfaction he felt after reading a copy of his letter was only matched by the concern he had shown and the aid he had given to many of the helpless emigrants he had so eloquently described. He could not help but reflect on one of his favorite idioms, *there but for the grace of God go I*, as he recalled the images of some of the people he was able to help and many that he could not. Not fifteen minutes after he arrived, the first of what seemed like hundreds of completely unexpected strangers passed through his door, most to offer their congratulations on what they viewed as his heroic efforts in the Carson River Valley. Judge Ralston was not a humble man but the admiration they expressed for what he had done truly overwhelmed him. He graciously accepted their praise while masking some feeling of guilt over the publicity effort so carefully orchestrated by J.

Sacramento 1850
Courtesy California State Library

Neely. Yes, there was no doubt he had put a full and sincere effort in helping the travelers and he had done as good a job as time and even the use of his own money allowed. Yes, he was glad that his efforts had ingratiated him in the eyes of the townspeople that might provide opportunities he otherwise might not have had, so, just maybe, his feeling of guilt was unjustified.

Near the end of the day James noticed a young man who had been standing patiently outside his office door as the people filed in and out. With the dinner hour fast approaching, the number of visitors finally abated and James was able to ask the man if he could be of any assistance. Tom Sunderland politely introduced himself to Judge Ralston and told him that he had read about the judge's tireless good deeds in the morning paper and that he was a bit embarrassed to ask. Was he the same man who had been an attorney for the Mormons in Nauvoo, Illinois a few years before? James thought for just a moment, then, with not the least bit of apprehension, he confidently told Mr. Sunderland that he was that man. When Tom told James that before he came to California he had been an attorney in Hannibal, Missouri, a relaxed conversation immediately followed. The two men exchanged their experiences well past the dinner they shared at the Sutter Hotel. Before the evening was over they had agreed in principal to form a law practice that would be situated in James' current office space. From Judge Ralston's perspective the highlight of the evening was Squire Sunderland's intriguing tale of his travel the previous year to California via the Panama isthmus, his brief time in the gold fields, and the Valparaiso, Chile *affair*.

In early February of 1849, while James was biding his time in Washington waiting for the auditors to review his work at the Alamo, four friends, including Tom, boarded a river steamer at their hometown of Hannibal, Missouri. The steamer would take them down river to New Orleans. The other three men, Tom's younger brother and attorney, Nathan[58], another attorney, Cook Campbell[59], and a grocery merchant, George Wiley[60] purchased tickets in New Orleans on the ocean worthy steam schooner *SS Crescent City*. It was bound for the mouth of the Chagres River, 1,600 miles south in central Panama.[61] The *argonauts* and their baggage were then put on native wooden canoes [*cayucas, called bungos by the gringos*] that were poled by the natives the 24-mile journey up the river to a jungle clearing at the hutted village of *Las Cruces*. From there, the travelers rode

Chargres River, Panama, 1850
bungo upstream

on mules the last 18-miles on the *Las Cruces Trail* to the 16th century walled town of *Panama* on the Pacific coast. The hot, humid, muddy, and insect infested crossing of the isthmus' jungle took 6 days. During the trip, Tom's brother Nathan, contracted malaria and the group had to wait another 2 ½ months boarded together in the small room of a *Panama* hotel. Joining them were all manner of native insects and animals, including alligators and snakes, while the disease worked its delirious and feverish course. Finally, on the 4th day of June 1849, 18 days after leaving *Panama*, Tom arrived in San Francisco.

After buying a wagon and two mules, Tom wasted no time in making his way to the gold fields. He stopped long enough at a Sacramento general store to buy all of the necessities a clerk said he needed to find a fistful of gold nuggets. He then drove what seemed like wagon to wagon with the other *forty-niners* up the foothills to gold country. Tom filed a claim in the gravel bank near the place James Marshall first found gold at Sutter's mill the year before. The claim was close to the boomtown of Mormon Island[62] where the north and south fork of the American River joined before winding its way down the foothills to Sacramento. Within two months of what Tom called *a sour venture,* he sold his claim, mules, and wagon for 1/10th of what he paid for them and went back to Sacramento.

Squire Sunderland then traveled by himself to the Chilean trading center and port of Valparaiso in early 1850 to negotiate trade arrangements for wool and flour with the Chilean government.

California Territory 1849

Mormon Island 1848

This venture failed to evolve into the profitable speculative investment he had hoped. On his way back to San Francisco, the leaking pile of logs, called a schooner, by its drunken captain, failed to negotiate the shallows near the Juan Fernandez Islands. Like Dafoe's fictional Robinson Crusoe, he was shipwrecked on the very same island. Fortunately, as Tom told his story, his stay only lasted a few days before yet another less than seaworthy vessel, the Sea Gull, picked him up, and somehow made it to San Francisco. He returned once again to Sacramento, August 10th. He spent the last month trying unsuccessfully to drown his disappointments with seemingly endless shots of rum at a seedy establishment near the Front street docks. Tom ended his account by thanking James for saving yet another poor emigrant soul.

Tom asked his new law partner when it would be best for him to start working and James asked if the next morning would be suitable for his younger friend. The two men shook hands in agreement and thus began a mutually beneficial friendship that would last well over a decade. Judge Ralston dropped by the Sacramento Transcript early the next morning to place an advertisement.

J. H. RALSTON.   THOS. SUNDERLAND.
Ralston & Sunderland.
Attorneys and Counsellors at Law,
Office, Fourth street, near J,
s12 1m   over the Court Room.

Sacramento Transcript, 9/12/1850

The four alternate routes, distances, and average travel time to reach California in 1850.

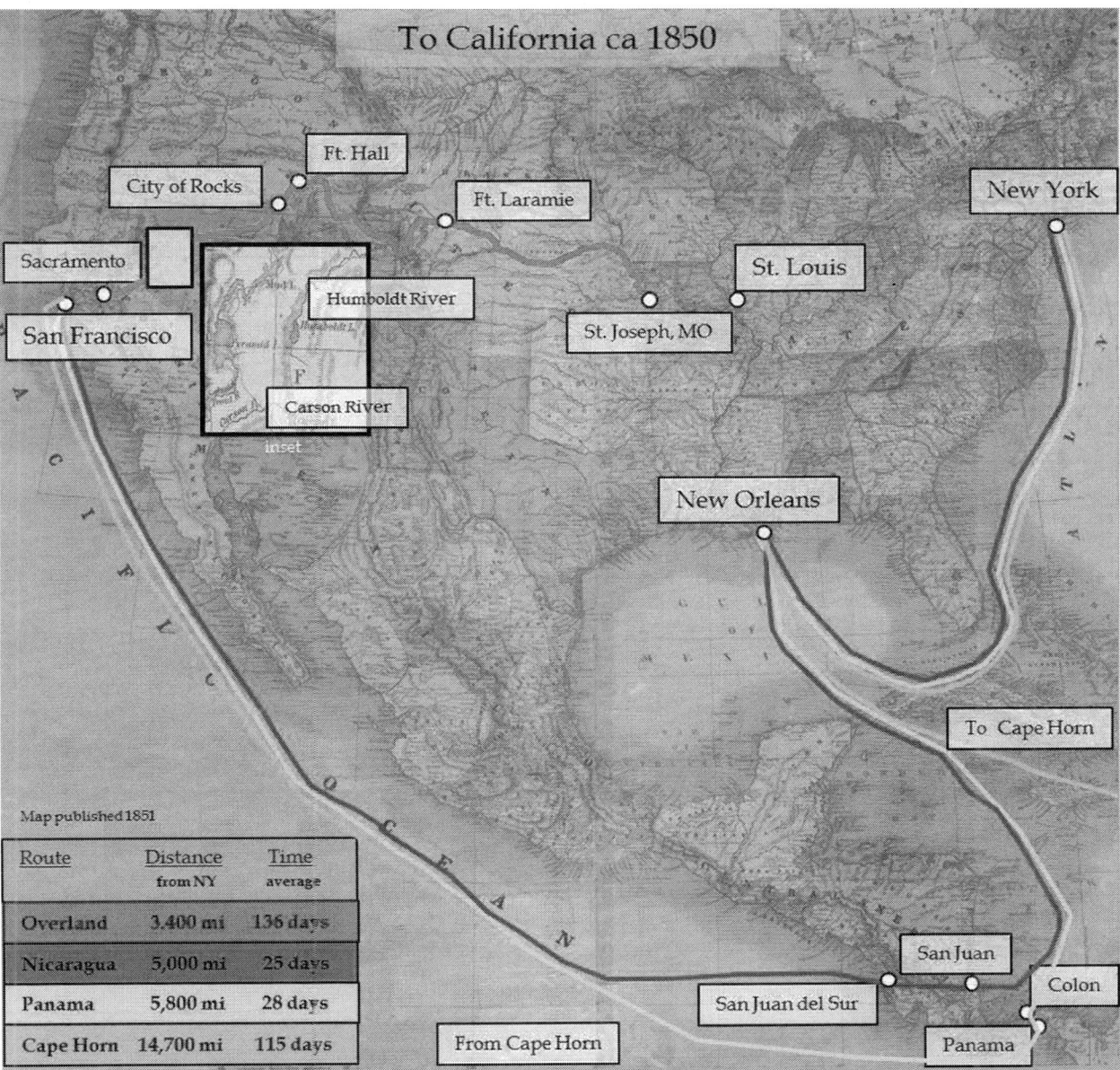

Route	Distance from NY	Time average
Overland	3,400 mi	136 days
Nicaragua	5,000 mi	25 days
Panama	5,800 mi	28 days
Cape Horn	14,700 mi	115 days

Chapter 12

A New Beginning

I am well pleased with this climate. It is much like western Texas. It must become a pleasant country to live in. This city only a year old contains 10 thousand inhabitants. It is being rapidly built up in neat framed houses. It does a heavy business. San Francisco is still virgin. If California is admitted into the Union, it will soon become a great state. It is no less rich in agricultural and commercial resources than in its minerals. But most men here are discontented, they are leaving by the thousands every week poorer than when they came. The reason why; they have left wives and sweethearts to mourn their absence and rejoice at their return. I have left neither so I feel pretty happy. Again, most men who have come here have wanted industry or business lost at home. Thousands of such are reduced to want hire and are leaving as fast as they can. In California, more than elsewhere, men must have mind, even an enlightened mind as well as health and industry to insure success. I know hundreds of men who for want of these qualities will be ruined by coming here. Whilst others apparently less the favorites of fortune will be enriched. I might name them but that would come too near home so I will forebear.

There is much drinking, gambling etc. in all this country. Say to Neely a vast field is open for Preachers. Why does not the church send them out here. They would be well fed and well paid, preaching is needed here as much as anywhere for in the absence of preaching business houses especially the gambling shops are left open all day Sunday.[63]

James smiled as he read two of the paragraphs of a letter he had just written to his youngest sister, Eliza Jane, a new bride of only six months to Professor James Dodd[64] now living near his brother in Lexington. He knew at the very first opportunity she had, his energetic sister would see her way to pay a call on her older brother, Reverend Thomas Neely Ralston, and share the contents of the letter with him. James had failed miserably to communicate his current state of affairs with his siblings and close friends and he decided it was time to correct that situation. This was the sixth letter he had penned, the next to last one he intended to write, on this absolutely crystal clear late September Sunday afternoon from his office in Sacramento. He finished writing and carefully folded the letter to Eliza then placed a blank sheet in front of him, dipped his pen in ink, and began to write the letter he had purposefully saved for last.

25th September, '50, Sacramento

Reverend Aaron Jackson and family
Quincy, Ills.

Dear Reverend,

I cannot find a suitable apology for waiting such a long period before sending this to you and your lovely daughters; therefore, I shall not try to invent one. Much has happened since last I saw you in Quincy. For fear of dredging up memories and completely exhausting my supply of ink, I will only say that I am glad the journey across the plains, mountains, and endless deserts came to a successful conclusion.

Since my arrival, I have been duly baptized by many inches or even feet of rain God sent to us all, requiring for a time the use of small boats and canoes to go from one place to another in the city. On more than one occasion, I was forced to plunge into the water to assure a safe but not a dry arrival at my appointed business. Without any great effort, I would like for you, on behalf of the many fine citizens of this city, to thank Him for the bountiful supply of water. Could we ask Him to consider a suggestion for bringing less. I would beseech that myself but I am convinced your prayer would curry much more favor than would mine.

My cousin J. Neely Johnson, who you may remember, has succeeded in making my presence known in Sacramento from the very top of society to the lowest, which may not be a blessing particularly on the low side. He involved my assistance in the effort to bring some relief to the emigrants coming to the gold fields that were in dire need of food and conveyance to ward off starvation before completing their journey. J. Neely saw to it that our joint efforts did not go without notice in the newspapers of the region. My office, and that of a newly found law partner, has been regularly visited by hosts of well-wishers and those who are generally curious about the features of the biblical Good Samaritan. For whatever reason the aforesaid was attached to my poor personage.

I saved writing this letter as the last of several I felt compelled to compose assuming that the sequence would make for a more informative message but alas, its contents seem eerily familiar to the others. There will be one original piece of news and that is my humble request for your permission allowing me to send a dispatch with the regularity afforded by my affairs to Miss Harriet. I have come to believe that my interest in doing so will do no harm and may be a respite in uplifting my spirits and mayhap hers.

I have frequently missed of our Sunday afternoon caucus. On more than one occasion I could well have used your sound advice and counsel as both a man of the cloth and a wise friend. I will freely admit that my decision, made with your help, to travel to this place to start anew is and will likely remain sound. Had or will it not be so, you, of course, will carry the full burden of my recriminations.

Pass along the best of my wishes to your daughters, one of whom I hope will see fit to write.

Your friend and fellow sinner,

[signed] *J. H. Ralston*

Though it had officially happened on the 9th of September 1850 in Washington's halls of congress three weeks earlier, the month of October saw statewide celebrations commemorating the admittance of California as a state,. The event in Sacramento was festively described in the October 21st, 1850 edition of the Sacramento Transcript.

The Mass Meeting on Saturday Night.

At an early hour on Saturday evening, our citizens began to assemble on the corner of J and Front streets, to commingle their rejoicings, and express their feelings at the present position of our State — our legitimately acknowledged State. All were filled with enthusiasm, and sought to show their patriotism in every conceivable manner. Bonfires were made, casting a lurid glare around the city and brilliantly lighting up the whole heavens. These, with the mass meeting, the illuminations, etc., constituted a picture never before equaled in our city. Fireballs filled the atmosphere, powder crackers were exploded in innumerable places and in numberless quantities, which, together with the huzzas of the multitude, formed a scene of life and animation characteristic of a great occasion.

J. Neely Johnson, Esq., who was the Chairman of the Committee of Arrangements for the grand celebration introduced one by one a list of speakers in the order of their political standing in the city beginning with Lt. Governor John McDougal. Judge Ralston's name was added to the distinguished list when it became known that he was a long time close friend of Illinois Senator Stephen Douglas. Douglas was currently popular among California citizenry because he, Daniel Webster, and Henry Clay had faithfully nurtured and ardently supported *The Compromise of 1850*, the very act admitting California to the Union.

The speaking was kept up till the night was far advanced, and many of the speeches were happily conceived, eloquent in delivery, and expressed the most patriotic sentiments.

Just a week later a much less enthusiastic mass meeting was held by the city's merchants at the corner of Front and J streets where, among others, J. Neely, Col. Zabriskie, and James again made speeches. This time the subject was in opposition to an action taken by the fickle U. S. Senate whereby Sacramento would be *excluded from the conveniences* of a California port of entry. Extensive lobbying in congress on behalf of the newest state reversed the ruling the following month. This and other early events in the history of California demonstrated the overall lack of knowledge and understanding about the new state's geography and its economic, financial, and political progress. This knowledge gap was due to the extensive distance between the east and west coasts and the lack of timely communication over the miles.

Squires Ralston and Sunderland soon made their mark in Sacramento's legal arena by gathering a substantial number of clients, a majority of them involving disputed land ownership. James' experiences in Illinois dealing with the military land tract claims involving naïve pioneers, greedy land speculators, and the federal government served him well. In his new setting, the disputes arose among another triad, composed of the holder of an official deed to land, the federal government entitlements as outlined in the Treaty of Guadalupe Hidalgo that ended the Mexican American War, and the Spanish records of legal land grants recorded before and after the treaty. James spent days mentoring his gifted partner, attorney Sunderland, in the fine art of proving land ownership then convincing the courts of their conclusion on behalf of a pleased and grateful client. James wisely avoided taking on clients involving gold claims. Cousin J. Neely warned him that those disputes were often settled with a bullet from a well-aimed revolver occasionally misdirected at the responsible attorney. The firm of Ralston and Sunderland's rising standing with the Sacramento bar and their burgeoning wallets attested to their combined achievements.

In Quincy, James' success had been built on his legal reputation, his social involvement, and his political accomplishments, in that order. In Sacramento he had rigorously pursued an identical strategy. His law practice now on a solid footing, he reached out using his experiences with the Masonic order and was a founding member of the newly formed Jennings Lodge #4 in Sacramento. He gave the principle address in front all of the city's Masons commemorating St. John's Day.[65] Judge Ralston was then called to chair a meeting at Sacramento's Orleans Hotel resulting in the official formation and platform adoption of the city's Democratic Party. Just as J. Neely had predicted, fellow democrats Judge Ralston and City Attorney J. C. Zabriskie had become close friends and key members of the party's activities. James had now solidly placed his foot on the doorstep of Sacramento society and he intended to proudly and successfully walk in.

New Year's Eve, 1850, San Francisco. James had never heard of, much less attended such a lavish affair. From his vantage point near the open veranda doors on the terrace level of the recently completed Jenny Lind Theatre, a spectacular panorama of San Francisco was presented. Inside the theatre, he counted at least a dozen men he quickly recognized as the *Crème de la crème* of the city's business and social circles including

Jenny Lind Theatre, San Francisco

his host and the current senator from California, Colonel J. C. Frémont[66] and his wife. A 20-piece orchestra seated with a backdrop of a red-satin-curtained stage, likely capable of playing any waltz that was ever written, serenaded a grand hall filled with couples of tuxedo-tailed men and lavishly gowned women. The couples twirled gracefully around the dance floor. In the wings, more people conversed in groups of four and five taking an occasional sip from a crystal champagne glass and waiting for their turn to *twirl*.

Two weeks earlier Tom Sunderland swaggered to James desk waving a letter in the air

and haughtily asking his partner if he was at all interested in attending a *soirée* in San Francisco to celebrate the last hours of 1850 and the first hours of a new year. All James could do was stare with disbelief at his partner who he was sure had relapsed to his days of throwing back continuous rum shots. Tom told James that he had just received an invitation to attend such an affair, a New Year's Eve party hosted by the Fremonts. Mrs. Fremont

Sen. John C and
Jessie A. Benton Fremont

was the former Jessie Ann Benton[67], daughter of Missouri Senator, and staunch democrat, Thomas Hart Benton. James then asked the obvious question as to how this had all come about and Tom responded that he was afraid his good friend would never ask.

It so happened that Tom had not shared every detail with James about his journey across the Isthmus of Panama or his lengthy stay in the city of Panama. He met Mrs. Fremont when he happened by and helped her and her young daughter from a boat on the Panama dock where they had returned from a picnic on a small picturesque island in the bay. He also had several lengthy visits with *Mrs. F.* while on board the steamer, *S. S. Panama*, that brought them both to San Francisco. Tom had made it a point of making sure Mrs. Fremont and her daughter did not encounter any problems on the final leg of their long journey. When they parted ways at the San Francisco docks, she thanked him for his kindness and attention during the trip and promised to do her best to stay in touch. Tom showed the invitation to James and, sure enough, there was a hand-written note on the bottom asking him to *please come* if he could and it was signed *Jessie*. James was impressed with Tom's heretofore-unknown friend in high places and promptly accepted Tom's request to join him if for no other reason than to see how the other half lived.

James mingled among the rich and famous and before the clock struck midnight he had introduced himself or been introduced to several important San Franciscans including his hosts, the Fremonts, Mexican War naval commander Commodore Robert F. Stockton who was, coincidentally, a good friend of Col. Zabriskie, California's first Governor Peter Burnett, Mayor of San Francisco, John Geary, real estate mogul Joseph Folsom, and Mormon entrepreneur Sam Brannan. James knew of Brannan from his days in Illinois and he had followed his accomplishments particularly after a *run-in* with the Mormon leader, Brigham Young. Young had sent an envoy from Salt Lake City to the coast to get a *tithe* from Brannan for the church headquarters. The wealthy businessman reportedly told the envoy's leader to, *tell Brigham Young that I'll give up the Lord's money when he sends me a receipt signed by the Lord.* When the news of Brannan's comment reached Salt Lake, his name was immediately stricken from the church rolls. After the grand celebration and fireworks at midnight had ended, James reflected on the year just passed as one of the most remarkable and memorable of his life, and he was resolute to have many more in the years to come.

The gold-rush-triggered exploding population and now California's statehood placed a premium on the delivery of mail to the newest state from all parts of the country. The profitability associated with the venture was undeniable. In April of 1848, a group of New York City merchants, led by William Aspinwall formed the Pacific Mail Steam Ship Company and wrenched the government contract for the right to transport mail away from its current holder.[68] By 1850, the company's newly built SS California, SS Oregon, and SS Panama led a fleet of ocean going sail and steam-powered vessels delivering mail by way of the Isthmus of Panama. One ship arrived at either the Caribbean or the Pacific Coast, the mail was taken over land by small boats and mules, and another ship on the opposite coast took the mail to its intended destination.[69] Despite the combined sailing and overland time of between 30 and 35 days between San Francisco and New York, actual mail delivery to and from specific locations, such as Quincy and Sacramento could take the better part of two months. Therefore, in early February of 1851, James received the first response to the various letters he had sent at the end of September the previous year.

3d December '51
Quincy, Ill.

Dear Judge Ralston,

You cannot begin to imagine my joy when Father shared your latest letter with me and my sister. We are all pleased to know that your are acclimating well to your new home in California. In a turnabout, I cannot begin to imagine what it is like in the Golden State though I have tried to gain a hint from the articles and the few and far between sketches that appear in the journals and newspapers. I hope that perhaps someday I can have the excited pleasure to experience first-hand what it is all about.

My affairs in Quincy remain on the whole rather ordinary and hardly worthy of spending the time and paper to make note of them. Were there a way, in my limited vocabulary, to embellish them to the point of worthwhile reading, I would do that. I will simply leave them to your knowledge when last you were here, for little has changed. I must, however, tell you that I so miss the joyful presence of Lizzie, as I am sure do you; I am happy in knowing she is well tended to in your brother and sister-in-law's Kentucky home.

Father continues to be busy in God's work and of course he and Amelia send their very best for your continued health and happiness. Father does not imagine that we will remain for over another year in Quincy, as three years is the usual pastoral assignment in one church. My little sister continues to pester me but since I am convinced she is the apple of our father's eye, I dare not respond in retribution. I have convinced father that we can celebrate Christmas this year in a like manner to the memorable event of last year though I know it will not be quite as joyous; dare I say because of you and your daughter's absence?

I have spent the better part of the last few hours carefully choosing the words of the brief poem I include, in the wish you will read it with interest. It is simply titled, <u>Absent.</u>

Sometimes in reverie the hours are lost
Tho' never the object of cause.
Clear memorable visions of conscious thought
Oft' makes my heartbeat pause.

A wish for the object to be here and now
Will not in the least make it so.
Replacing that wish with prayer and the hope
That one day the absence will go.

Before Father became a minister he earned his living as a blacksmith. I will close this letter with three words of wisdom taken from that profession he has often shared with me when I am sad; <u>always forge ahead.</u>

I am wishing for you the very best, and I remain your dear friend [signed] *Harriet*

There was now little doubt in James' mind that his wish to strike up an ongoing correspondence with Miss Jackson was shared. He reflected on Reverend Jackson's comment, *perhaps someday.*

Chapter 13

Working Things Out

Though there is disagreement as to when American settlers first viewed the glorious Yosemite Valley in the central high Sierras of California, opinions about its abundant scenic beauty and serenity are of a single mind. One of the earlier accounts of viewing the valley was written by a member of the Mariposa Battalion that visited the valley in March of 1851. The battalion was formed and sent to the area by the recently appointed second California governor, John McDougall, on the advice of his assigned envoy, Sacramento city attorney J. Neely Johnson, to quell an uprising of several Indian tribes in the vicinity. The

Yosemite Valley California

outnumbered and out-gunned tribes were quickly dispatched by the battalion in an affair that became known as the Mariposa Indian War that for all intents and purposes lasted only from March through June of 1851. The valley did not become widely known or visited for another few years and soon became, and still is, perhaps **the** most visited *off the beaten path* location in the state. A few years later, the Ralston and Johnson families accompanied a larger group from Sacramento to the valley. James could not keep from laughing out loud when, at their entrance to the valley and in all seriousness, his cousin proudly claimed sole responsibility for its discovery and made matters even more ludicrous when he fell just short of adding Yosemite's natural beauty to that dubious accomplishment.

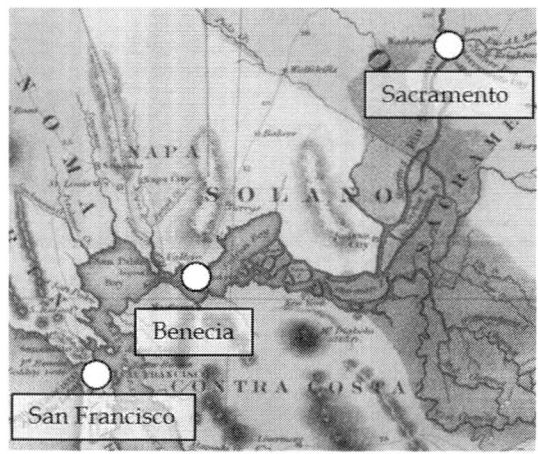

California 1852

In 1851, the Sacramento County Democratic party had several meetings in March and April. An overflowing crowd at an early May torchlight procession beginning at Lee's Exchange then parading a large party banner through the Sacramento business district were all in preparation for the party's state convention. Benecia was to be the convention site and May 19th was the date. At the convention the party would choose its candidates for various state offices and adopt a party platform. Judge Ralston was a leading party *politico* from Sacramento. He was recognized statewide as an experienced politician and effective orator, both of which James proudly wore as badges of success. He was subsequently elected as a vice-president of the convention.

James had known for some time that his cousin had been *seeing* the oldest daughter of his good friend and fellow democrat, J. C. Zabriskie, 21 year-old Mary Brevoort Zabriskie. He had even on occasion, for reasons he never fully understood, provided an alibi to Col. Zabriskie on behalf of the impetuous J. Neely when his cousin was trysting with the proper *Miss Mary B.* Judge Ralston was overjoyed and relieved with the news that the couple had become betrothed. The date chosen for the affair was June 26, 1851, a Thursday, at Sacramento's First Church of Christ Congregational, with the church's pastor Reverend Joseph A. Benton[70] officiating.

For the past two months the lack of rainfall had made the city a dustbowl. The American river on the north side of town was so low that people had taken to fording the river to avoid having to pay a toll to use Lisle's drawbridge. Reports had been received from the Sacramento valley to the north all the way down to the San Joaquin valley in the south that crops would fail if rain was not soon forthcoming. James rose on the morning of the Neely and Zabriskie wedding to a virtual deluge that had turned Sacramento's J street into a torrential stream of water making its way quickly west to the Front street docks and the Sacramento River. People could be seen madly scrambling for higher ground. James suspected that the smiling men he saw still sitting oblivious to the downpour on the boarded sidewalk dangling their feet in the raging water were likely area farmers or citrus orchard owners. About two hours before the blessed affair, the rain left as quickly as it had come. Though the streets resembled a muddy pig sty, the knee-deep water had completely subsided. Then, lo and behold, the sun was shining brightly. James knew his cousin well enough, that any connection between the clearing skies and J. Neely's wedding had to be purely coincidental and not in the least the result of any heavenly interdiction on Neely's behalf..

The standing room only assembly at the church witnessed J. Neely and Miss Mary B. quietly exchange their vows. While sitting in a front row pew, James wondered how the smiling couple kept any signs of mud from their elegant footwear. Standing with Neely was his brother, William, and a good friend David Douglass, and for Miss Zabriskie, her sister Elizabeth, and a Miss Rice. It soon became clear to Judge Ralston why a Thursday was chosen for the nuptials. He heard members of the wedding party mention they were boarding the side-wheel steamer Wilson G. Hunt for a trip down the Sacramento river to San Francisco where the celebration would continue.

Wilson G. Hunt

J. Neely needed to be back at his desk bright and early Monday morning. James finally had the chance to congratulate his cousin, the new bride, and the proud father of the bride at which point Zabriskie asked Judge Ralston if he was planning to join them on their junket to San Francisco. James casually pulled his timepiece from his pocket, opened the case, looked at the dial, and told J. C. that there would just not be enough time left after he cleaned the mud from his shoes. Zabriskie laughed, shook his head, and followed his daughter and new son-in-law to a horse drawn sleigh, an ingenious idea, that would take them sliding through the mud to the waiting steamboat.

For the statewide election in September 1851, the Democrat party officially named Judge Ralston as its candidate for state senator from Sacramento's 11th district in early August. Shortly thereafter, the Whig party nominated the well-known American river drawbridge owner, Daniel J. Lisle, as his esteemed opponent. The two men spent the month of August visiting every corner of the county. They never passed up an opportunity to *say a few words* about their own stellar qualifications and abilities and their dreary opponent's lack thereof. Judge Ralston believed Lisle succeeded in achieving a new low. A week before the election and with *Vote Lisle* posters plastered from truss to wooden truss on his drawbridge, its owner creatively lowered the toll to $ .00 in exchange for a vote. James was sure a case could easily be made for ballot box bribery. However, he feared voters would view such a last minute action as just another example of a two-timing politician trying to line his own satin pockets at the expense of the righteous citizenry.

The election day weather cooperated to the fullest extent of its most congenial ability and long lines formed at the polling stations all over the county. James stationed himself at the Orleans Hotel, doffing his top hat and shaking the hand of each voter before they entered the confines of the first-class establishment. At day's end neither candidate was convinced of a win because the two parties were both well membered in the city. Perhaps the Democrats had a slight edge coming from the county's mining districts. The newspaper had made a generous additional allowance in the number of papers it printed. Within an hour's time of its placement at the outlets, a copy of the September 6th edition of the *Daily Sacramento* containing the county's election results was nowhere to be found. By hook or by crook the Democratic party leadership had an abundance of the valued item. Among the party's celebratory results, James H. Ralston would be one of the newly seated Senators at the third session of the California legislature in Vallejo. Judge Ralston had garnered a 232-vote advantage over his opponent in the Sacramento City wards and he had added to that total from the results of the outlying mining camp polls.[71] James was by far happier with the result of this election than any of those in Illinois. This single outcome confirmed James' belief. The personally devastating contempt he encountered on his return to Quincy was indeed based on the hatred of Mormons as opposed to a basic flaw in his professional ability or in his personal character. It was a proud moment in his life.

Since he first arrived on the coast, to the present time, James had focused relentlessly on building his law firm and building his political reputation. He had not taken full advantage of any opportunity in his busy schedule to rest and relax by doing something, just anything, that did not involve the law, making speeches, or attending countless meetings. J. Neely and Tom Sunderland on several occasions had invited James to join them on *back to nature* forays involving fishing, hunting, and generally enjoying the abundance of scenic beauty that surrounded this place. On every occasion he had artfully but not convincingly declined and the offers stopped. He had also once again fallen seriously behind in keeping his distant family and friends up-to-date on his current affairs. He knew full well he could likely fill a sizeable journal with the details of his activities and accomplishments since his time in California. Now that Senator Ralston had reached a status he had worked so hard to achieve he, at last, seriously considered what was missing in his life. He had not reached very far in this self-examination when he realized what he had really known since the time Jane had passed away and when he last left Lizzie in Lexington. He missed loving companionship and a place to call home. For the sake of his personal happiness James was determined to do something about it.

The judge had written a brief and *polite* response to Harriet's first letter in which she had carefully skirted the issue of building an ongoing relationship with a man 21 years her senior. She had nonetheless made her feelings quite clear. He believed the first task at hand was reading and responding to the unopened letters that were in a neat pile on the corner of his desk. Letters he feared may ask something of him that at the time he was not yet ready to give. He told Tom that he planned to take some time away from the office and get caught up on the affairs he had been altogether neglecting. James saw the relieved look on his partner's face who quickly observed that *it was high time.*

James packed a few of his things in a bedroll. He carefully placed the unopened letters, a pen, several bottles of ink, and several sheets of paper in a satchel that, with the bedroll, he attached to his horse's saddle. He mounted, and rode north along the Sacramento River. He had no particular destination in mind other than to find a spot far from the pressures of his daily routine where he could literally just enjoy the scenic beauty of his new state. He could listen to the sounds of serenity, write, and plan a future that he knew needed to include in the least a home for Lizzie and someone to help him look after her.

For the next ten days he camped in the foothills under the majesty of Lassen Peak with its occasional billows of steam rising from the deep natural fissures in the earth near and around its summit. At last count he had written a dozen lengthy letters to his friends in Quincy, including Dr. J. N. Ralston and his wife Maggie, and a letter to Rev T. N. Ralston and his wife Josephine. He lastly finished a special letter just for Lizzie, in Lexington. Then, he opened a four-page letter from Harriet Jackson who wrote that she and her family were doing well, they were keeping busy, and still awaiting word as to when they would leave Quincy for a place presently unknown. The last two short paragraphs of her letter were of special importance to James and he read them several times over.

I have read and reread your letter of April last, looking for the slightest hint of any feelings you may hold for me in your heart or mind and found none. My twenty-third birthday is fast approaching. Tho' it would not be expected of you to begin to understand the desires of a young woman of age and how her status is generally viewed by the society around her, I must, with some hesitation and dread, help you understand.

With a boldness that is not in my true nature, I will make my feelings for you as plain and clear as I am possible of writing. Since the first time I met you 18 months past, I unashamedly admit to you I was captivated. Father and I have emotionally spoken often on this matter. He, trying to help me see what future, if any, there may be in following the feelings of my heart to fruition or trying to cope with closure. I am compelled to tell you my feelings for you cannot be ended as simply as breath can quell a candle's flame. I would like, no, I must know if there is a place within your being that may share a whit of my feelings.

I am, praying for more than a friendship, your [signed] Harriet

James had at last come to a clear conclusion about a relationship with Harriet and decided that she, with Lizzie, should be an integral part of his life in California, and he wrote to her at some length, telling her that very thing.

Judge Ralston returned to Sacramento as invigorated as he had ever remembered being, looking forward to having Lizzie and possibly Harriet by his side and ready to take his seat in the 1852 legislature at Vallejo. Tom noticed Judge Ralston's new frame of mind and he recommended that his esteemed partner make a regular habit of such absences.

Chapter 14

Meet Me in Manhattan

On New Year's Eve, 1851, the loud shriek heard from the Jackson home in Quincy, brought a response from every alert canine in the block. It could likely have also been heard by attentive listeners in far-away Sacramento. The entirely unladylike sound erupting from Harriet's lungs was in response to the first few lines of the letter she read from James that was delivered just minutes earlier. She wept and whimpered with happiness and sat alone repeatedly reading the letter until at last she was tearless. Harriet shared the news on the arrival of Amelia. The two of them held hands dancing the entire width and breadth of their parlor several times before Harriet breathlessly collapsed on the settee, still in utter disbelief of her news from the West Coast. Amelia laid out a menu of Harriet's favorite foods for a celebratory evening meal. At top speed Amelia was out the door with a list of groceries, nearly knocking over her father on the front steps as she charged by to complete her sole mission of getting to the general store. The inquisitive Rev. Jackson walked through the door and he was again nearly toppled by Harriet's rush to his arms. After tearfully sharing her news, her father gently smiled and told her it appeared as though, *perhaps someday*, may actually be a nearing reality. Then he cautioned her not to be too enthusiastic because, he said with a sly smile, men too are known to be fickle. He then thought to himself that Judge Ralston had never been known to break a promise, even if he suffered mightily for it. The words James used from the letter that meant the most to Harriet, she would keep in a pendant locket around her neck; *could you consider standing by my daughter's side and mine.*

Monday morning, January 5, 1852, the 3rd California legislature convened in what was expected to be a new capital building and attendant lodging overlooking Vallejo's San Pablo bay. Instead, newly seated Senator Ralston, the other senators, and the lower house of assembly, found the buildings promised by General Mariano Guadalupe Vallejo, the benefactor of 156 acres of land and $370,000 in building costs for use as the state capital site, had not yet been built. After spending 11 days in a leaking wooden structure using whiskey barrels for makeshift seating, the legislature picked up lock, stock, but no barrel, and promptly reconvened at the Court House in Sacramento on Friday, January 16th. Senator Ralston was appointed to the corporation and library committees of the senate and later in the session he was added to the judiciary committee.

On the 28th of January the senate and the assembly met in joint session to elect a United States senator from California. After statehood was gained in September of 1850, the first senator, Colonel John C. Fremont, was elected by the state's legislature for a term expiring March 4th, 1851. At the expiration of his term, the 2nd legislature had failed to elect another senator and the state's seat in the United States senate had gone unfilled since that time; it would now be filled. James knew that his name had been mentioned as a candidate for the prestigious position but he also knew his chances of being elected were somewhere south of none. Senator Ralston was still pleased when his name, among eight others, was placed in nomination. The total number of votes in both the senate and the assembly was 89, and a simple majority of 45 votes was required to elect a senator. By the fourth round of voting, Senator Ralston received the 4th highest number of votes, nine. The following day James withdrew his name from contention and gave his endorsement to fellow democrat, John B. Weller, the former United States Senator from Ohio; the lesser of the two evils[72] of the remaining Democratic front-runners. The legislative session ended on the 5th of May and James returned to leading his law firm on a full-time basis, now more widely known and admired than when he first entered the senate chamber.

At about the mid-point in the just ended legislative session, Judge Ralston received a letter from his brother in Quincy telling him that Dr. Ralston's son Virgil Young[73] had decided to make the overland journey to California. V. Y. was James' favorite nephew in spite of the fact he was as ardent a Whig party member as his uncle was a Democrat. His brother had asked James to keep an eye out for his son's arrival likely sometime in August. Uncle James was not surprised when his nephew strolled into his office in early September and he was very glad to see that he had made it to the safe confines of Sacramento. The two men embraced and James was anxious to compare experiences with V. Y.'s account of his arduous trek halfway across the continent.

James could not refrain from laughing when his nephew shared his account about his 4th of July oration on the Sweetwater River near Devil's Gate, Indian Territory. V. Y. and several of his young traveling companions had visited Independence Rock earlier in the morning to carve their names on the granite outcropping and had celebrated their achievement with a bit too much fermented liquid refreshment. They arrived back at the wagon train just in time to join in honoring the women's handmade *Old Glory* nailed atop a makeshift forty-foot pole. The travelers were singing Key's Star Spangled Banner, accompanied by two accordions, a violin, and

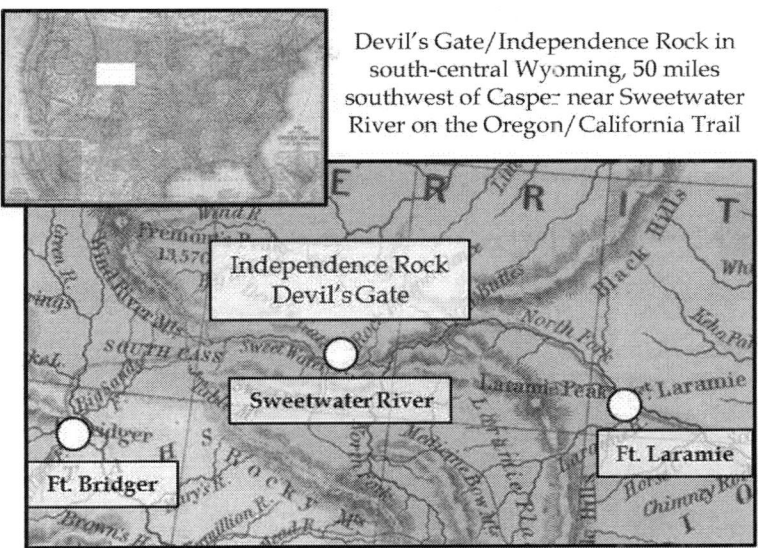

Devil's Gate/Independence Rock in south-central Wyoming, 50 miles southwest of Casper near Sweetwater River on the Oregon/California Trail

United States 1853

several harmonicas. The gathered crowd then demanded a speech in honor of the special occasion and several of the pioneers nominated the well-spoken Ralston, not being aware of his present state of non-sobriety. V. Y. was lifted on the shoulders of his drinking mates to the back of a wagon where it was reported *he spoke for over a half an hour, and delivered, off-hand, an excellent oration.*[74] James' nephew summed up his trip with words that his Uncle believed rang quite true, *if there is anything in this world that will bring to the surface a man's bad traits, it is a trip across the continent with an ox team.* James asked V. Y. about his plans and he jokingly responded he thought he would try his hand at picking up nuggets barehanded along the American River then make a sizeable deposit at the local bank before claim jumpers *got wind* of his good fortune. He added seriously that he and his friends would head to the foothills to pan for any gold that might still be left. James wished his nephew luck and reminded him that he would help if ever the need arose. James kept in touch with V. Y. who would settle for a time in Diamond Springs, west of Sacramento, before returning to Quincy.

Second term Senator Ralston entered the 4th session of the California state legislature on January 3, 1853 starting the session in Vallejo. If the still ongoing construction was not completed, it was agreed the senators and assemblymen would move the proceedings to nearby Benecia. Senator Ralston suffered a brief illness during the session but nonetheless still found a way to be the chairman of the legislature's Judiciary Committee and was again a member of the Corporation Committee. The session ended on the 19th of May 1853.

At the mid-point of the ended legislative session, an event occurred that corresponded almost too perfectly with James' personal intentions to marry Miss Harriet Newell Jackson sometime in the near future. Harriet now lived on Staten Island, a short distance across the upper Hudson River bay from New York City. The three members of the Jackson family moved to the island coming from Quincy in early November of 1852. Reverend Jackson had been called to the island's North Baptist Church on Staten Island where he faced the challenging duty of closing a serious rift in the congregation caused by a truly minor difference in the interpretation of the biblically described life of John the Baptist. Aaron Jackson was considered among the pre-eminent biblical scholars in the denomination and he was confident he could mitigate the differences in short order.

Harriet had recently written in one of her many letters to the man she loved about her move to what she called an island not unlike that of Robinson Crusoe. Save for her father and her sister, Harriet felt isolated and alone in her new surroundings despite the huge populous of the surrounding cities. She wanted her knight in shining armor to rescue her. James could not wait to write Harriet telling her of his latest news and hoping that the letter would arrive in New York in time for the needed arrangements to be made.

18th March '53
Sacramento, Cal.

Dearest Harriet,

The news I have to share with you should soon brighten your spirits and provide a clearly lit pathway to our future.

Yesterday, I received a communique from Governor Bigler asking me if I would accept his nomination for me to attend the New York Exhibition of Industry as a representative from this great state. His words expressing confidence in my cordial manner and speaking ability that he believed would favorably represent his dominion, were kindly received. I did not waste a moment in composing a written reply accepting his generous offer.

My plans, as yet, are incomplete tho' it would be my intent to leave from San Francisco in mid-June or very early July, depending on the steamship schedules, and arrive at the port of your fair city not later than the third week of July. Joining me on the trip will be Captain Douglas Ottinger, a fine seaman of earlier California exploration in Humboldt Bay. I have had the pleasure to meet him on one occasion. He, along with representatives of Adams and Company will be escorting a gold exhibit destined for the exhibition that the governor's letter says has a worth in excess of $80,000, making me generally unsettled. I am hopeful you can regularly join with me as a partner in my exhibition assignment.

After my time at the exhibition, my thoughts are that I would travel to Quincy by way of Lexington with the express intent of gathering my beloved Lizzie and returning with her to New York. With your agreement, I would be the happiest man in the world if you would become my wife! In more direct language, will you marry me? After the happy nuptials the three of us could then book passage to return to San Francisco and Sacramento where a surprise awaits you; no, I will not say what it is.

I will patiently await your answer to the primary question posed in the letter, hopeful that it will arrive prior to my departure. In the event it does not, God willing, you can speak your answer to me on the passenger ramp at the New York docks.

I am wishing to be your husband & most obt. svt.

[signed] James

James letter was greeted at the small Jackson home on Staten Island in May with the force of a *nor'easter*, mercilessly battered and flooded by waves of Harriet's joyful emotions. She faintly remembered hearing her sister begging to join the newly wedded couple on their return trip to the western most coast of the continent and the look of abandonment on her father's face that forced a faint smile. She did not particularly care when her love's ship arrived in port. She was more than willing to make her new home at the docks, if necessary, waiting to catch the first glimpse of his face and running to his open arms. She added the words *will you marry me,* in her locket knowing for certain her *knight* was now on his way.

The secret James would not share with his intended was the result of a purposeful search he had completed less than a month earlier. In the hopeful anticipation of having a family to care for in a home of their own, he purchased 175 acres[75] of meadowland east of Sacramento about ¼ mile south of the American River. He knew the land might flood but he also knew from his time in the legislature a levee was planned for that area to encourage homesteading. James thought this should be more than enough land for father and daughter horseback rides, planting of grape vines, and the privacy he so much needed to be able to enjoy his time away from the office. He would leave the naming of the property to Harriet after they built their home.

Judge Ralston kept the memories close of Tom Sunderland's story about his 1849 journey from New Orleans to San Francisco by way of the Panama Isthmus and about the malaria that plagued his brother. He nervously stood on San Francisco's Pacific dock on July 1st next to Captain Ottinger about to board the Steam Ship Sierra Nevada. His trip was of the same nature as that of his partner, only crossing from the Pacific to the Caribbean by way of the Nicaragua Isthmus and steaming to New York's harbor. He knew the uneasiness he felt was a foreboding trifecta of Sunderland's tale, his first open ocean voyage, and the $80,000 in gold he knew was stored somewhere below decks. When James overheard two crewmen discussing how good the ship looked despite its collision with the SS Golden Gate in early May, his anxiety was nearly over the top. Captain Ottinger noticed the pallor of his traveling companion's face. Ottinger told him that in his many years at sea he had never seen such color until after boarding the ship and rolling to-and-fro for a few minutes on the open ocean waves. Seeing that Judge Ralston was not in the least encouraged by his words, he added that the same experience also resulted in such a voyager usually finding his *sea legs* in a very short time. Matters did in fact get worse for James with Ottinger's emphasis on the word *usually* as the judge politely excused himself for the short walk to the dock's edge to heave the sumptuous breakfast he now wished he had not eaten. James knew this was an auspicious start to the nearly 5,000 miles yet ahead. He returned to the captain's side determined to have nothing but positive thoughts starting with the image of a joyful Harriet coming to greet him on the docks in New York.

At the top of the passenger ramp, Judge Ralston was heartily greeted by the ship's captain, J. H. Blethen, wishing him the best of luck on his trip to the New York exhibition. The Sierra Nevada, under steam and sail, passed through the Golden Gate narrows heading for open sea and a trip of about 10 days south to the Nicaraguan port of San Juan del Sur [southern]. The ship would make three stops along the way to pick up coal for the twin-engine steam boilers that powered two propellers and a large water wheel on each side of the ship. The newspaper description of the first-class cabin James and Captain Ottinger entered was not in the least misleading. It was roomy, above deck, and had two windows that on a clear day provided a magnificent view of the hazy outline of the far-distant mainland. Staying true to his oath of being positive, Judge Ralston was also glad the $350 stateroom cost was being paid from the limited coffers of the California state government. About two days out from their destination, Captain Blethen spread the word that there were no reports of illness in Guatemala, the roads were in excellent order, and the stage of the river was satisfactory for the isthmus crossing. Words that James' greeted with pure delight.

On the 12th of July the ship docked and Judge Ralston and Captain Ottinger among the other 450 passengers began their trek of 135 miles from the Pacific to the Caribbean. The first twelve miles was covered by wagon on a plank road to the western shore of Lake Nicaragua where river steamers boarded passengers and luggage across the lake and down the San Juan river. At the Castilian rapids there was a 900-foot portage around the rapids where more river steamers took the travelers to the Caribbean port of San

Juan del Norte [northern], known to the gringos as Greytown or just San Juan. A few
hours short of four days and
three nights on the journey,
sleeping in primitive quarters,
dining on meals of unknown
origins, and swatting legions of
attacking   fingernail-size
mosquitoes,   the   *argonauts*
caught   the   first   welcoming
sight   of   their   destination.
Moored   at   the   dock   was   the

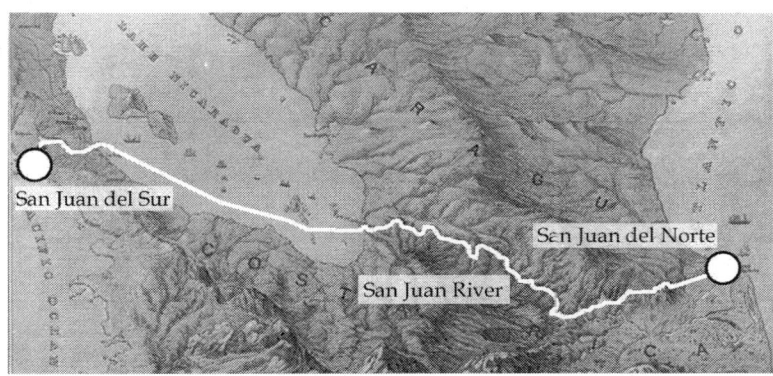

Isthmus of Guatemala

dark green painted wooden hull of the 254-foot three-mast ocean going steamship,
Northern Light. Given fair winds and calm seas, the ship would deliver them to the
port of New York in just a week's time.

The Northern Light with Captain Thomas Minor at the helm left San Juan del Norte on
the 17th of July heading for New York under full steam and sail. The warm breezes and
calmer waters of the Caribbean more favorably suited Judge Ralston's taste in ocean
travel than the Pacific. He spent more time roaming the main deck and stopping
occasionally to gaze mindlessly at the horizon from the ship's rail, until the afternoon of
the second day at sea. Dark rolling clouds began to gather and in the distance James
saw frequent streaks of lightning from cloud to water. The ever-closer sounds of
thunder chased him to the safety of his cabin, arriving just in time to hear a deafening
clap of thunder immediately followed by the horrifying sound of wood splitting.
Ottinger quickly recognized the agonizing sound as one of the ship's masts failing to
endure the direct hit of a lightning bolt. He ordered James to take cover under his bunk
in the event the massive solid oak spire fell on the cabin ceiling. James' quickly followed
orders and fearfully waited for the *sky to fall*. He relaxed his white knuckle hold on the
floor to bunk wooden post when Ottinger said he would go survey the damage and
return to the cabin with a report. He returned moments later. The lightning had indeed
split the top half of the mainmast, the crew was in the process of lowering the sail, and
James was cleared to emerge from his positon of safety. Within hours the crew had
securely wrapped the damaged mast with thick-chorded rope, the sail was set. With the
storm having passed, the Northern Light, thankfully proceeded on its course only
slightly the worse for wear. James discovered that the dreadful encounter with Mother
Nature's wrath had occurred just off Cape San Antonio on the westward most tip of
Cuba. He made a mental note to be at his best attention at that spot should the return
voyage pass the same location.

On the 24th of July, every passenger, including James and Douglas Ottinger lined the main deck rails as the ship made its way toward New York's harbor. At James' request, Ottinger pointed out each-and-every landmark as the vessel made its way toward the

Hubert Sattler, New York, NY 1854
View Northwest from Williamsburg in the Borough of Brooklyn, the site of the 1870 Brooklyn Bridge

wharf on the Hudson River just above Battery Park. There, it would anchor off shore in the quarantine area for a full day to assure no contagious diseases, contraband cargo, or stowaways were onboard. James took immediate advantage of the Nicaragua Steamship Company's service of delivering messages to those wishing to meet loved ones and acquaintances dockside the next day.

24 July '53
SS Northern Light
New York harbor

Deliver to North Baptist Church, Richmond, Staten Island, New York
Attention to Rev. Aaron Jackson

I have arrived in New York and will be disembarking on the morrow.

[signed] *J. H.*

James was just sure the combined weight of the large gathering of ship greeters could send the wharf, to which the Northern Light was securely moored, crashing into the Hudson River. The eagerly awaited passengers slowly began to descend the long passenger ramp to *terra firma*. He knew his turn would come to take the first few giddy steps on land. He hoped that his inner ears equilibrium, used to being on the rolling sea, would

Among the passengers by the *Northern Light* are Capt. D. OTTINGER, U. S. N., and Judge RALSTON, of Sacramento, delegates appointed to represent the State of California in the World's Fair Convention at New-York

New York Daily Times, 7/26/1853

soon discover its new surroundings and quickly make the necessary adjustment. He slowly scanned the assemblage from his vantage point at the wharf-side railing looking for any signs of the Jackson three or more specifically the one love-letter-writing Jackson he had not seen for over three years. Finally, standing purposefully apart at the far reaches of the mass of humanity on the wharf, he barely made out the figure of Harriet standing between her father and sister, furiously waving the brightest red neck scarf he had ever seen. The closer he came to the top of the ramp, the closer the scarlet scarf came to the ramp's bottom resting on the wharf. When he could clearly see her face, he more calmly returned her still excited salute. Judge Ralston's first step on the wharf was predictably unsteady then, much like the parting of the Red Sea, a path between James and Harriet was cleared. Nearly identical to his image of the event, his *all grown up* lovely fiancé came rushing to his arms loudly repeating the single word, *yes!*, until her voice was quieted in a tender embrace.

Chapter 15

I Do

James had never seen such a magnificent structure. The so-called *Crystal Palace* had been painstakingly constructed in 1853 with no expense spared specifically for housing the Exhibition of the Industry of All Nations. It was truly a world's fair that the bustling city of New York gladly agreed to host. The building was directly

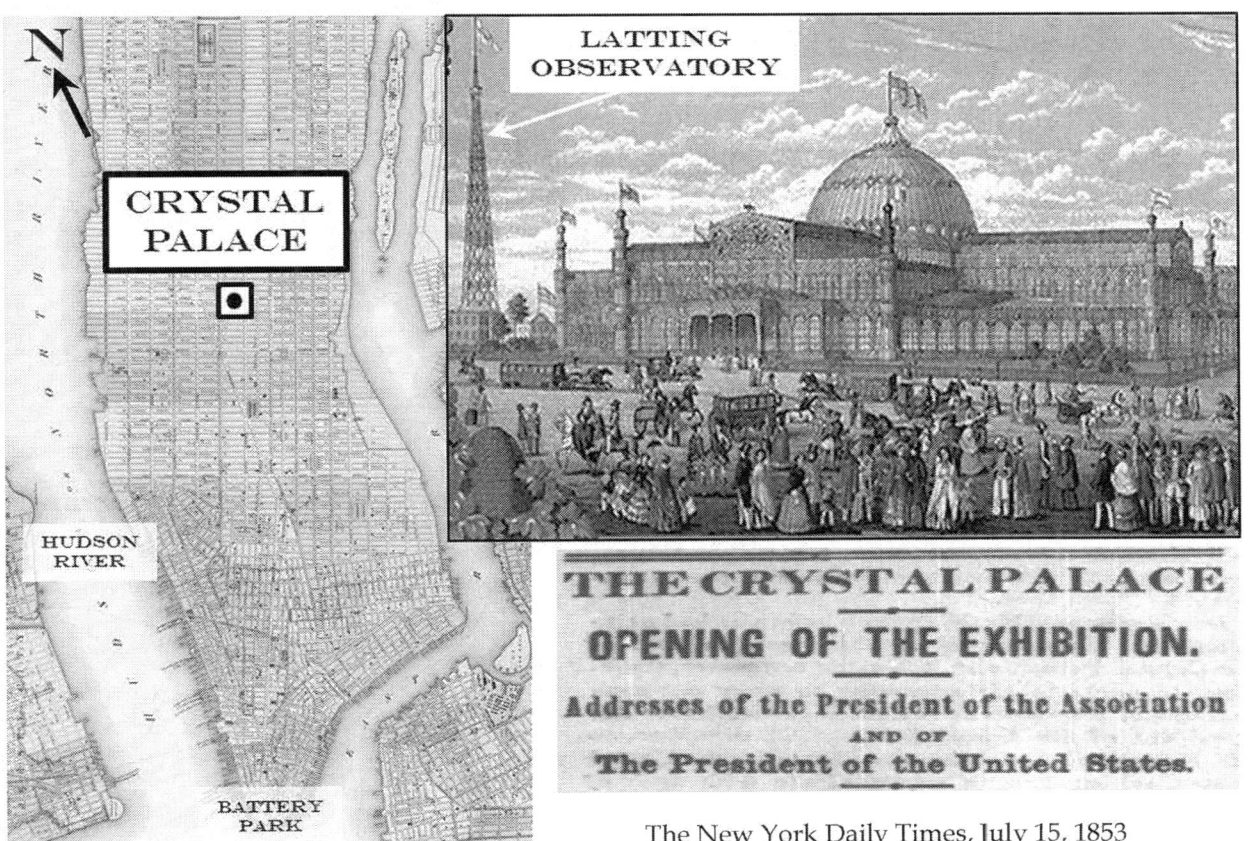

The New York Daily Times, July 15, 1853

inspired by the site of the highly successful *Great Exhibition* held in London's Hyde Park two years before. New York's version, built between 5th and 6th Avenues on 42nd Street behind Croton Reservoir[76] was in the shape of a Greek cross crowned by a dome 100 feet in diameter. Like the London building, it was almost completely made of glass, framed with iron beams. The adjoining 315 foot wooden *Latting Observatory* allowed visitors a scenic panoramic view of Manhattan Island, Brooklyn, Queens, the Hudson River Bay, 18 miles to the southwest to Staten Island, and beyond.

Harriet stood by James' side nearly every day for the next two weeks as his *assistant*. She took the early morning Staten Island and New York Ferry Company's steamer to Manhattan island , then a carriage to the Crystal Palace and reversing the trip in the late afternoon. Judge Ralston had never shaken so many hands or kissed so many babies over such a long period of time. Wave after wave of exhibition visitors gazed in wonderment on the glittering display of California gold and quartz guarded, mostly for show, by four of New York City's finest armed police officers. He had arrived at the world's fair too late to join in the festivities of the grand opening ceremony and the opportunity to meet fellow Democrat, President Franklin Pierce. Nonetheless, he still shared with an excited and awestruck Harriet the occasional visit of an important diplomat or capitalist from places in the world he never knew existed. Both James and Harriet found the experience to be wonderfully tiring.

Wedding plans had been first and foremost on Harriet's mind since her future husband arrived in New York. When, at a break in Judge Ralston's duties at the exhibition, they both agreed that the third week of October would be the date of the long-awaited event, she joined her fiancé in a happy celebration.

James' agenda, without Harriet, for the next few weeks included plans to visit his brothers and friends in Quincy then on to Lexington, Kentucky for a much-anticipated reunion with his daughter Elizabeth. Lizzie had taken up residence with his brother Thomas and his wife Josephine shortly after he had left for California four years earlier. The letters he received from the childless couple described in detail the loving care and attention they gave his daughter.

For some time James' pondered the question of Lizzie joining Harriet and him in New York for the wedding and traveling with them on their return trip to Sacramento after the nuptials. His concern was not who would care for his daughter while he worked, since Harriet had repeatedly expressed her happy wish to be a loving mother to Lizzie. Rather, he was worried about the arduous lengthy trip , the suitability of Sacramento's evolving, yet in many ways still primitive rough and tumble setting, and the absence of a comfortable home for his 8 year-old daughter. During his trip to Illinois and Kentucky he planned to gain more advice on the subject from his brothers.

The much-improved combination of railroad and overland travel from New York to Quincy allowed James to arrive in his former hometown in less than a week after his August departure. Judge Ralston returned to Quincy much more a celebrity than on his return from the war nearly 4 years before. Since his time in Sacramento, word of his accomplishments had spread throughout the area and there were many more than just a few relatives who were anxious to *meet and greet* J. H. Ralston's return to the town high on the Mississippi bluffs. After all, California state senator Ralston had nearly succeeded the storied explorer Col. J. C. Fremont as the United States Senator from the country's newest state. Moreover, he was bound to have first-hand knowledge and could no doubt provide sound advice as to the wisdom of still striking it rich in the California goldfields. The size of the crowd that stood patiently waiting for his arriving stagecoach took James completely and pleasantly by surprise. James' eyes filled with tears as he embraced his siblings and shook the many hands of well-wishing friends who reaffirmed his standing as one of Quincy's favorite sons.

> ☞ We learn that Hon. James H. Ralston, of California, (formerly of Quincy,) arrived yesterday. He is one of the Commissioners for the State of California at the World's Fair.
>
> The Quincy Whig, 8/29/1853

James could not believe his eyes when he saw Lizzie a week later in Lexington. The tallish young girl standing in front of him was nearly a perfect image of her mother. She was barely recognizable from the five-year-old that he kissed and cradled tightly in his arms before he mounted his horse and fell into line behind a wagon train headed west. The many years of her life away from James were evident as she shyly approached him and hesitatingly gave a hug to the stranger she barely knew as her father. He could also tell that the Reverend Thomas and Mrs. Josephine Ralston had coached their niece when she asked, with genuine interest, for him to tell her all about California, the World's Fair, the Crystal palace, and how her friend Harriet was doing. The discussion of those subjects and others lasted well into the evening as Lizzie's uncle and aunt approvingly watched her slowly warm to stories told by her long absent father. For the next week father and daughter were inseparable, sharing nearly every waking moment on horseback rides in the country, walking hand-in-hand to see her school in Lexington, and sitting on Thomas' front porch just talking. James was nearly unable to cope with the many tears of sadness Lizzie shed when she discovered that a little more time needed to pass before she could permanently join Harriet and her father in Sacramento. He may have been able to find the words to convince state legislators, governors, and army generals to agree with his point of view, yet he could not find the right words to make his daughter feel the least bit better about his departure to New York and then to California without her by his side.

Amidst the billowing steam from the locomotive, Harriet ran to meet James as he stepped from his passenger car to the train depot platform. She immediately looked around expecting to see Lizzie and she was upset when she learned of his decision that his daughter would join them in Sacramento in the not-too-distant future. He had trouble explaining to his intended why the decision was made, without giving away his secret land purchase and the plans of building a home for Harriet and Lizzie. He was finally able to change the subject when he asked how the wedding arrangements were progressing. Harriet's frown turned to a smile as she told him the marriage would take place at her father's church in Staten Island, her sister Mary would be her maid of honor, and that Rev. Jackson would perform the ceremony. When she asked about who would stand with her fiancé as his best man, James believed that Captain Ottinger would agree to make the wedding party complete.

On the 21st of October, the first full day of their lives together, James and Harriet, with a stunning diamond ring predominately displayed on her left hand, stood at the railing of the steamship Star of the West waving good-bye to her family. The ship would take them on their honeymoon to their new home in Sacramento, stopping first in San Juan,

10/21/1853   **Passengers Sailed.**
In steamship *Star of the West,* for San Juan, Nicaragua.— J. H. Ralston and wife

Nicaragua [Greytown], crossing the isthmus, and connecting with the same steamer, Sierra Nevada that James was aboard in July. Then, to San Francisco, boarding a river steamer to Sacramento. James had thoroughly briefed Harriet about what to expect on the 27-day journey. Watching out for storms off the west coast of Cuba, doing her best to keep the Nicaraguan jungle mosquitos from carrying her off to South America's Cape Horn, and personally making sure that the captain avoided ramming another ship. The two *steamer* trunks full of Harriet's *bare necessities* were aptly named. Not that the trunks were to be loaded on a steamer, but because lashed together they could serve as a backup vessel, the *SS Harriet Ralston's trunks*. Needless to say, the two brawny deckhands who lugged them to the Ralston's first-class cabin had few good words to say about their task, not to mention the miniscule gratuity James gave them for the effort. Unseen by James, Harriet added a substantial amount to the gratuity to avoid any possibility of his mysterious and unsolved disappearance at sea.

Every aspect of the uneventful journey was of excitement and eye-opening discovery for Harriet. She particularly enjoyed stationing herself at the bow of the ship with the wind blowing her hair and watching an occasional dolphin pod escorting the vessel toward its destination. Or, viewing the flying fish that seemed to remain endlessly airborne just above the waves. James was not sure how to corral Harriet's reaction to the site of a breaching humpback whale in the Monterey Bay though at a minimum he made sure she did not somersault over the railing. Passing through the Golden Gate strait and viewing the hundreds of ships of all sizes and shapes anchored in the San Francisco harbor nearly took her breath away. At trips end, she was just sure there  could never be another experience to match this most glorious journey. James knew then and there his new wife's adventurous spirit would allow her to feel quite at home in Sacramento.

The very moment Harriet stepped from the river steamer to the Sacramento dock she turned to James and asked him what surprise he had in store for her. James was taken aback because he had incorrectly assumed that his wife had completely forgotten about the brief mention of his secret. He barely remembered the faint memory of promising her he would share it with her in Sacramento. They were now officially in Sacramento and Harriet wanted to know about the surprise; another lesson learned about his new bride.

Oh yes, the surprise. James and Harriet took a carriage ride that ended about two miles east of Sacramento. The judge helped his new bride from the carriage and told her to fix her gaze directly in front. He asked Harriet if she could imagine a Spanish style hacienda facing the foothills of the Sierra Nevada. She could not, saying that to her best recollection she had never seen or heard of a hacienda. James cleared his throat and rephrased his description. Could she image a spacious home where she, Lizzie, and he could live with lots of room for a growing family. Harriet screeched with delight and gave James a big hug and a kiss. *Yes*, she responded with a broad smile, *I could very clearly see that!*

Chapter 16

Home Comings

At the beginning of 1853 James and Thomas Sunderland decided it was in both of their interests to end their two and a half year partnership and, still the best of friends, go their separate ways.[77] Now, in late November, James purposefully did not see a single client nor open a law book spending the better part of the next two weeks helping Harriet to become familiar with her new surroundings. They needed to find a place to live while construction was underway for their new home. Just when the couple were sure they would find nothing that would meet their temporary housing needs, the manager of the Orleans Hotel took pity on the Ralstons and offered them a room at a monthly rate far below the total amount of 30 nightly stays. *Pity* was not exactly the word best describing the manager's action since Senator Ralston knew well and was well known by the hotel's owner and present Mayor of Sacramento, James R. Hardenbergh. The bottom line was that Harriet had very comfortable though somewhat cramped accommodations, James would be near his office, the stay, based on their builder's estimates, might be at the very most six months, and the cost was very affordable.

J. Neely and Mary B. Johnson were the first to make a call on the Ralstons at the Orleans after their return to Sacramento. They came bearing gifts for the newlyweds that included one of the finest and largest silver sets Harriet had ever seen. She was just sure that the ornate teapot would hold enough liquid to satisfy the whole of Sacramento's citizenry. Mary B. told the couple that she and her husband would very much like to plan a grand social occasion at their new home to introduce Harriet to the *movers and shakers* of the city. J. Neely was humorously quick to add that he could also use the event to rub elbows with his important Whig party friends while, on the other side of the room, James could mingle with the Democratic Party elite. Harriet wanted to know who would keep the two sides from quarrelling and James suggested that special care should be taken to invite Colonel Fremont who could no doubt arrange for a militia to be standing nearby at the ready. The four laughed and the Ralstons said they would be delighted and honored to attend the social soirée.

Some of the finest carriages in the state carrying a select group of dignitaries with their wives began to arrive at the Johnson home on Sacramento's F Street about seven in the evening on Saturday, December 3, 1853. Mary B. had spared no expense in tastefully presenting her lovely new home in an inviting warm glow. Luminaries lined the circular carriage path and leading up the steps to the front door. Candles softly lit each of the four tall windows facing the street and evergreen branches formed a garland hung from the railing of the second floor balcony. Few introductions were necessary as each of the couples entered the door to the living room where they were greeted by the formally

J. Neely Johnson home
in Sacramento, built in 1853

attired Johnsons and Ralstons. From the back of the luxuriously appointed living room, a pianist seated at a grand piano imported from New York accompanied a distinguished violinist softly rendering the favorite classical music of the day.

The guests in attendance were the crème de la crème of Sacramento's wealthy. John Sutter whose extensive land holdings included the site of the mill near the spot of discovery on the American River that spawned the gold rush. John Bigler the state's

Living room's 19th century square grand
piano in the present-day Johnson home.

current Governor, John B. Weller, U. S. Senator, Sacramento Mayor Hardenbergh, the Ralston's landlord. Neely's father-in-law and attorney, Judge James Zabriskie, Josiah and Leland Stanford, two of the six brothers in the process of amassing a fortune as general merchants, and Johnson's law partners Ferris Forman, and James' good friend Tom Sunderland. The evening's festivities included a multi-course French cuisine candlelit dinner, dancing, and the expected discussions of the pressing financial and political topics of the day. On the Ralston's ride back to the Orleans, Harriet was still in a state of joyous disbelief over her good fortune of attending her first ever formal affair let alone in the company of so many important people. James asked her what the most memorable part of the evening had been and with no hesitation she answered, *being by your side.*

A letter arrived in mid-December from James' brother Thomas with further details about the possibility of Lizzie joining her father in Sacramento. The judge and Reverend Ralston had discussed in general terms what options may be available for such a trip when James stopped by Lexington on his way back to New York from Quincy. Since that time he had been unsuccessful in forgetting the tears and the look on his daughter's face when she learned he would leave without her.

27 Nov. '53

Brother,

A brief note for you in consideration of Lizzie's trip to her new home in California. Good news I believe!

My good friend and fellow clergyman Joshua Soule[78] shared with me his plans to travel by ship from New Orleans to San Francisco to preside at the statewide gathering of the Methodist Episcopal followers at Stockton in mid-February next. With your approval, he, and his fellow travelers, would be pleased to escort Lizzie on their upcoming trip. His entourage will include his personal physician should a need for his assistance arise. Please respond at your earliest.

Neely

Before he had time to share the glorious news with his wife, James' affirmative response was on its way to San Francisco destined for the next mail steamship leaving the port. When she learned of the plan, Harriet was ecstatic and immediately rushed to the Orleans front desk to reserve an adjacent room especially for Elizabeth, three full months in advance of her arrival.

In early February of 1854, Judge Ralston was so consumed by his practice that it became evident he sorely needed to find a new law partner. A young attorney from Missouri, George May, had recently given up his backbreaking and financially fruitless practice of panning for gold in the Sierra foothills. He joined James as an apprentice in preparation for being officially admitted to the California bar. For nearly two months after being

> J. H. RALSTON.   GEORGE MAY.
> **RALSTON & MAY,**
> Attorneys at Law.
> Office, Read's Building, between I and J streets, on 3d.
> No. 15, up stairs.   r6
>
> Sacramento Daily Union, 2/6/1854

admitted, he and the judge worked closely together until it was time for May to test his wings and open his own practice in nearby Marysville. The search was again underway, this time for a more experienced partner.

On February 17th, 1854, James and Harriet were dockside in San Francisco as the familiar view of Pacific Mail Steamship, Sierra Nevada, made her way to port. Three months before, they had been travelers on Captain Blethen's vessel and this time they were greeters, anxious to catch first sight of Lizzie. They both knew she would be at the ship's railing taking in the many sights and sounds of the arrival as they had been. Not a hundred yards from the wharf Harriet tugged on James arm. She pointed to the figure of a young girl near the ship's bow holding hands between two distinguished men unmistakably dressed in clerical garb. James confirmed his wife's sighting of Lizzie and they both waved until they were spotted and their greeting was joyfully returned. Bishop Soule was the first traveler to descend the passenger ramp still tightly holding Lizzie's hand. Before he even considered acknowledging the half-dozen or so news reporters and a large assembly of the church faithful, the stately cleric purposefully walked to James and Harriet. He told the couple that Reverend Thomas Neely Ralston sent his best wishes. He was pleased to complete his most delightful duty of delivering a charming intelligent young lady to the waiting arms of her father. Harriet curtsied and with Lizzie now in James' arms, he freed one hand for a firm handshake to greet his Eminence. He thanked the Bishop for a job well done and assured the popular religious leader that he would not allow the next Methodist Episcopal collection plate he encountered to pass by him unfilled. The Bishop laughed, wished for God's blessing on the Ralston family, and returned to greet the crowd. Harriet was thrilled that Elizabeth remembered, or was coached to remember, her, from their days together in Quincy and the three of them left the San Francisco dock hand-in-hand; next stop, Sacramento.

William Cyrus Wallace had come overland to California from Missouri in 1849 with his law books stacked in his oxen-pulled wagon. In 1850, he was elected Sacramento County's first District Attorney, and he had recently returned from his home state where he was married to his childhood sweetheart in December of 1853. When James first learned of W. C.'s desire to get back into private practice, he made a point of seeking out the experienced 31 year-old. He was glad when W. C. agreed to join him. Like his first partner Tom Sunderland, William was a Mason and he had strong ties to the Whig Party, a shortcoming James had overlooked with Tom and was sure he could find a way to do the same with W. C. During the first year of their partnership, Wallace also conveniently served as

William C. Wallace

Sacramento's City Attorney and W. C.'s wife, Mary[79], and Harriet became the best of friends.

Now that Lizzie joined them, Judge Ralston's insistent and head-strong young wife had made it quite clear to her beloved husband that he could no longer spend the number of hours at work to which he was accustomed. He needed to spend less time meeting with clients, scouring the books in his law library, and preparing his patented non-flowery to-the-point speeches. He, in company with her and Lizzie, occasionally needed to devote time to affairs of interest to his female family members, though she clearly understood Sacramento was not by any account the hub of the societal and entertainment universe. In March of 1854, there were two events unusual to the city that happened to be planned for the same period. Harriet was determined, however reluctant James might be, to have all of the Ralston family in attendance.

English born prima donna, Madam Anna Bishop, one of the finest operatic sopranos of

Madam Anna Bishop

the time, performed worldwide with her second husband, French harpist Nicholas-Charles Bochsa. The two had just completed a critically acclaimed standing room only three-week engagement in San Francisco. The couple and their agent had agreed to perform in the much smaller venue of Sacramento's Congregational Church and whether by hook or by crook, whether seated or standing, the Ralstons would be there! From their fourth row center seats, Harriet gazed at the beauty of the church's spacious sanctuary and the temporary accoutrements placed in support of the performance. Just prior to Madam Bishop's entrance, James whispered to Harriet that they were seated almost exactly where he sat at the wedding of his cousin, Neely Johnson.

The Sacramento Daily Union critic, March 11th, 1854:

The superior adaptation of the human voice to musical expression is acknowledged and complete. It is susceptible of modulations of most touching effect... That Madame Bishop possesses the necessary acquirements to give the voice this full and extended power was manifested to everyone that was so fortunate as to be present at the splendid entertainment given by her last evening.... The tones of the harp, under the truly wonderful touch of M. Bochsa, made us fear that all we had claimed for the superiority of the voice was vain. This veteran displays a delicacy and rapidity of fingering in connection with this, his favorite instrument, that is almost incredible.

When Harriet read the critique of the performance she could not keep from commenting that those words did not begin to adequately describe Madam Bishop's angelic presence and magnificent voice she had witnessed and heard in the church.

The second event that both Harriet and Lizzie wanted to attend was at the opposite end of the entertainment spectrum. When James saw the posters announcing that the circus was coming to town, he immediately knew the nature of the second attraction requiring his presence. The judge arrived at the Orleans that evening and announced to Lizzie, with Harriet nearby, that they should make a point of attending the circus. His daughter's joyful reaction and the gleefully intriguing look on his wife's face confirmed he had dodged what was likely a rehearsed dialog. The two would likely have explained why they should attend a performance of Lee and Marshall's National Circus and Hippodrome. Neither of the Ralston women had ever been to a circus and from the moment they entered the large canvas tent to well after the end of the performance,

they were both in delighted childlike awe of the whole affair. Former state senator Ralston chuckled when he read the short *Sacramento Daily Union* item about the convened state legislature in Sacramento being interrupted by the circus' promotional efforts.

11 March 1854: *Mr. Colby introduced a resolution against Lee & Marshall's circus band, providing for the appointment of a committee to confer with the Common Council* [of Sacramento], *and see if the practice of serenading the Senate could not be stopped. Laid on the table.* [No action taken.]

Lee and Marshall's
National Circus and Hippodrome

Shortly after Lizzie's arrival, James and Harriet took the opportunity to enroll her in Miss Doty's boarding and day school. Mary Doty[80] had established a similar school in Quincy in 1847 and all of the members of the Ralston family, including Lizzie, were well acquainted with her excellent work. Ms. Doty knew that Judge Ralston now lived in Sacramento though she was pleasantly surprised to learn that he had married Harriet Jackson. She was even more pleased to see that Lizzie had joined them and would again be one of her students. If Mary succeeded in Sacramento, she had plans to construct her own building, but for the moment she rented space in the home of Rev. and Mrs. O. C. Wheeler. Reverend Wheeler was the minister of Sacramento's Baptist Church and was presently the chaplain of the California legislature. James gladly accepted Mary's offer for him to be among the members of the school's board of visitors and Lizzie was happy to be at school again. From the *Sacramento Daily Union*, 30 March 1854.

Seminary for Young Ladies. — We are much pleased to learn that a school for young ladies is to be opened on Monday next, at the residence of the Rev. O. C. Wheeler. It is to be under the charge of Miss Doty, late of Quincy, Illinois, in which city she taught a similar school for some seven years. All the higher branches, including music, will be taught by Miss Doty. A seminary of this character is much needed in our city, and we trust Miss D. will receive such encouragement as will induce her to make this enterprise the nucleus of a female seminary of a high order. Miss Doty has several pupils in the city who received their education with her in Quincy. The boarding department will be under the charge of Mrs. Wheeler.

There was a controversy on the horizon for the remaining months of 1854 that was to affect J. H. Ralston in more ways than he could ever have imagined at the time. In early January his longtime friend, U. S. Senator Stephen Douglas of Illinois, introduced the Nebraska Bill[81] in the Senate. Simply stated, the bill called for extending Nebraska's territorial border to the 49th parallel, the northern most United States border. Unlike previous legislation, this bill would allow any state or states subsequently admitted from this territory and the current Kansas Territory to decide by popular vote whether slavery would be allowed. Well before the furor in California and elsewhere began to rise, James made a personal decision to support his friend and the Democratic Party in favor of the bill's passage. The bill was passed on the 30th of May and the legislation had several unintended but predictable consequences. A bloody border war began between Missouri's *border ruffians* and Kansas *jayhawkers*, the demise of the Whig Party replaced by the Republican Party, and more fuel to the already flaming issue of slavery. Judge Ralston's support of the controversial bill was the beginning to the end of his political career in California.

To avoid the stifling heat of the summer, the Ralstons took an extended and relaxing high Sierra sightseeing trip in June and July. They visited many of the places where James had faced some of his more interesting experiences since his time on the coast. They traveled to the Carson Valley along the trail where James and J. Neely had organized help for the many weary and destitute emigrants allowing them to complete the last few miles to their destination. Along the way Harriet and Lizzie saw the gold seekers fluming and panning along the rivers and living in the squalor of the mining camps. The miners suspected that at this point their arduous efforts to strike it rich were too little too late. At Diamond Springs, Harriet again met James' ever bubbly and loquatious cousin, V. Y. Ralston. Harriet was sure James' cousin could not have sprung from the same blood lines as her conservative and tight collared husband. They all camped under a starlit canopy of stars near clusters of pine spires seeming to touch the stars and met friendly *real live* Indians whose ancestors were the first to see the majestic beauty of this land.

The threesome returned to their newly completed home that Harriet named *Shady Branch Farm*, east of Sacramento reinvigorated and ready to take on whatever challenges their future might hold. James' first offical fatherly act at Shady Branch was his much anticipated horseback ride with his daughter. A beaming and giggling Lizzie was seated on the saddle in front him. Her wind blown hair brushed his face as he raced his black stallion to every corner of their 175 acre farm. Lizzie would frequently accompany her father on future rides in the saddle of her new pinto pony she fondly named *Patches*. Farmer Ralston spent the next few months with the help of their new neighbor, James Burns, who preferred the moniker agriculturist to that of fruit farmer, with planting what would eventually be a grape vineyard containing nearly 4,000 vines. Meanwhile, Harriet shopped for furniture and accessories to make their comfortable

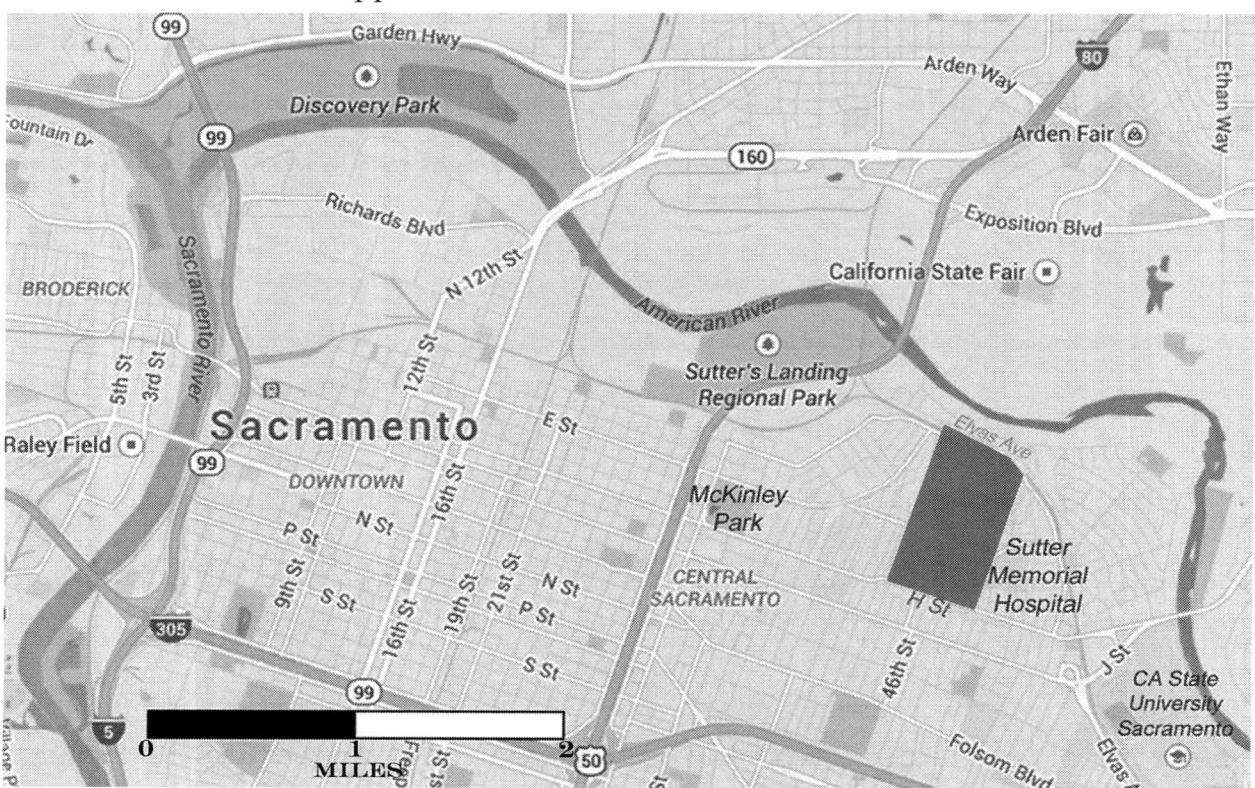

The location of the 175 acre Shady Branch Farm superimposed on a current Sacramento map.

new woodframe and adobe *hacienda* a home.

Much like a bee visits flower to flower collecting its pollen so had the location of California's State Capital proceeded. From Monterrey to Vallejo to Benecia to Sacramento, back to Benecia and Vallejo, to San Jose, and back to Sacramento. The joke of the period was that half of the time the state legislators spent in session was in determing what location they would next conduct the state's business. The third time in Sacramento was apprarently the charm the legislators needed in February of 1854 to once and for all designate that city as the state capital. The plans were immediately begun for a permanent building that would serve as the site for the governor, legislature, and the courthouse for Sacramento county's offices and legal affairs.

On the 27th of September a ceremony was planned to lay the cornerstone for the new structure and it had fallen to all five of Sacramento's Masonic lodges to organize the affair. Worthy Master of the Union Lodge, J. H. Ralston, was chosen as one of the keynote speakers and Harriet and Lizzie were among the hundreds of spectators assembled at 7th and I streets to witness the grand and historic event.

From the *Sacramento Daily Union*, 28 September 1854:

It has rarely been our fortune to witness a more interesting ceremony than was performed yesterday in the laying of the cornerstone of a new courthouse by the Masonic Fraternity of this city.... In conformity with the arrangements, at about five o'clock p. m. the Sutter Rifles, the Masons, the Sons of Temperance, the State and City Officers, and a large body of citizens formed into line on Second street....and preceded by an excellent brass band, proceeded up J street to Sixth, through Sixth to I, up I to Seventh, and through Seventh to the northeast corner of the edifice. A commodious platform, which had been constructed for the accommodation of those who were to take an active part in the ceremonies, was then taken possession of by the Fraternity [Masons], and three lighted candles placed near the stone.

The orator of the day, Judge Ralston, W. M. [Worthy Master] of Union Lodge, was then introduced and spoke as follows :

The work is commenced — the cornerstone is laid for the second temple of Justice erected upon this spot. This event will be chronicled in our history. The early history of Sacramento will show how a city sprang up, as if by magic on the plains — first by the erection of tent houses and small trading shops, soon replaced by more spacious wooden structures. They, in turn, were speedily

swept away by the contending elements [floods], and hundreds of their inhabitants fled to the Court House — then standing upon this spot — as to a house of refuge, where they hoped they and their effects would be secure....

May we hope to soon to see it completed — perfect in strength, symmetry and beauty — well adapted to the purposes intended. May justice be forever administered in these halls, without sale, denial, or delay — according to the principles of eternal truth. These halls may for a season be devoted to the more

Sacramento Courthouse
begun in 1854

important purposes of legislation. May wisdom forever guide our legislative councils! May more than a common eloquence ring through these halls in the advocacy of truth and right. May order prevail through their precincts, and the present as well as future generations be blessed by the wise laws here enacted....

We must walk uprightly before all mankind, on the platform of equality, remembering that we are traveling to that bourne whence no traveler ever returns — the great level where we shall all meet. Let us square our lives by the rules of truth and virtue, so that we may become living stones in that temple not made by hands eternal in the heavens. As the trowel unites the whole building in one common mass, let us spread the cement of brotherly love and affection, so as to unite our fraternity as one band of brothers, seeking the common good of all — nay, our affection should extend to the whole human family — we should seek to unite all by the ties of sympathy and affection forever indissoluble.

Chapter 17

Brother-In-Law and a Governor

The role of matchmaker had never been seriously undertaken by Mrs. Judge J. H. Ralston though in this particular circumstance she had made an exception. Since first she met the ruggedly handsome Tom Sunderland after her arrival in Sacramento there was no doubt in her mind that he should be a leading contender as the perfect partner for her sister Mary Amelia. Harriet had moved aggressively on the matter with both participants involved in her objective. Firstly, she had on several occasions *cornered* the unsuspecting Squire Sunderland and made subtle efforts to gauge his level of interest in pursuing the general possibility of marital bliss. In the latest encounter, she had even produced a picture of her attractive young sister explaining that Amelia was now living in New York and caring for their father. Sadly, she mentioned, Amelia had often written to Harriet expressing her wish to join her sister in the California adventure, which was actually true.

Mary Amelia Jackson

Sunderland's expressively favorable reaction on viewing Amelia's picture did not escape Harriet's attention.

Each letter Harriet had sent to her sister extolled every aspect of her new life on the opposite coast. Harriet insisted that, if Father would allow, she should consider making the journey west and joining James and her in Sacramento. Rev. Jackson married for the second time to Martha Quigley in early February of 1854 in New York and moved to Oyster Bay on New York's Long Island. Harriet accelerated her matchmaking efforts. In her latest letter to Amelia, she pointedly reported that she had *happened upon* a handsome young attorney that was at one time a partner in her husband's law practice. He was completely taken by a picture of Amelia she had coincidentally *taken the liberty* of showing him. Harriet was more than just delighted when Sunderland asked her if it would be appropriate for him to correspond with Amelia; romance, Harriet hoped, was in the air.

On the 14th of October 1854, the steamship Sierra Nevada made its way through the golden gateway on its most recent trip from the Nicaraguan Isthmus and docked at San Francisco's Jackson Street wharf. James and Harriet, accompanied by none other than the distinguished Tom Sunderland, waved when they first sighted Reverend Jackson who had accompanied his youngest daughter to her new home. There was an awkward moment when Tom and Amelia, who had exchanged letters for nearly six months, first met face-to-face. Both wanted to share an embrace though in the presence of the good reverend, they settled on a warm friendly handshake. Reverend Jackson returned to New York, Amelia took up residence at Shady Branch, and, after a short courtship, Amelia agreed to become Mrs. Sunderland in May of the following year.

In late October the passing of the highly respected associate California Supreme Court Justice, Alexander Wells, was met with much sadness. His passing sparked speculation in the Sacramento press that there were two city residents that could very capably fill the vacancy. One of which was Judge J. H. Ralston. James and Harriet both believed that his appointment to this position would be the top most rung of his legal career marking the end of the lengthy work days needed to support his private practice. The vacancy would be filled by an appointment of Governor Bigler. Though James and Bigler were good friends, he did not get his hopes too high. When it was announced in late November that the governor had appointed C. H. Bryan from Marysville to the position, the Ralstons felt as though the air had escaped from their celebratory balloon. James found it much easier to handle the disappointment of the news than his wife, who eventually came to grips with the situation. It was just another addition to a growing list of *might have beens* to which James had reluctantly become all too accustomed.

Two days before the Wednesday, May 30th, 1855, wedding of Miss Mary Amelia Jackson to Mr. Thomas Sunderland, esquire, at the Ralston's Shady Branch farm, an article appeared at the top of page two in the Sacramento Daily Union newspaper. The previous Saturday night, a rowdy meeting of the Sacramento County Settlers Association was held in front of the Noyes House on 10th and I Street at Sacramento's public square. The paper reported that the large angry gathering had been hastily assembled in response to a growing uproar from homesteaders. A land agent of John Sutter was moving to evict settlers from their homes on what was documented to be public land. The Sacramento Daily Union reported the event the next day:

Judge Ralston, being loudly called for, then took the stand. A long time had elapsed since he had addressed a public meeting of his fellow citizens; his own taste rather inclined him to the peaceful walks of private life; it was when there arose a necessity for public consultation in regard to some prominent interest, that he felt impelled to turn aside from those walks. Those present doubtless supposed that their homes — their castles of defense — were to be invaded, were to be taken away from them. He [Judge Ralston] thought, however, there was no occasion for alarm; let us be calm and collected, and prepare for the approaching storm, like good citizens, law-abiding citizens. What are we and our possessions without law? We have our redress; when men determine to adhere to and insist upon their legal rights, they will maintain them.

Most settlers knew that James was experienced and grounded in the laws of private land ownership on public lands. The judge had himself thoroughly researched the Mexican land grant that John Sutter claimed gave him the outright ownership of nearly 80,000 acres when James bought 175 acres of that very land early in 1853. Attorney Ralston found the grant to be well intentioned but in his opinion not legal under the sale of the California land to the United States as part of the treaty that ended the Mexican-American War. Judge Ralston knew that there would be more legal troubles ahead and he again urged the settlers to be peaceful as the wheels of justice ground ever slowly forward hopefully in the defense of their concerns.

Two days later, Harriet beamed as she and James quietly watched Lizzie spread flower petals in advance of the bride and groom. A short time later, dashing tuxedoed Thomas and the beautiful Amelia, adorned in her mother's wedding dress, exchanged their wedding vows before Reverend Jehu Lewis Shuck. Reverend Shuck was a longtime Baptist missionary in China who had recently come to Sacramento to minister to the needs of the large resident Chinese population. After the ceremony, the wedding guests were treated to a delightful reception featuring wine made from the grapes of the Ralston vineyard, Harriet's acclaimed homemade bread, and cheese. Then the wedding party escorted the newlyweds to the Sacramento docks where the couple boarded a river steamer for a gala honeymoon in San Francisco.

Will wonders never cease! After nearly a quarter of a century of believing in and faithfully supporting the tenets of the Democratic Party, James had more than had enough! The absence, until recently, of Judge Ralston from the public eye was due in part to his newly confirmed belief that the Douglas led Democrats had done no favors to the American people in passing the Kansas-Nebraska Act the year before. James' last straw came when the Democratic led California legislature took no action in support of the settlers land issues. At another Settlers Association meeting on July 17th, Judge Ralston boldly announced to the applause of the gathering that he was now a proud member of the American State Party [aka the Know Nothings] and would support its platform in the upcoming elections. With the virtual collapse of the Whig Party and the complete public disgust for the Democratic Party, the American State Party held much more than a small chance of a strong showing at the polls.

At the August 9th,1855, American State Party convention held at Sacramento's Presbyterian Church, delegates nominated several candidates for governor including J. H. Ralston. On the convention's first ballot, the top four candidates garnering votes were Baldwin 82, Johnson 77, Wade 44, and Ralston 42. The Johnson receiving the second highest number of votes was none other than James close friend and cousin, attorney J. Neely Johnson! On the second ballot, Johnson received 118 votes, Baldwin 82, Stow 38, and Ralston 37.

Prior to the third ballot, James withdrew his name from consideration and asked his delegates to cast their vote for Johnson. On the fourth ballot Neely was nominated as the party's candidate and in early September John Neely Johnson was elected by a large margin of the state's voters to a two-

Sacramento's J Street looking east from Front Street, 1855

year term as California's fourth governor. Several days later, Governor-Elect Johnson's celebrations filtered down to a quiet evening dinner for four; Mr. and Mrs. Johnson and Judge and Mrs. Ralston. James and his 30-year-old cousin reminisced about their experiences of the last six years and about their common family heritage until the early hours of the morning. Perhaps even more so than his cousin, Neely wanted to see to it personally that James garnered the public recognition and status he so richly deserved.

The Sacramento Daily Union, 9 January 1856, described Governor-Elect Johnson's inaugural ball held the evening before at Sacramento's newest theatrical venue, the Forrest Theater. The Ralstons had of course attended and Mrs. Ralston was simply awe-struck by the grand affair.

The Ball. — The inauguration terpsichorean [dancing] festival last evening exceeded in splendor all that have ever preceded it in this the Capital of the State. It was a flattering compliment to the Governor elect, and reflected infinite credit on the Chairman of the Committee of Arrangements and efficient committees under his supervision. The evening was rainy, but despite the unpropitious [unfavorable] weather, carriages were rolling up and discharging their fair occupants for an hour or more after that designated as the one for "the hall to open". The immense stage and parquette had been handsomely, conveniently and tastefully arranged as a dancing floor, and from the first until the hour of our going to press, was festooned with chequered groups mingling in the mazes of the merry dance. The dress circle throughout the evening was crowded with an array of loveliness and manliness seldom seen congregated on similar occasions. The spectacle presented to one on looking down from the upper tier of boxes was a truly brilliant one and could not but call forth expressions of delight. Although the spacious edifice was filled, yet there was no crowd, and so admirably conceived and carried out were the plans of the committee, that not a single murmur of complaint was heard, but all testified to their successful exertions in rendering the entertainment more than everything that could be desired. At 12 ½ o'clock, the band sounded a march, when all formed in procession and passed up the spacious saloon above, which had been converted into a supper room. On entering the room, the eye fell upon four or five tables, laden down with viands of every description. The dishes were elegantly ornamented, and so arrayed as to produce the most pleasing effect. The pyramids of confectionery added greatly to the beauty of the tables, and were universally admired. There was room enough for all the guests, and that, too, without crowding; and, more than this, there was a profusion of every delicacy, and those of the very choicest description. The chef d' cuisine was Monsieur Raynald, and in all the appointments of the feast his taste and skill were exhibited. Day had begun to dawn ere the last of the guests of the Inauguration American Ball retired to their homes.

A few short months after newly elected Governor Johnson was comfortably seated in his office at the Capitol, one of the darkest clouds in the history of the state began to billow in San Francisco. It took little time in spreading its dread to Sacramento. The city near the golden gateway previously known as the sleepy coastal village of Yerba Buena was transformed in two short years. San Francisco became a ship filled thriving port bringing thousands upon thousands of gold fevered amateur miners close to their eureka in the western foothills of the Sierra Nevada. The recognized need for law and order fell woefully behind the establishment of saloons, hotels, general stores, banks, and assay offices. Many of these businesses made enormous profits from fraudulently providing the much sought after services to their unsuspecting and naïve patrons. Graft, corruption, and lawlessness were the orders of the day. When the state legislature, the court systems, and the municipal governments did begin to form, the positions of the latter were filled to the brim with the worst of the worst who wanted to protect the means of their ill-gotten gain. Well before 1856, the citizens were fed up with the situation and were joined at the hip with newspapermen who did not hesitate in voicing their fervent demands for change.

The Vigilance Committee of San Francisco was originally formed in 1851 and in its brief existence the aptly named group unsuccessfully tried to curb the criminal violence plaguing the city. The committee's resurrection was immediately undertaken after the cold-blooded murder in mid-May 1856, of the editor of one of San Francisco's newspapers by the editor of a rival paper. The dastardly deed was done because of the slanderous accusations the mortally wounded man had published about his shooter. The constitution of the re-formed committee was now expanded to include political corruption in addition to the earlier committee's focus on civil crimes. This expansion poised a truly explosive combination of objectives given the city's current state of municipal chaos.

The Vigilance Committee's first order of business was arming its claimed 6,000 members to the teeth, heavily fortifying their headquarters building several feet deep

with sandbags, and with cannons strategically placed at the ready on the rooftop. The vigilante members then wrested two men from the city jail, one of them the editor murderer and the second an unsavory local character awaiting a second trial for the murder of a federal marshal. The two men were tried before a committee formed and closed-door kangaroo court. Minutes after the court finding of guilty, punishable by

Committee of Vigilance, San Francisco
Membership Certificate, May 1856

death, the two men were hung in full public view on the street in front of the committee's headquarters. When news of the mob action reached Governor Johnson's office, he immediately formulated a badly needed plan of action.

The Governor summoned a small group of respected and influential Sacramento citizens led by his father-in-law attorney, J. C. Zabriskie, and Judge Ralston. He asked the men to travel to San Francisco as his representatives and find a way to negotiate an expeditious end to the violence. The group of negotiators agreed with Governor

Johnson that the actions of the Vigilance Committee were no better than those of the men they summarily executed. After the lengthy and sometimes heated discussions, the meeting with the *vigilante* committee's leadership failed to produce any conciliatory results; it was time for Neely's Plan B.

The Governor became aware that a man working for the San Francisco banking firm of Lucas, Turner, and Company, William T. Sherman[82], a promising United States Army captain, who had resigned his commission in 1853. Sherman now made his home in the City by the Bay. A few members of the negotiating group, including Judge Ralston, accompanied the Governor to San Francisco where he met with Sherman

William T. Sherman

and offered him command of San Francisco's 2nd division of the state militia if he would agree to end the Vigilance Committee's stranglehold on San Francisco's municipal court system and police force. Sherman accepted. The new militia commander then met with General John E. Wool, Captain Ralston's commanding General at the Alamo, and gained Wool's unofficial agreement to provide the militia with breech loading muskets from the Benecia arsenal and cannons positioned at Rincon point. Three days later Wool reneged on his promise of supplying arms and Sherman promptly resigned his militia appointment. Fortuitously, the Vigilance Committee took one-step over the line when it jailed a respected justice of the California Supreme Court. The *reign of terror* ended in August of 1856 when cooler heads of the committee leadership finally prevailed. The continued unfair lambasting by the press of Governor Johnson's handling of the whole affair haunted him for the remaining sixteen months of his governorship making California's youngest ever elected top official ineffective in completing many of his worthwhile objectives.

Chapter 18

The Family Grows

James was seated comfortably at the dining room table in the Ralston home at Shady Branch. Between sips of coffee, he had just finished reading an article in the mid-August, 1857 edition of the *Union*. The paper reported the Vigilance Committee's release of Supreme Court Justice Terry that he knew would mark the end of the committee's rampant lawless actions. Harriet walked from the kitchen to the dining room and quietly asked him for the third time in the last five minutes if she could pour him another cup. After looking at his full to the brim cup, he glanced at his wife with a bothersome smile and thanked her for her relentless service. He once again occupied himself with the news of the day. Harriet still stood next to her husband and cleared her throat. James again diverted his attention and before kindly asking his wife to just leave him in peace with his paper, he noticed Harriet's nervous smile. On the many other occasions James had seen this smile he knew that it was her way of letting him know she had something she wanted to say. He immediately put the paper on the table, turned his full focus of attention to Harriet, and waited. Harriet again cleared her throat and in a barely audible tone she meekly told Judge Ralston that he was again going to be a father. Before his wife could tell him that she did not know how he would react to the news, James impatient frown turned to a broad smile as he sprang to his feet, embraced his young wife, and whispered that these were the happiest words he had heard in quite a long while. Harriet and James' tears were those of pure joy.

The howling north wind of Sacramento's second coldest day of the winter, 6 February, 1857, did not in the least take away from the warmth and joy of the early morning birth of Jackson Harvey Ralston. Dr. Morton pronounced mother and son to be in the best of health, though when James joined them in the bedroom, mother had tears of joy and newborn son had tears of hunger and general dissatisfaction with the whole birthing affair.

Lizzie had been purposely backstage since her stepmother began her contractions and the doctor had arrived. James immediately went to look for her and found her lying on her bed with her back to the door. When she turned to look at him he knew she had been crying. Judge Ralston's public reputation as a stern relentless *just-the-facts-please* attorney was well earned. Privately he displayed a

Sacramento Daily Union

SATURDAY MORNING, FEBRUARY 7, 1857.

COLD SNAP - Friday night was the coldest we have experienced since the 9th of January, the mercury having fallen to 30 degrees....A cold north wind prevailed throughout yesterday, rendering an overcoat a comfortable companion.

BIRTHS

In Sacramento, Feb. 6th, the wife of Judge J. H. Ralston, of a son

softer more understanding side, particularly with his children. He knew that his daughter mistakenly believed that with the arrival of her infant brother, her father would set her aside as chaff from the wheat, never again to enjoy the hours of bliss being by his side. James knew that he now needed to invoke his power of persuasion and leave no doubt in Lizzie's mind about his feelings on the subject. He sat next to her on the bed and gently put his hand on her shoulder.

James described to her how she had been her parent's miracle child after four heart-breaking attempts to bring a new life to the world. He told her how, each day, she afforded him a mirror image of the beauty, understanding, and grace of her mother who he had loved so deeply. He told her about the promise he had made when she was born and that nothing on the face of God's green earth would ever sway him from loving his daughter. James added that he needed Lizzie to be by his side and help him raise and love her brother as Jane would have wanted her to do. A faint smile began to appear then, followed by tears of happiness. Lizzie embraced her father and promised him that she would do her very best to help him. From that moment, Lizzie kept her promise and became as much a second mother to her brother as a sister.

At the end of the previous year, Jewish Supreme Court Justice Solomon Heydenfeldt announced his resignation from the court effective in 1857. The judge stated a desire, primarily for financial reasons, to return to private practice, the opposite direction once sought by Judge Ralston. J. H. was again mentioned in many corners of the state to be the leading contender for the position. However, James knew his recently broken ties with the state's Democratic Party rendered his election nearly impossible to attain. In April of 1857, James wrote a letter to the Sacramento Daily Union addressing his reported interest in the position.

Sacramento Daily Union, April 11th, 1857:

We have also received the following card from Judge Ralston, which speaks for itself:

Editors Union: With surprise I perceive my name mentioned in the Union as a candidate for Judge of the Supreme Court. As I am not a candidate for that or any other office, I wish you to correct your list of candidates by dropping my name.

The country has been long and sorely afflicted by an excess of office-seekers, and my name cannot go to swell the list. If I could do anything to restore the government to pristine purity, and to reestablish it on pure Democratic principles, I would gladly do it at any sacrifice, but I do not believe the use of my name in this connection would aid that high purpose. I am therefore constrained to deny to my friends the right to use my name as a candidate.

Knowing the country will not suffer for want of candidates, and hoping that the choice may fall on some better suited than myself for the office, I subscribe myself truly
Your Obt. Servt, J. H. Ralston.

James meant every word he wrote in his note to the *Union*, though Harriet had a different idea. Despite his many earnest attempts to explain his action, she could not understand why her husband would simply throw away his *and through him, her* opportunity to achieve fame on California's grandest judicial stage. James was merely *along for the ride* when Harriet convinced lame duck Governor and cousin Neely Johnson to join her cause. Neely saw to it that James gained his American State Party's nomination for the judgeship. It was heartache for Harriet and not the least bit surprising to Judge Ralston when he finished a distant second in the election for Supreme Court Justice to the Democratic Party nominee, Stephen J. Field. James hoped that Harriet would learn from her ambitions for her husband and herself and be more careful in picking her future battles.

The year 1857 was glorious for the Ralstons on the family front and inglorious from Harriet's standpoint on the political front. James was personally satisfied with his continuing efforts during the year to help the Settlers and Miners Association with their land claim struggles. Yet, he had little to show for his efforts other than to gain the complete trust, respect, and confidence of the association's widely diverse membership. He was particularly proud of a letter he had written earlier in the year.

Sacramento Daily Union, 24 June, 1857

[excerpts from a much longer letter detailing the historical and legal basis for the rights of public landowners in California]

… I deeply regret that the Democratic party [in California] *has adopted an erroneous policy in regard to public lands in the State of California. Its consequences have entailed upon the State much of the misery, degradation, and immorality that now pervade the country* [California]. *…*

We alone are responsible for it; therefore, whilst I adhere to the national Democracy, I shall continue to oppose the party in California. ... In my anomalous position I may have no party. For that I care not. I would rather be right than President!

These are my views, fully and frankly expressed. They are, my friends, written for your own private use, but I cannot object to any use you may make of them, as I have no opinions I wish concealed from the public.

Very truly, your ob't serv't, J. H. Ralston

In mid-February of 1858, James received a letter from his brother William who was living with his family in Leavenworth, Kansas Territory, just south of the army fort.

12 Jan. '1858, Kansas Territory

Dear brother,

Since not having communicated for some period, a pressing matter confronting our community about which I am in need of your view, has provided a bona fide reason for ending my inattention. Firstly, I must in all good conscience provide news on the family front.

Mary's [wife] health of late has not been good and she plans to take an intermission from her motherly duties in this place for a visit to her mother's home in Fairmont.[83] *Our domestic and I will do our best to manage the children in her absence. Your namesake flashes with your brilliance yet being a young male uses that inherited acumen to be a constant source of devilment to his three younger sisters; they are all flourishing in spite of the conflict.*[84] *My legal and other various enterprises fortunately continue to challenge me, keep the wolves away from the door, and places food on our dinner table.*

As you are no doubt aware, my fellow Kansans attempted through the Lecompton Constitution to have our territory admitted to the Union as a slave-holding state. I am glad your friend Douglas supported and won its defeat in Congress a few days ago. That action will no doubt forestall our statehood objective though now as a convert to the free soil movement I would rather reside in a free territory than a slave state.

However, many of us are tired and fearful of the Missouri border ruffians continually trying to extend their beliefs and their state boundaries to our peace-loving territory. My request, legislator Ralston, is to provide me your insight as to how the Californians who have an interest, view the turmoil in our besieged territory and can foresee a time, short of civil war throughout the land, when it can be made to end.

Please pass along my best wishes to your lovely wife and your children for their continued full health and happiness. I trust the activities of my infant nephew [Jackson] have not caused him to overstay his long awaited and loving welcome.

[signed] Will

James responded to his brother's letter with all of the vim and vigor he could muster as an anti-slavery and anti-Lecompton Democrat though he could not rule out the possibility of his brother's portent of a dreaded civil war.

In a brief unheralded report, the *Daily Alta* carried a news item from Washington that the country's attorney general, J. S. Black, had decided to send a federal agent to

New Almaden Mine, ca 1856

California. The agent was sent to prosecute a land ownership dispute between the United States and the New Almaden Quicksilver[85] Mining Company in Santa Clara County just south of San Jose. This was the first major case Judge Ralston knew of, where the federal government was disputing the private ownership of public land that was supported solely by a Mexican land grant. This case might well set a precedent for the rights of the area miners and settlers he ardently supported. He intended to follow its progress closely.

On March 20th, 1858, Edwin M. Stanton[86], the agent assigned by Attorney General Black,

Edwin M. and Edwin I Stanton, ca 1855

and Stanton's young son, master Edwin, arrived in San Francisco on the S. S. Sonora. Attorney Stanton established an office in the city. Judge Ralston made several trips to visit Stanton over the next few months to gain information about the progress of the case. When it was resolved in favor of the government, James disappointingly discovered that unlike John Sutter's Mexican grant, the mining company had forged its supporting documents. On the brighter side, the government gladly accepted a multi-million dollar settlement from the mining company to gain the outright ownership to much of the company's fraudulently claimed land. Stanton was immediately recognized as a force in the legal and hence the political circles of the nation's capital.

W. C. Wallace and Judge Ralston had dissolved their law partnership about five months before Jackson was born. It would not be accurate to say that James had given up the practice of law, far from it, he had just decided he should spend more time at home with his family. However, it would be fair to say that a portion of attorney Ralston's current income now came in the form of stock dividends from his investments in area companies[87] and from an occasional land sale. Harriet had mildly voiced her concern to James about this practice though she did not bother to mention why. In early May, on James' return from one of his San Francisco trips to see Stanton, Harriet nonchalantly mentioned to her husband that the Ralston family of three would soon welcome a fourth member. A now attentive Judge Ralston anxiously asked his wife to repeat what she said and when she did a celebratory shout filled the room followed by a tender embrace. When asked the expected date of the new arrival, Harriet believed that sometime in October would as good a guess as any. Lizzie came in the room wondering about the cause of her father's uncharacteristic outburst and she too shared in the celebration. In the background Jackson contributed his displeasure with the ruckus.

There were occasions when James was a little slow in catching Harriet's reactions to certain circumstances. When he finally put two and two together he immediately began the search for another law partner. James would celebrate his 49th birthday the same month as the new arrival. He encountered some difficulty in finding a bright

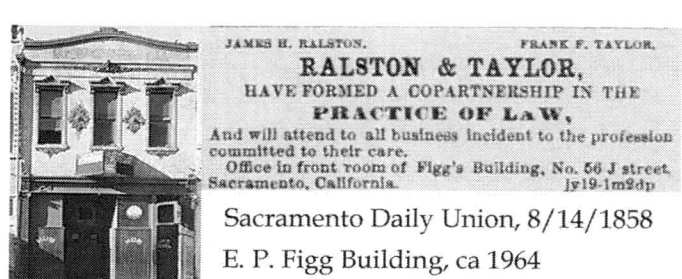

Sacramento Daily Union, 8/14/1858

E. P. Figg Building, ca 1964

experienced attorney who was willing to share a practice with an *old hand* at the law. Judge Ralston visited several attorneys interested in joining him and he finally settled on Frank F. Taylor[88] as his new junior partner. James decided that Taylor's current office on the first floor front of the E. P. Figg Building on J street would be as good a location as any. Frank purchased the building from Figg when Figg decided to close his general store in favor of investing in mining interests. Figg had lost everything in the Sacramento fire of 1852 but he had persevered and built his business back better than before. Most of the Sacramento citizenry, including Judge Ralston, knew and thought highly of Figg who was one of the original 49ers and who, in the greater opinion, had the finest store in the city. The joke around town was to avoid Figg's first floor pile of flour sacks unless one wanted an unexpected visit to the store's basement. On two separate occasions the weight of the flour had caused the floor to collapse, fortunately with no injury to life or limb.

The first newspaper-to-newspaper telegraph between San Francisco and Stockton, California was received by the *Daly Alta* from the *Stockton Journal* on the 24th of October 1858.

Daily Alta, 25 October 1858:

About 10 minutes after 9 o'clock, yesterday evening, we were gratified by the reception of the following dispatch (our first) by telegraph from Stockton: ...Please receive the compliments of the Stockton Journal. May that lightning which alike serves to awe the superstitions and to cleave the forest oak serve but to link us closer in those bonds of friendship that should even unite and actuate all honorable members of a free Press.

To which we replied: ... Compliments of the Alta California. The music ol your Tabor is grateful to our ears. Truly our lines have fallen in pleasant places, and we have a goodly heritage. May inspiration be drawn from this and the kindred events of a mighty age as freely as our great Franklin drew lightning from the clouds.

Though the telegraph had long been in use east of the Mississippi River, this marked the first use over any distance of consequence in California. When James read the news on September 17th, 1858, that the first successful use of the Atlantic Ocean telegraph came in the form of a message between England's Queen Victoria and President Buchanan the month before, he could not help but laugh. California's accomplishment paled in comparison.

There he sat in the country's 30th state, first discovering the success of a major world communication event a full month after it happened! News of the rest of the country reached Sacramento with its age based on the number of days from Panama, New Orleans, or New York that it took a Pacific Mail Company steamship to arrive in San Francisco. *Isolation* was the first word that came to his mind. Today, if he stood next to a telegrapher, James could find out in a few short minutes about the current news of a friend in Carson City, Nevada, and reply. For a friend in the nation's capital, he would need to wait at the very least, 24 days, not including a reply. The judge knew that based on the technology of the time, it would not be long before the great expanse of mountains and deserts separating the land of milk and honey from the rest of the country would be spanned. Telegraph poles, railroad tracks, and roads would be put in place simply because there was more than reason enough to do so.

Harriet had been under the care of Sacramento's tall and thoroughly proper English born bachelor, Doctor James Blake[89]. When the signs of a difficult pregnancy had first been diagnosed, he was by her side late in the evening of October 5th. Harriet was due to give birth at any time. The doctor decided to spend a sleepless night with James and Lizzie at Shady Branch frequently checking on the expectant mother. At first light, with help from her three attendants, Harriet gave birth to Mary Aurora Ralston. After a careful

BIRTHS.
At Shady Branch Farm, Sacramento county, the wife of Judge Ralston, of a daughter.

Sacramento Daily Union, 10/7/1858

examination from the doctor, he pronounced mother and daughter to be *fit as a pair of fiddles*. James knew that with the much more than able knowledge of Doctor Blake, there could have been a far different outcome. He could not express enough gratitude for the doctor's extraordinary care. Within days of the happy event, Harriet was up and about and with Lizzie's help, seeing to the needs of her infant daughter and young son.

Attorney Ralston was again practicing his profession without a partner. He *hung his shingle* in a new location on the 2nd floor above the St. Louis Clothing store owned by David Kohn and Charles Robin at 160 J Street at the corner of 6th. His new office was across the street from the popular and well-appointed saloon owned by Jacob Kruhler. The saloon was the source of disagreements that occasionally spilled onto J street. A meeting with one of Judge Ralston's clients was briefly interrupted by such an occurrence. As his client started to get up from his seat to see what was going on, James casually commented that there was no cause for alarm. The Judge predicted the vociferous altercation would shortly end with a saloon employee's well-placed blow to the groin of the offender. However, he added with a straight face, if a pistol shot rings out we shall both proceed to the full view of the window sure to witness a scene that would likely lead to the need for a good defense attorney.

Chapter 19

Twists and Turns

As a prelude to the 1859 U. S. senatorial election in Illinois, the two remaining candidates, both of them Judge Ralston's acquaintances, squared off in a series of seven debates in the fall of 1858. James followed the encounters between Democrat Stephen Douglas and Republican Abraham Lincoln to the extent the limited news reports of the events allowed. The country's growing divisive sentiments on the subject of slavery had to be the leading topic of the debates, and it was. James' longtime friend Douglas advocated that whether thumbs up or down on slavery, it should be determined by the choice of the people at the ballot box. Lincoln on the other hand, frequently repeated the sentiments he first expressed in June at the Republican convention that nominated him, *a house divided against itself cannot stand*. Politically, James was now a borderline supporter of Senator Douglas because of his friendship and his former party affiliation, though he personally believed that attorney Lincoln was in the moral right. James learned in late January of 1859 that by a slim margin Douglas

Douglas and Lincoln 1858

had retained his seat in the Illinois senate. He knew that Lincoln's outspoken stand against slavery may well vault him to his new party's presidential nomination in the upcoming election. He thought that if by some glimmer of a chance, *Honest Abe* should become president, may God be pleased to help us all.

At half past two on the 2nd of August 1859, Judge Ralston was among the nattily dressed dignitaries at the Sacramento depot boarding a railroad passenger car for the short 40-minute ride from Sacramento northeast to Folsom, California. The assembled group, including the leader of the arrangements committee, Judge J. C. Zabriskie, and his son-in-law ex-Governor, J. Neely Johnson, were scheduled to meet New York Tribune editor, Horace Greeley[90]. The famed editor was on the last leg of his overland journey. Greeley had traveled by rail to St. Joseph, Missouri, then by overland stagecoach through Denver City and the Colorado Rockies, Salt Lake City, Carson City, and had stopped the night before at the Cary House in Placerville. At Folsom, the greeters found no sign of their heralded guest and most of them left the depot to visit with the citizens of the town.

Sacramento Daily Union, August 2nd, 1859:

… [the committee] learned that the "Man with the White Coat" had not yet made his appearance…the cannon was brought out, and soon a thundering report, which must have wakened Greeley a mile distant …. announced that the friends of the great expected were ready to receive him with open arms. At a quarter to four, a carriage drawn by a pair of roan-colored ponies drove at a pretty smart pace down the main street and straight up to the depot. By this time most of the committee had wandered off …. so that when the proprietor of a little old glazed traveling bag, marked "H. Greeley, 154 Nassau street, New York, 1855" a very rusty and well-worn white coat, a still rustier and still more worn and faded blue cotton umbrella, together with a roll of blankets, were deposited from the carriage, there was no one present of the committee to take him by the hand. The crowd about the depot, however, closed in so densely that Greeley was fain to make for the first open door that presented itself. This, unfortunately, happened to be the barroom attached to the ticket office, and here some of the committee found him, with his back turned defiantly against the sturdy rows of bottles and decanters….

James told Harriet all about his meeting with Greeley and he accompanied her to Rev. Benton's church in Sacramento that evening to hear a speech by the New York newspaperman. Greeley extolled the virtues and the overwhelming need for a transcontinental railroad joining the east with the *golden state*. He received a standing ovation from the Ralstons and the rest of the church's overflowing crowd.

Horace Greeley

In early September, James shared his events of that day with Harriet. He highlighted a lunch he had with a friend, Judge J. P. Jones, and the judge's one-time partner in a hotel venture, Duane Bliss[91], accompanied by Bliss' young daughter. The more James told her about the conversation, the more Harriet was saddened by the tragic story. Bliss was married to a woman named Mary Elizabeth Healy and they had two daughters, the youngest of whom was only two months old when she died in Sacramento in 1857. The oldest by two years, Lucia Mary, named for Bliss' mother, was currently staying with her father in Sacramento after his wife's premature death in San Francisco just two weeks earlier. The widower had returned to Sacramento to find a temporary home for his young child. He had received a lucrative offer to work at a new mining company in Virginia City. He dared not expose his little Mary to the rough and tumble life of the new boomtown just east of the Sierras. James ended the story by telling Harriet that the four year-old was an intelligent and well behaved little girl and he felt sorry for her circumstance. As it turned out, not as sorry as his compassionate and decisive wife.

With her husband's help, Harriet and James sought out and found Mr. Bliss in one of Sacramento's less than finest hotels. The precious little sad-eyed girl that answered the knock on the door caused Harriet to choke back her tears. Mrs. Ralston managed a friendly smile and she introduced herself to the child who called herself Mary. The child recognized Judge Ralston from earlier in the day and she politely asked the couple to come in. The three were soon joined by Mary's father who was surprised by the Ralstons unannounced visit and asked how he could be of assistance. Harriet dispensed with formal introductions and pleaded with Bliss to allow her and her husband to make the arrangements necessary for his daughter to live at their home for whatever period was necessary. Mrs. Ralston knew immediately that Bliss' joyful reaction to the offer would make it possible for the motherless child to leave with the happy couple. Mary gave a big hug and kiss to her father telling him she would see him soon and with no hesitation turned and walked hand-in-hand with the two strangers to the waiting carriage. James placed the small bedroll containing all but one of Mary's every possession in the back of the carriage. Holding tight to her favorite possession, a well-worn cloth doll, Mary joined Judge and Mrs. Ralston in the carriage waving good-bye to the forlorn tearful father.

Name	Age	Sex		Occupation			Birth Loc.
3	4	5	6	7	8	9	10
J. H. Ralston	51	M		Lawyer			KY
Harriet	30	F					NY
Lizzie	15	F					Ill
J. [Jackson]	3	M					Cal
A. [Aurora]	1	F					"
M. Bliss [Mary]	3	F					"
Simon Hack	20	M		Farm Labor			Ill
Geo. Brown	20	M		" "			Canada
L. Penny	24	M		" "			Ohio
Chas. Switzer	53	M		" "			Germany

1860 U. S. Census Sutter Twp., Sacramento Co., CA

It was the first of October, the judge had left for work dropping Lizzie off at school on his way. Harriet had finished the breakfast dishes, and her new eager helper, Mary Bliss, was *minding* Jackson and Aurora. Harriet played for a while with the children then she reluctantly decided that she would celebrate the arrival of the new month. She would undertake one of her least favorite chores, a thorough housecleaning. Harriet, with broom in hand, was on the front porch taking out the displeasure of her duty by vigorously thumping the dirt and dust from the large living room rug. Suddenly, from the corner of her eye, she saw a man running toward the house. By the time one of the Ralston's farmhands, George Brown, arrived at the porch he barely had enough breath to ask Harriet to follow him to the barn. Just inside the barn door another farmhand, Charlie Switzer, was lying on the ground barely conscious and moaning. Brown told her that his friend had fallen from his horse and hit his head on the top rail of the hay storage bin. Harriet bent over Charlie and noticed a large gash just above his forehead. She told Brown to get Switzer into the back of the nearby wagon while she bridled a horse and they would take him straight away to Dr. Blake's office.

Harriet and George sat silently in James Blake's office waiting for news about Charlie. She fondly remembered the time her husband first introduced her to the soft-spoken hard-working German. James explained that George had lost everything

SERIOUS ACCIDENT.—A German in the employ of Judge Ralston, who resides just beyond the city limits, while engaged on Monday in securing a mare and colt that had wandered off, was thrown accidentally from a gentle horse and sustained a fracture of the skull. He was attended by Dr. Blake, who, at last accounts, had but little hope of his recovery.

Sacramento Daily Union, 10/5/1859

but the shirt on his back in the gold fields and in the old country he had been a master gardener. She prayed he was not badly injured. Dr. Blake emerged from his back office and Harriet knew the prognosis was not good. He explained that Mr. Switzer fractured his skull as a result of the fall and if there would be a large amount of swelling to the brain, his chance of recovery was slim to none. Harriet remained calm and asked her good friend what would happen next. The doctor said that he would have him taken to the hospital where he would regularly tend to him until an outcome could be determined. On the way back to Shady Branch, Harriet and George stopped by James' office with the news about Switzer. Contrary to the published report of his probable demise, Charles Switzer regained his full health and continued his work on the Ralston farm.

He told himself he would give public office one more try. Just before the end of an eventful 1859, Judge Ralston was asked to fill a vacancy in Sutter Township as Justice of the Peace, a part-time job that kept him within earshot of Shady Branch. It also meant that his law practice would receive less of his attention and neither he nor Harriet wanted that to happen. For what seemed like the hundredth time, J. H. was again on the hunt for a law partner. The judge knew full well his best bet would be a young lawyer without much legal experience, perhaps a carbon copy of George May. At the Anti-Lecompton Democratic convention earlier in the year he remembered a discussion with attorney William Weeks about a bright young man living in his boarding house who Weeks was tutoring that had a great deal of promise. In mid-January of the New Year, he made a point of dropping by Weeks' office in Sacramento's Union Hotel to get the *rest of the story* about the young attorney.

The business of finding a junior partner was getting old and he did not expect the Weeks visit to amount to much. Just inside the office door a young man sprang to his feet from behind a small desk and asked Judge Ralston if he could be of any help. James almost always recognized the face if not the name of anyone who called him by his title though this was one of those rare exceptions. He made no attempt to hide the fact he did not know the young man he faced and he extended his hand asking whom he had the pleasure to meet. *M. C. Tilden* was the immediate reply. He added that his given name was Marcellus though he did not know if his parents had taken the name from a family member or they were fascinated with Rome or Shakespeare. James laughed noting the young man's sense of humor and knowledge of history. The judge wondered aloud if M. C. was the legal apprentice Weeks had used such glowing terms to describe and the quick reply from M. C. was that he hoped so. The two men talked for about an hour covering a broad range of topics that centered primarily on the law when Weeks returned from business at the courthouse. Weeks asked James if he had yet succeeded

> J. R. RALSTON,   M. C. TILDEN.
> **RALSTON & TILDEN,**
> **Attorneys and Counselors at Law,**
> Office—One door south of Court Block, Fourth street.
> fe12

Sacramento Daily Union, 2/13/1860

in luring his protégé to his practice. Judge Ralston noticed the surprised look on M. C.'s face and gave himself a mental pat on the back for successfully masking an interview process. Four weeks later, James placed an advertisement in the *Union* announcing the new partnership. Unknown at the time to both men was the much greater role M. C. Tilden would soon play in the future of the Ralston family affairs.

During the third week of a particularly warm Sacramento July, Harriet noticed a marked change in Mary Bliss' behavior. At mealtime she showed little interest in her food though when questioned she insisted she just was not hungry and felt just fine. The next day Lizzie noticed on Mary's bed sheet that sometime during the night she had been sick and immediately reported the finding to Harriet. The Ralston household was on full medical alert when Mary showed the signs of a low fever. Dr. Blake was summoned to determine what the problem might be. The doctor examined Mary from top to bottom. He was alarmed with her low-grade fever and redness he found on her tongue, and calmly suggested it would be best for her to be hospitalized. He told the Ralstons that his recommendation was simply a precautionary measure in the remote possibility that she was suffering from a nasty bout with some sort of a contagious illness. Blake added that it was likely nothing more than a sore throat. He knew better.

Though he had not yet seen a rash on Mary's neck, he knew it was coming. The only question that remained was whether the otherwise healthy five-year-old could withstand the onslaught of scarlet fever.

Harriet accompanied Dr. Blake and Mary to the hospital. When the doctor asked that the child be placed in an isolated area and denied Harriet's request to be by Mary's bedside, Harriet knew the worst was yet to come. She returned to her duties at Shady Branch. Later that evening James' consoled his distraught wife trying unsuccessfully to convince her that Mary was in the best of care and she would be fine. Early the next day Judge and Mrs. Ralston visited the hospital and waited for Dr. Blake to finish his morning patient rounds. The doctor met the Ralstons and shared the news that Mary had a confirmed case of scarlet fever and reminded them that many children survive the disease. He suggested a prayer for the best possible outcome. Harriet kept her composure though the tight grip she kept on James' hand revealed the true depth of her concern and fears. After a short though valiant struggle, Mary passed away ten days later.

James knew that Duane Bliss was mining somewhere in the hills around Virginia City though he had no specific address or even a mining company name. He sent a telegram simply addressed, D. L. R. Bliss, Virginia City, Utah Territory, hoping against hope that Mary's father would receive the news of his daughter's death. The judge knew the length of the trip to Sacramento would prevent him from attending the funeral. Few attended the service conducted by Reverend Benton at Shady Branch that celebrated the life of a beautiful child. Like her mother and sister before her, she was taken too soon from this earth for a reason known only to God. She was laid to rest next to her sister in Sacramento's City Cemetery[92]. Harriet wrote a short poem in remembrance.

DIED.
In Sacramento, July 30th, of scarlet fever, LUCIA MARY BLISS, aged 4 years and 26 days.
[Funeral to-day at 9 o'clock, A. M., from the residence of Judge Ralston. Friends and acquaintances are invited to attend.]

Sacramento Daily Union, 7/31/1860
Note: Lucia Mary's age s/b 5 years 26 days

For Mary

So joyous now among the angels
Oh, child of beauty and promise and grace.
Hand-in-hand with the past beloved
and smiling at us from a heavenly place.

by Harriet Jackson Ralston

There was about to be a major turn in J. H. Ralston's life that for the present only he contemplated. For about a year, rampant rumors of a new silver strike near the small tented and *borrowed* wood built mining shacks of Virginia City had spread across the Sierras to the nearly defunct gold fields of the western slopes. Rumors evolved to fact based on published assay reports and by early in 1860 another new frontier in the far

THE COMSTOCK LODE.—From late advices the Placerville *Observer* learns that much richer silver ore had been struck in the Spanish claim than has ever before been found. The Spanish is a part of the Comstock lode. The rich ore was found at a lower depth than had been reached heretofore.

Sacramento Daily Union, 11/24/1859

western reaches of the Utah Territory was soon to be bombarded by experienced *get-rich-quickers*.

For the last few months, James had frequently reminisced about his travels. The sights and sounds, over 30 years before, of the rudimentary cabins and wood-frame structures he saw from a wagon on a rise overlooking Springfield nestled in Illinois' Sangamon Valley. The even fewer abodes in Quincy on the bluffs and the number of cabins he could count on one hand in Chicago on the shores of Lake Michigan. He remembered the dusty paths of the army's fort in San Antonio and his first office in a canvas tent near the Sacramento River just a decade ago. All of these places had become flourishing centers of commerce and prosperity due to the diligence of people just like him who were in the right place at the right time with the right amount of money. He often regretted never even attempting to kneel by a stream swashing the contents of a tin pan and patiently looking for golden reflections. Now, another opportunity to seek real fame and fortune was less than a week's ride from the chair where he sat. The strands of gray among the auburn hair he saw in the mirror every morning were a constant reminder that the number of such opportunities remaining may well be counted with a single finger. Is there silver in *them thar hills*? James needed to find out firsthand. How would he go about telling Harriet about his latest fantasy for another frontier foray. Careful deliberation was clearly in order.

Chapter 20

Something New, Something Borrowed

Since August of 1860, many of the notable names in Sacramento's law circles had made an exodus from the *plains city* east to the considerable heights of Carson and Virginia City. One of those defectors was none other than Neely Johnson, from who James was surprised to receive a short, but to the point, serendipitous letter in early October.

26 September '60
Carson [Utah Territory]

Cousin James,

I awoke this morning and was able to confirm that my current residence in Carson City was not some form of a delirious dream. Though, at some point in time I may determine my change of address to be a nightmare. With the notable exceptions of a river that periodically deposits a foot of mud in the town's streets and becoming winded on my early morning stroll, the tents and shanties here are a vivid reminder of our early days in Sacramento. But enough of my personal recollection.

THE BAR IN WASHOE.—We doubt whether any Court in California can show as brilliant an array of talent, as is now engaged in the trial of different cases before the U. S. District Court, in Genoa. We notice among other members of the Bar, Judges Baldwin, Terry and Bryan, present or ex-Judges of the Supreme Court of California; Stewart, Thornton and Kirkpatrick, of Downieville; Anderson and Lansing, of Nevada; ex-Governor J. Neely Johnson, and a host of others.

Marysville [CA] Daily Appeal, 9/20/1860

This place [Carson City], *and indeed the entire territory of Utah, including the Mormon stronghold near the Great Salt Lake is in need of capable attorneys whose services can attract a lucrative sum; I would add physicians to the list were I to mistake you for your brother. However, I was unaware that to ply our trade in this country requires substantive proof of residence in the same, a shortfall I have overcome at the expense of 30 days of not plying my trade.*

My request is simple, come to Washoe[93]. I, along with many of your friends now here, will welcome you with open arms and holstered pistols. Proof of my sincerity lays in the fact that my wife Mary, and our two children, will be joining me before the snow falls of which the aforesaid, as we have both experienced, is ample enough in this country.

Cousin Neely

When the time was right, this letter conveniently provided James with the facts he could use to frame a discussion with Harriet. He desired to pursue a life, including his family, in the endless deserts and high mountains of the frontier territory to the east.

A week later Judge Ralston decided to arrive early at his 4th street office to put the finishing touches on a brief he was to present at court that afternoon. He was surprised to find his 27 year-old junior partner, M. C. Tilden, already seated at his desk quickly turning the pages of a document as if he was looking through them for a particular passage. The judges greeting was met with a polite but nervous response and James asked his fidgety assistant if he could help with the work. M. C. finally looked up from the papers and uncharacteristically stumbled through a reply saying he thought he could find what he was looking for. James was now intrigued about what was bothering Tilden and he said as much. With a combined look of fear and dread, his partner stood from his chair and with perspiration dripping from his forehead he told the judge that he had a question he very much needed to ask. James handed M. C. his handkerchief and suggested he wipe his brow and try to calm down before he spoke. The Judge doubted there could be any subject he could think of that should cause such obvious anxiety on this cool pleasant morning. Tilden placed his hand on the corner of his desk as if bracing himself against a gale-force wind and blurted out a request for permission to marry Lizzie.

James stood motionless, reconsidering his previous thought about *any subject.* Before he could form a reply that in no uncertain terms would inform his junior partner that his daughter was only a child of 15, Harriet entered the room. She had secretly followed her husband to work in the event she was needed as a character witness for Squire Tilden. For the first time in a great while, James was speechless only asking himself what form of a conspiracy was about to unfold. Harriet asked James if she could explain the circumstances that led to this moment and all he could do was nod in agreement. She told him that some months ago, shortly after the couple first met, Lizzie had confided in her that for both she and M. C., their meeting was love at first sight. She asked Harriet what she should do. Harriet told her that she well understood that feeling because she too had felt that way when she first met her father though she knew at the time the feeling was not shared. Harriet's advice to Lizzie was to be patient and in a few years if she and her beau still felt the same about each other they could marry. With a tear trickling down her face, Harriet pleadingly looked at James and added that his daughter was in tears as a result of her advice. Lizzie had more to say.

Lizzie knew her mother had passed away well before her time. Because of her own frail nature, Lizzie firmly believed she would meet the same fate but not before she fulfilled her dream of becoming a mother. Further, with or without her father's approval, she and M. C. would marry as soon after her 16th birthday as possible. James felt the air leave his lungs and his stern expression became a soft smile directed first at his persuasive and loving wife. Then, adding an affirmative nod, he extended his hand in friendship to his soon-to-be son-in-law, Marcellus Crane Tilden. The satisfied silence in the room was broken when a joyful Lizzie rushed through the door and, starting with her father, she tearfully embraced each participant of the early morning meeting.

Harriet hosted a gay though small party at Shady Branch in October of 1860. She wanted to share with a selected few friends the occasion of her and her husband's 7th wedding anniversary, James' 51st birthday, and the official announcement of the marriage of Lizzie and M. C. Tilden in the coming year. The guests included Tom's wife and Harriet's sister, Amelia Sunderland, the proud parents of a new daughter born just a month before. Her good friend Mary B. Johnson whose husband, J. Neely, Harriet knew was off doing something in the wilds of primitive Washoe [the Nevada portion of the Utah Territory]. William C. and his wife Mary Wallace, and of course, M. C. Tilden. James toasted his lovely wife on their anniversary. Though not with a single breath, he blew out 51 candles on a multi-tiered frosted cake. M. C. placed an engagement ring on the finger of a beaming Lizzie. Jackson too participated, *borrowing,* then playing hide-and-seek for a time with Harriet's only solid silver cake spatula. Near the end of the party, Mary Johnson was talking with Harriet and mentioned her plans to join Neely, with their children, in Carson City in a few weeks. She wondered if James had completed his plans to make a similar trip. Harriet simply replied with a questioning look, *not to her knowledge.* A good time was had by all though Harriet was anxious for her guests to leave so she could *speak with James* concerning Mary Johnson's parting comment.

After the last guest departed, James made a beeline for his favorite chair and assumed a relaxed position after an unusually long day. Harriet returned to the sitting room from making sure that Jackson and Aurora were tucked in and asleep and she sat in her chair near James. After Harriet was comfortably seated, she casually addressed her husband as *Judge Ralston* and asked him when he was planning to let her in on an idea he may be entertaining to travel to Carson City. It would be an understatement to say that James found himself in the precarious position between a rock and a hard place though he was still hopeful of an escape. He truthfully shared with Harriet his reminiscences and his one last chance to be rich and famous on a new frontier. He took from his pocket the folded letter from Neely, a telegraphed message he had sent to Neely in reply, and handed them to Harriet.

Telegraph message, 3 October '60 to J. Neely Johnson, Carson City UT

Neely [stop] I can only respond to your offer after I have spoken with Harriet [stop] J. H. [stop]

Harriet carefully read the two documents. She looked at James and rhetorically asked him if he thought for one moment that she would stand in the way of anything he believed he needed to do as long as the rest of the family could be by his side. She added from her standpoint, his age never had been and was not now an issue in any decision they made. James rose from his chair, leaned over, and gently kissed his wife on the forehead. He promised to never again doubt the unflagging support of the woman he loved.

The first order of business allowing Judge Ralston to invade the new frontier required that he establish residency in Washoe so that he could practice law while he searched for his very own rich vein of silver. Three days after Harriet's *grand party,* he boarded a Pioneer Stage Company coach in Sacramento for the 2-day trip to Carson City. He borrowed a horse from cousin Neely and rode another day northeast to Virginia City nestled at 6,600 feet on the eastern slope of Mt. Davidson. With *somewhat bogus* paperwork he had prepared before he left Sacramento, J. H. Ralston filed a speculator's mining claim at the city offices of Atwill and Company's Agency for Mining Claims that showed he resided at the site of his purported claim. Harriet was glad to greet her husband on his return five days later. Life at Shady Branch returned to normal, at least for the time being.

In early November of 1860, the Sacramento countryside stirred with the anticipation of the presidential election to be held on the 6th of that month. All over the country bands played, speeches were made, bets parlayed, and politicians unstaid in every attempt to curry the favor of the voting public. The leading contenders were Abraham Lincoln, heading the Republican ticket, Stephen Douglas the *regular* Democrats, John Breckinridge the *southern* Democrats, and John Bell the Constitutional Union candidate.

On election day, Judge Ralston placed an *x* on his ballot next to Douglas' name, reasoning that his friend's election might forestall or even prevent an irreparable rift in the country between the north and the south on the slavery issue. The subject of slavery in the southern states was disguised as each state's right to self-govern and to preserve

its heritage that included the ownership of slaves. As early as the 15th, the San Francisco Daily Alta, and the Sacramento Daily Union declared Lincoln as president-elect. Those papers based their reporting on the early returns from the populated northern states including Lincoln and Douglas' home state of Illinois. On the 28th of the month, California finally had an official tally from all of its counties showing Lincoln with a 681 vote margin over Douglas and a 4,999 margin over Breckinridge, out of over 120,000 votes cast. During and in the days following the election, rumor of secession in southern states was already being publicly reported. In James' view, it was merely a matter of *when* and not *if* that action happened. Interestingly enough, the election

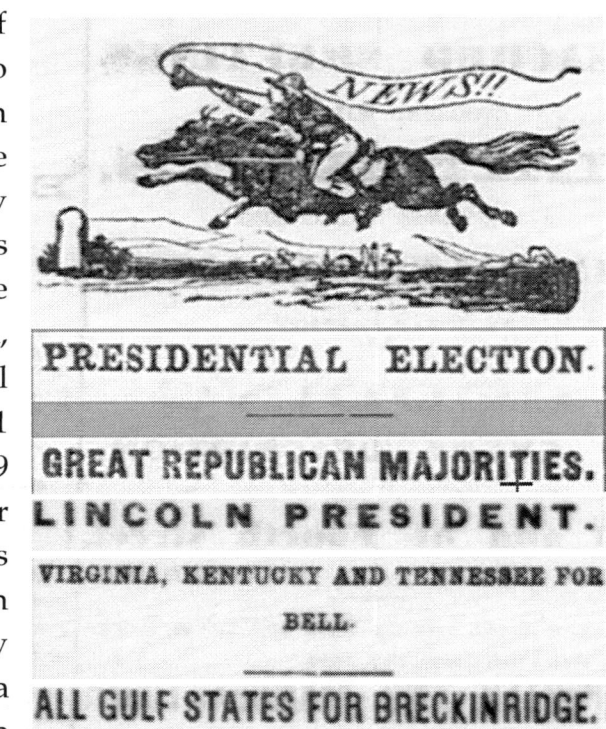

San Francisco Daily Alta, 11/15/1860

news throughout the country reached the west coast in the form of telegrams sent to St. Joseph, Missouri that were delivered at the then hefty cost of $2.50 per ½ ounce to Sacramento, a distance of over 1,600 miles, in just under 8 days by the recently formed *pony express*[94].

After a tearful departure and with James promising to be back in Sacramento in time for his daughter's marriage, Judge Ralston left on horseback for the Carson Valley. Though the terrain, mid-November's light snowfall, and the compass direction were the opposite, J. H. felt much of the same excitement and anticipation as he did on his departure from Quincy to California ten years earlier. This next new frontier he hoped provided another opportunity to succeed.

He had arranged to meet Mormon Colonel John Reese[95] and his family in Carson City then join them in crossing the desert to Salt Lake City. Attorney Ralston would represent Reese in a suit tried before the Utah Territory Supreme Court in the thriving Mormon city by the Great Salt Lake. Assuming the weather cooperated, James was confident of an uneventful journey because Reese knew the route like the back of his hand. Also, his client was on friendly terms with the various Pah Ute[96] Indian colonies inhabiting the desolate mountainous desert terrain. However, as it turned out the trip was anything but uneventful.

The 9-passenger overland stagecoach left Carson City on the 14th of November 1860, pulled by a team of six horses carrying Judge Ralston and the Reese family. The coach dutifully followed the route used by the *Pony Express* that Col. Reese and his brother knew in detail years before during their frequent re-supply trips between Salt Lake and their general store in Genoa. Seven days east of Carson City and about 280 miles of rough and tumble riding, ascending and descending one desert mountain range after another, the travelers arrived at the Ruby Valley express station. They spent a restful quiet night on the southern shore of Ruby Lake.

Early the next morning under a clear sky, the passengers were again headed eastward on the trail and by mid-morning they arrived at the Mountain Springs station for a brief respite and a change of horses. The coach would next negotiate the treacherous climb over the Butte Mountains and half-way down the eastern slope to the Butte Station. On the narrow trail leading to the pass, the horses began to shy, sensing something out of the ordinary was about to happen, which it did a few moments later. Just behind the coach, a loud rumble marked the beginning of a rock slide that moments later sent rocks of all shapes and sizes cascading down the mountain side, covering the trail they had just passed. Gaining momentum and magnitude, the slide continued to send tons of debris to the valley below. The episode was over in less than a minute, the driver brought the coach to a stop, and set the brake to see what harm, if any, the rock slide had caused to the passengers or their mode of transport.

Everyone emerged safe and sound and they all surveyed the massive amount of mountain that the effect of gravity had sent to the valley floor. Col. Reese glanced up the mountain side to insure that no more rocks were on their way when his eye caught the sparkling reflection of the sun's light from the slide's crater. Reese cautiously made his way about fifty feet up the mountain to verify what he suspected caused the rainbow colored reflection. Confirming his suspicion, he summoned Judge Ralston to the spot. The rockslide had uncovered a nearly five-foot vein of quartz and by the time James had joined his friend, Reese was sifting through a handful of the quartz and commenting that it contained

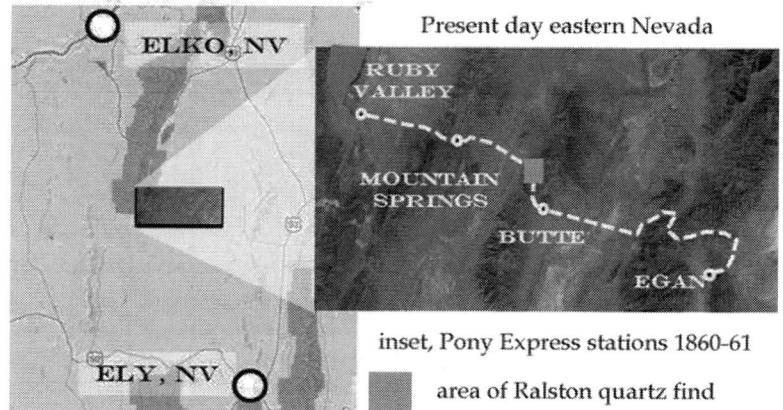

Present day eastern Nevada

inset, Pony Express stations 1860-61

area of Ralston quartz find

recognizable flakes of silver and gold. James had heard stories of valuable ore found as a result of such slides. His heart skipped a beat when Reese shared his opinion that this one might just be a paying find, worth, in his experience, assaying a sample and possibly filing a claim. In the least, he suggested that the judge carve his name and the date on a sizable rock and place it at the foot of the vein indicating a potential owner had surveyed and marked the spot. When James asked Reese if he wanted to be part of the discovery, his client said that he was a *mercantile man and not a miner*. James eagerly scrawled *Ralston Nov 22 '60, Thanks-giving day* on the face of a large rock with his pocket knife. With Reese's help he rolled it to the foot of the vein, filled an empty burlap feed sack with samples from several places in the vein. With a boyish wild-eyed enthusiasm, he reluctantly took his seat back in the coach. During the rest of the day's journey to Butte Station and on to Egan station for the night, Reese shared with James his many stories of instant riches.

Ten days later when the travelers arrived at the Salt Lake station, James mind was still spinning in wonderment over what he was sure was *the find* he had waited years to discover. That evening he could not resist penning a short letter to Harriet with the news of their great impending wealth.

2 Dec. '60
Salt Lake City

Dearest Harriet,

I cannot bring to bay my enthusiasm over my adventure on the trail to this city. On the 22nd last, our coach barely escaped an avalanche of rock while climbing the pass to the Butte express station. During a brief inspection of the calamity, Col. Reese brought to my attention a quartz vein uncovered by the slide that in his most experienced opinion was laden with silver and gold. On the Col.'s recommendation I inscribed a rock at the sight with my name and the date of its discovery and replaced a burlap bag containing oats with rock samples from the same.

I shall have an assay carried out in this city to either confirm or deny the bountiful riches we may receive and keep you appraised of the findings. I will readily admit to you that my aged curiosity is piqued at perhaps its highest point and keeping my mind to the purpose of the Law will be a task worthy of a better man.

J. H.

[BY PONY EXPRESS.]
LETTER FROM SALT LAKE.

[FROM OUR SPECIAL CORRESPONDENT.]

Judge J. H. Ralston, of your city, arrived here on Wednesday Evening. He left Carson with a small company coming to this city, among whom were Colonel Reese and family .... The Judge had extensive acquaintance with the Mormons in Illinois, in the days of Joseph Smith, and seems to have no difficulty in recognizing and being recognized. He comes here on [legal] business appealed from Judge Cradlebuagh's Court to the Supreme Court, which will be held in early January.

Sacramento Daily Union, 12/10/1860

Judge Ralston kept very busy in Salt Lake City while he anxiously awaited the assay results. When he was not diligently preparing for his first appearance in the territory's supreme court, he made a specific effort to renew the old Mormon relationships he had in Quincy. Starting, of course, with Brigham Young. Young called together a select assembly of the men and women who had known Judge Ralston. For nearly a week, they reminisced about the *old days*, described their arduous journey to the Great Salt Lake, and accompanied him on an extended tour of *their* city in the desert. At the end of the week, James was feted to a banquet in his honor where he was toasted for his efforts allowing the *Saints* to recover from their Missouri ordeal in the relative safety of Nauvoo and to renew their strength for the migration west. Though it had cost James his personal and professional status in Illinois, he took great satisfaction from the fact that his efforts were recognized and appreciated. He was glad to see the Mormon's had found their true *Zion* at last, a place that he knew would endure for generations to come.

James received the assay the week before Christmas and the results showed the presence of large quantities of both gold and silver. The report clearly stated that the true worth of the claim can only be determined when the extent of the vein is known. He was eager to return to the site. He knew the completion of the obligation to his client, Col. Reese, and the weather would prevent him from making the journey any time soon. A realization that caused anxiety and many sleepless nights. The Supreme Court session began in the city on the 6th of January 1861 and despite the nearly overwhelming distraction, Judge Ralston's courtroom demeanor and effectiveness was perhaps better than it had ever been. He believed his performance was driven by the tidy sum he would receive for this work and even much more by his visions of abundant wealth as the territory's new gold and silver *baron*. A new found level of confidence, he reflected, at the ripe *young* age of fifty-one.

Before mid-January, Judge Ralston knew that the agonizingly sluggish progress of the trial, the severity of the high desert winter, and his intense desire to get back to his claim would make his presence at the February 3rd wedding of Lizzie and M. C. Tilden a virtual impossibility. He wrote a lengthy letter addressed to both Harriet and Lizzie. He explained as best he could why he could not be present, profusely apologizing for his absence at perhaps the most important event in Lizzie's young life, and telling them how much he cared for and loved them both. The spots of tear stained ink were dry, though not unnoticed, by the time the sealed envelope was opened and read in Sacramento.

Harriet exceeded her expectations in preparing Shady Branch to host the nuptials of her step-daughter, Lizzie and M. C. The guest list included everyone that Harriet, Lizzie, and M. C. knew or *thought* they knew. On the day of the life-changing occasion, every corner of the Ralston home was full, with many of the attendees spilling onto the front porch. To say the event was standing-room-only would have significantly understated reality. Four-year-old Jackson even tried his best to put his learned numerals to the test in counting the number of carriages and horses arrayed near the barn all the way to the house, but tearfully succumbed to an unknown number.

Justice of the Peace, Charles Pettit, assumed his position near the front windows of the living room soon joined by M. C. Tilden. The crowd parted the way for two-year-old Aurora who, with her mother's help, dropped rose petals from the kitchen all the way to where Justice Pettit stood. Then, to the accompaniment of a violinist, a smiling Lizzie, arm-in-arm with good friend Tom Sunderland made her way through the living room. She carried a small bouquet of her favorite violets and was dressed in the same pale-white laced linen gown her mother wore to marry Judge Ralston almost 30 years before. She joined her already tearful step-mother and her smiling betrothed in front of the Justice of the Peace.

Before Lizzie kissed her new husband, she kissed Harriet on the cheek, blew a kiss in the air announcing it was for her absent father. Hand-in-hand the couple joyfully acknowledged the surrounding well-wishers. Everyone in attendance tried their best to catch a glimpse or, for the lucky ones, a full view of the couple exchanging their vows.

Harriet sat alone in the quiet of the evening satisfied with her deeds for that special day then fell asleep tearfully hoping that her man so far away was safe from harm.

Marcellus Crane Tilden   Elizabeth "Lizzie" Jane Ralston Tilden
Courtesy of the descendants of James H. and Jane Alexander Ralston

Chapter 21

Silver Baron?

Nearly the same time Lizzie said *I do* in Sacramento, Judge Ralston completed his closing arguments in his case before the Supreme Court in Salt Lake City. A few days later the court adjourned. James made arrangements to travel with a small group going west to Carson City though he would disembark at the Butte express station and travel by horseback to his claim about five miles farther west. On the 8th of February 1861, Judge Ralston boarded the overland stage in Salt Lake City with his traveling companions Major Egan[97] and Edward Creighton[98]. Miner Ralston neglected to account for two related obstacles before arriving at his claim a little over a week later. In mid-February and for the two months prior, at well over a mile-high elevation, the temperature rarely, if ever, reaches above freezing. Hence the

Major Howard Egan

Edward Creighton

ground is frozen to a depth of over two feet. James spent nearly a week with pick and shovel and freezing at night with no tent, he slept in a cave he found near-by. The hole he dug around the quartz vein was about 4 ½ feet deep at a 45-degree downward angle. The good news was that the full breadth of the vein extended that distance and, he still had feeling in his face, fingers, and toes. The bad news was he realized he would need help in digging deeper, and he returned to Salt Lake.

The judge found it difficult to locate experienced mining labor to assist him because the proven miners were already reaping the benefits of their labor at the Comstock Lode near Virginia City nearly 400 miles to the west. The knowledge of the miners in Salt Lake was limited to Mormons who had been unsuccessful during the height of the

California gold rush and returned to Zion to farm. Though they were hard workers, many of them were not anxious to leave the warmth of home in exchange for the freezing temperatures at higher altitude 250 miles west. None of them had experience with the use of black powder needed as a blasting agent for the mainly granite rock in the area of the mine. He did however find a group of about a dozen men with questionable experience, currently out of work, who were willing to accompany him with the promise of riches beyond their wildest dreams.

[BY PONY EXPRESS.]
LETTER FROM SALT LAKE.
[FROM OUR SPECIAL CORRESPONDENT.]

GREAT SALT LAKE CITY,
March 2, 1861.

Hunting for Silver Mines.

In a former letter I noticed that Judge Ralston, of your city, had gone west to examine what he supposed to be a rich silver mine. The Judge returned on Monday or Tuesday, formed some relations with parties here, took out some help, and started back again on Wednesday. I had no talk with him during this visit, but I learn from a gentleman with whom he spoke that the article had been discovered, spirits were light, and pleasant day-dreams were the result.

Sacramento Daily Union 3/12/1861

Two wagons that James *borrowed* from Mormon friends lead the convoy of horses heading for their first stop at Fort Crittenden [formerly Camp Floyd] about 50 miles south southwest of Salt Lake. Here they would turn due west for the rest of the 7-day journey. Ten miles from their first destination a light snow accompanied by darkening clouds portended one of the infamous winter snowstorms that struck the high desert. These storms, with unimaginable ferocity, created a virtual *white out* of wind driven snow. These very conditions existed just as they arrived at the fort. The caravan barely had time to stable their horses before the visibility turned to less than five feet. The wind howled and the snow fell until just before daybreak. At first light, the troop examined the white landscape covered with about a foot of new snow. Most of man had already had enough, their silver fever dipped to normal body temperature, and they were ready to head home. Three of the company committed to proceed with James though he knew that would not be enough men to meet the task. He sent them all back to Salt Lake lead by one of the two wagons containing their camping and digging equipment.

Later that day, Judge Ralston tied his horse to the back of the remaining wagon and, undaunted, slapped the team of horses in a westerly direction. For the next five days, James only company was the occasional pony express rider, each one stopping long enough to warn him of the proven dangers of proceeding alone. They all mentioned calamitous storms that approached without warning. More importantly, the occasional whims of the Pah Ute Indians to attack a lone rider particularly one with a wagon full of tradable goods. James safely arrived at the comparatively luxurious Deep Creek Pony Express station. He decided to stop for a time and send mail on the pony trail to recruit workers for his all-consuming cause. After James mentioned his friendship with Major Egan, the station manager's boss, J. H. found himself in a comfortable room with double rations of food. In exchange for the manager's kindness, Judge Ralston volunteered to help with the station's chores, including cooking meals for the riders and shoveling a copious amount of the foul smelling byproduct of the equine digestive system.

The Sacramento Daily Union published an update on the Judge's progress to getting rich on April 11, 1861.

I had almost forgot to mention the absence of Judge Ralston at the silver mines he thinks that he has discovered... The Judge's company only went out part way, and a heavy snowstorm turned them eastward again... since their return I have not heard the first one avow that he had ever gone further than Fort Crittenden, or ever intended going further. The judge has lost none of his faith, though his disciples have deserted him... the mail agents, aware of the danger from Indians, urged upon taking up quarters with them at Deep Creek [Pony Express station]... He is there at the present time and safe enough.

While at Deep Creek, the miner examined his alternatives for proceeding. He determined he would need more funding if he was to gain the level of expertise he needed to fully probe his discovery. On more than one occasion, James had used the newspapers to sway public opinion, why not this time. With the pony express riders

Deep Creek Pony Express station, Utah Terr. ca 1862

literally stopping at his front door, he decided to write some letters. His first letter was to Harriet so that she knew where he was and that he was safe. The second letter was to J. Neely to see, if by way of the newspaper, his cousin could arouse some level of interest in the mining investment circles. A third letter, to the Sacramento Union extolled the virtues and possibilities of his discovery. As a result of his letter to J. Neely the following article appeared in the Sacramento Daily Union, on March 29th, 1861 in the *News of the Morning* section:

A report is in circulation, among dealers in Washoe stocks and others interested, that Judge Ralston, formerly of this city, has discovered a silver lead of remarkable richness near Salt Lake City. We have ascertained from good authority that the mine in question, like a thousand others existing in the same region, is only of supposed richness. It is situated two hundred and fifty miles this side of Salt Lake City, directly on the pony route. Judge Ralston is taking measures to practically demonstrate its value.

Thirteen days later the letter he wrote directly to the newspaper, supposedly written from the *Ralston Mines*, dated April 1st appeared in the Sacramento Daily Union, April 11th 1861, under the heading *Discovery of a Rich Mine in Utah Territory;*

.... I found one of the most magnificent veins of quartz I have ever seen, of the most perfect crystallization.... indicating either gold or silver, or both.... On further examination, made when the surface of the earth was enveloped in snow, I found several other veins, from two of which I took specimens and have tested them---one proves the existence of gold, the other, gold and silver mixed. In a few days I shall commence work in earnest on these mines, and have no doubt of finding them equal to any in Carson Valley. We are about 400 miles east of Carson City and two hundred [250] miles west of Salt Lake on the great Central Mail Route.... I shall keep you advised of the further result of my operations in these mines.

Alright, he told himself, the bread is on the water.

O joy of all joys, he had a taker! On the 6th of April, James received a letter from his earlier travel companion, Edward Creighton. Creighton wrote that he had an eastbound telegraph pole setting crew coming by Deep River station on the 8th. He went on to write that they had all of the tools and explosives necessary to *side bore and shore* a small tunnel next to his vein to determine its depth. If he wanted their help they would be available to him for no longer than a week. Creighton, ever the opportunistic businessman, added that in the event the mine looked promising he would require a 20% ownership option and if not, James could consider the work a favor to a friend. The short ending paragraph read that Mr. Green was the crew foreman and if he was interested in the offer, *let him know.* There was absolutely no doubt in Judge Ralston's mind that an affirmative response would be forthcoming when the crew arrived.

For the next two days James repeatedly glanced at his watch hoping that unlike a *watched pot* the time would quickly boil away. It did not. The longest two days of his life eventually passed when three wagons and a nine-passenger coach pulled into Deep Creek. After the shortest conversation Mr. Green had ever experienced, James tied his horse to the trailing wagon, climbed into the coach, and patiently waited for over two hours while the men ate lunch and watered and fed their horses. Finally, they were off.

On the 13th day of April 1861, a Saturday, not a Friday, Judge Ralston was officially told that his vein, called a *pocket find* by Green, abruptly ended at 8 feet from the surface. Though there was quartz containing mainly silver and some gold, the cost to mine the claim far exceeded its ore value. He handed James a six-inch quartz crystal that in Green's opinion was worth a $20 gold piece in any bank in the country, as a memory of his find. The men shook hands, and Green proceeded with his crew west to the Mountain Spring station leaving James sitting by his horse on the side of the mountain in perhaps the most remote spot in the desert. For a while James looked with utter disappointment at the crystal, then smiled and thought to himself, *I am worth $20 more* *than I was before I came.* He mounted his horse and rode in the opposite direction, east to the Deep River station.

In those days, word about the worth of mining claims traveled as fast as a speeding horse could carry its rider. The following article appeared in the Sacramento Daily Union on the 26th of April, dated from the 18th of April.

The Ralston Discovery: *In my correspondence I noticed that Judge Ralston had supposed himself the discoverer of a rich silver mine, about 250 miles west of this* [Salt Lake]; *and noticing that it is somewhat credited in Sacramento, it may not be amiss to add that the Judge's efforts to produce ore have, it is reported, been a perfect failure. I have just seen a Pony Letter from Deep Creek, where the Judge was temporarily located, and the writer states that his Honor had fired his last blast, and "fiasco" was written on the scattered rocks.... Had the Judge been supported by the company that started from here with him, but who turned back at the first snowstorm, it might have been different.*

Chapter 22

Virginia City

The *mining* judge had been busily infatuated with his silver mine during the first four months of 1861 missing out completely on two other events of importance. One event, unknown to him at the time, would provide the stage for his next production. In late February and early March, the United States Congress sequentially passed two bills officially forming the Colorado Territory from a western portion of Kansas. The second bill formed the Nevada Territory from the area in western Utah Territory called Washoe. Departing President James Buchanan left the naming of the new Nevada Territory officials to his successor Abraham Lincoln. On March 22nd, Lincoln named New York Attorney James Warren Nye as the first governor of the Nevada Territory. A few days later, Lincoln appointed an ardent campaign supporter and little known Hannibal, Missouri newspaperman, Orion Clemens, as the territory's secretary of state.

The other event that captured headlines across the country and eventually around the world was the commencement of the event most everyone predicted and feared, civil war.[99] Confederate General Beauregard's bombardment of Fort Sumter in the Charleston, South Carolina, harbor, on April 13th 1861, lead to Union Major Anderson's surrender of the fort. This action triggered a flurry

The New-York Times.

NEW-YORK, SATURDAY, APRIL 13, 1861.

THE WAR COMMENCED.

The First Gun Fired by Fort Moultrie Against Fort Sumpter.

THE BOMBARDMENT CONTINUED ALL DAY.

Note spelling of Ft. Sumter

Daily Alta California.

SAN FRANCISCO, THURSDAY MORNING, APRIL 25, 1861.

Attack on Fort Sumter!

Surrender of Maj. Anderson!

CIVIL WAR COMMENCED

Note: first printed in an Alta extra 4/24/1861, 11 days later.

of events culminating in Lincoln's proclamation to conscript 75,000 men from the states still in the Union in an effort to quell the rebellion. When James finally became aware of the conflict's outbreak, he was even more determined to protect his family and himself from the political fallout and out of harm's way by residing in the safety of the Nevada Territory, far from the war's epicenter.

For a while, James continued to *dally* in the area of his mine knowing full-well that there would be no intervention, divine or otherwise, that would make his vein spew forth copious amounts of silver and gold. He was just not quite ready to let go of his evaporated dream. On the 26th of May, James wrote a letter to his son-in-law M. C. Tilden from the Antelope Springs express station, 178 miles southwest of Salt Lake, describing the remaining vestiges of that dream.

…. In my mine we have not reached pure ore …. The men working with me in the mine found, a few miles distant a place where …. Silver can be gathered up without digging. They have all gone there leaving me alone. In the mine we have gone through the outer covering at a depth of thirteen feet, and come to clear moist crystalized quartz …. but not in good workable quality.

In July of 1861, Judge Ralston packed his belongings in two carpetbags and boarded an overland stage west to Carson City. From there he traveled 17 miles northwest where he intended to establish a law practice and make a home for his family in Virginia City[100].

The same month, Governor Nye finally arrived in the Nevada Territory he was appointed to lead. A few weeks later he was joined by his secretary of state, 35 year-old

Samuel Clemens

Orion Clemens

Orion Clemens. Orion traveled to Nevada with his younger brother Samuel. The younger Clemens had saved the money necessary for the journey from his job as a Mississippi River steamboat pilot. Samuel came along on the trip ostensibly as his older brother's unofficial secretary, though it would, a year later, lead to more than that. Nye and Orion Clemens began the process of organizing the territory's first legislative session scheduled to be held in Carson City in October of 1861. Meanwhile, the more congenial Samuel filed a timber claim, took options on mining company stocks, and had ore assayed from a number of speculative mines, all of which promised much and yielded nothing.

Harriet received a letter from James writing about his arrival in Virginia City. He wrote that once he was well settled in his law practice he would make the arrangements necessary to sell Shady Branch and move her and the children to Virginia City. She meant exactly what she said when she told James she would never stand in the way of anything he wanted to do as long as his family was with him. However, to say she was thoroughly pleased with the latest news would be a stretch of the truth. His plan to sell the family's comfortable home in Sacramento in exchange for the life in a rough-and-tumble mining town on the side of a desert mountain in the middle of nowhere would be a test of *stand by your man*. Harriet sent a return letter innocently asking James if he was sure this was what he wanted do and again repeating her pledge. She knew what his answer would be and she started preparing herself to follow her husband to one of the nearby *ends of the earth*.

Judge Ralston followed his *modus operandi* by letting as many people as possible know of his arrival and law practice in Virginia City. He managed to arrange to be one of the featured speakers at a political rally in his new home. He eloquently extolled his support for the Union in its armed struggle against the secessionists willing to divide the country at whatever the cost.

Sacramento Daily Union, 8/29/1861:

Later from Nevada Territory: A political meeting was held at Virginia City last Saturday evening, and Union speeches were made by Judge Ralston.... After the meeting had adjourned the friends of the Secession candidate for Congress, gathered around the stand. He [the secessionist] compared Jeff Davis to [George] Washington, and according to his idea Jeff Davis was rather the greater and better man of the two....The confusion was so great that the speaker could barely be heard.... Three cheers were then proposed for Davis but the secessionist voices were drowned by cheers for the Union.

A little over a month later, October 1, 1861, the judge was present as an interested spectator when Governor Nye convened the first Nevada territorial legislative session at the Warm Springs Hotel on the outskirts of Carson City. The hotel had been loaned by its builder and owner, Abe Curry as a temporary meeting place for the legislature while a permanent meeting place was sought.

Warm Springs Hotel ca 1864

In 1924, James' son, Jackson, wrote about a five-year old's vague memories of the trip Harriet, Aurora, and he made to Virginia City to join his father in November of 1861.[101]

....[It was] in the month of November, that my mother with her two children, little more than babes, resolved to leave Sacramento for Virginia City, where my father in the first flush of the Comstock [Lode] days, had begun the practice of law. My mother was warned of the hardships and dangers of the trip .... for her, meaning a month of trouble.

In spite of all terrors, however, my mother with her children set out on the adventurous trip. Vaguely I can picture stops among the trees in camp at night. For some reason our original conveyance [likely a stagecoach] *was abandoned for another wagon with a strange driver....*

A memory comes back to me of being snowbound in a sawmill, in one end of which privacy was secured for us by putting up blankets for curtains. High up in the Sierras I seem to see a moment of danger when the wagon is apparently about to go over the steep outer side of the road, while the boulder clad mountain rises high on the other, with snow all about. My sister and myself are dropped out of the wagon while my mother in terror jumps for her life. When the wagon is righted we proceed on our journey....

The latter part of the journey was for a short distance by stage, which took us to Carson, where we were joined by my father. Thence the trip to Virginia City was a short and unadventurous one.

James was again in the loving company of his family that he had last seen almost a year

Virginia City
Nevada Territory
1861

Nevada Territory
1861

VIRGINIA
CITY

CARSON
CITY

ago and when he asked Harriet about their trip she smiled and modestly replied *not much of a bother.*

The Virginia City that greeted the Ralstons in late 1861 was carved out of the slope of Mt. Davidson, a location that best served the Comstock miners and the hundreds of other smaller mines with their telltale tailings that seemed to dot the entire landscape.

The city was divided into wards, and the straggling cabins formed parts of connected rows.... Substantial wooden and brick buildings lined the main business streets and wooden platforms or sidewalks were laid in front of the stores and saloons.... On the upper streets were the residences of the mine superintendents and the leading merchants.... At the foot of Mount Davidson was the Chinese quarter, and below this crowded section were a few rickety huts, which sheltered Piute or Washoe Indian families.... Gambling and eating were occupations; work, an unpleasant interlude....the city, set in a desert, had something prison-like in its encircling wall of barren hills, and few thought of straying beyond the circle of lights.[102]

Despite the setting, the Ralston family thrived as described by Jackson:

Three years of life in this famous mining town have left few memories. I recall somewhat of a house clinging to the steep side of Mount Davidson, in which we first lived and through which the water rushed when the spring snows melted, and then removal to a house nearly opposite the Episcopal Church.... I recall with some little cousins [the Sunderland family also moved to Virginia City] *finding a few grains of wheat which we sowed and watered with the greatest of care and were rewarded by the shooting up of tender spears of green.... These were flush times in mines and among the mining attorneys.... From its earliest days Virginia City boasted a public school, and at that time boys of my age were taught that when we looked to the North, the East would be to our right and the West to our left and the South behind us.... Hooky was popular and its glories described to me so vividly that I took one day off from school to study it, wandering with other errant boys over the desert, chasing lizards, eating pine nuts and wild onions, while doubtless dreaming ourselves great Indian killers or road agents* [bandits] *according to the then popular term. The game did not seem to me worth the candle* [the high price paid] *and the experiment was not replicated.*

Judge Ralston was successful in gaining a good price for Shady Branch just before Harriet traveled to Virginia City. Edward F. Aiken, an agriculturist of some reputation, renamed Shady Branch, Glen Gardens, and began a nursery business selling many varieties of fruit trees and fruit and grapes from his personal orchard and vineyard; until the rains came. In the winter of 1861-62, Sacramento was inundated with the greatest amount of water in its recorded history and nearly a third of Glen Gardens and its planted contents were mercilessly engulfed by the raging American River. In late December of 1861, M. C. Tilden wrote to his father-in-law. His home was completely surrounded by water and he was only able to post the letter because of the kindness of some friends who checked on his family's well-being. They arrived using canoes they had borrowed from a friendly Indian Tribe. James was glad his daughter was high and dry and even more thankful that the rains had come after the sale of his land and Harriet's journey over the Sierras.

The extensive barren surroundings of Virginia City coupled with the unusual odors that occasionally wafted from town up to the Ralston's mountain side home were just two of the many reasons Harriet was bound and determined to make the Christmas of 1861 a special event. She started the work by locating, with her children's help, a particularly spectacular Douglas Fir in the forests leading to Lake Bigler [Tahoe]. A silver dollar persuaded the wagon driver to cut *the magnificent find*, load it into the wagon, and carry it back to Virginia City. For another *two-bits*, he nailed the tree's base to a couple of short two-by-fours and helped Harriet positon the evergreen *just so* in the middle of the living room. She spent the next few hours in the Chinese neighborhood of the city bargaining for candles. Returning home, she adorned nearly every branch on the tree with something colorful to put the finishing touches on her Christmas masterpiece. When James came home at his usual early evening hour, he was greeted by luminaries that were in every window of the house and lit his path to the front door. Once inside, Harriet placed a blindfold around her husband's head. Jackson and Aurora took Father by the hand leading him to the living room for the grand presentation of this year's version of Christmas in the high desert. The blindfold removed, James was nearly overwhelmed by the scene that brought back the pleasant memories of James and Harriet's first Christmas as good friends in Quincy, and the Johnson's gala, as newlyweds, in Sacramento. Beside the warmth of the fireplace, the Ralston family raised three wine glasses, a baby bottle filled with hot chocolate toasting one thing then another, and ending with a toast to the wife and mother they all loved. There was a mad scramble to the living room the next morning for the grand opening of gifts under the tree. Dinner featuring roast turkey, warmed pine nuts, and custard, more than succeeded in satisfying Harriet's Christmas wish and far exceeded any expectations of her family.

The rain that flooded the rivers of the Sacramento and Joaquin Valleys to far beyond anything previously remembered turned to snow by the time the moisture laden storms repeatedly visited the eastern slopes of the Sierras. The mud on the streets of Virginia City froze solid. The only good that came from the worst winter the *old-timers* could ever recall was the superb condition of the sledding runs that threaded among the mines down the slope of Mt. Davidson. When no snow fell, children escaped from school and their academic toils at the ending bell. From that moment until the sunset hour, the mountainside was filled with the joyous sounds of frolicking sledders and snowballers. It seemed to Harriet she was in a constant state of being housebound and Judge Ralston often needed over an hour to reach the law offices of Ralston and

Griffith[103] in neighboring Gold Hill less than a mile away. The signs of spring in 1862 were never ever more welcomed.

Cousin J. Neely was a well-established attorney in Carson City by 1862. In the spring he was in the middle of a project that had nothing at all to do with the law though it had a great deal to do with his social standing. Nearly a year earlier, Neely and his wife Mary, had struck up a friendship with *Sandy* Bowers[104] and his new wife Eilley Cowan Bowers[105]. The couple were two of a handful of speculative mine investors to strike it very rich. They were the first official millionaires from the discovery of silver mined from the Comstock Lode. Sandy was an *unlettered* [illiterate] teamster who came to Nevada from Missouri

Sandy Bowers ca 1864   Eilley Bowers ca 1867

where he met and married Scottish-born Eilley, of the same educational achievement. In later years Sandy was described as *spare, boyish and given to roistering,* and *a gentleman without trying and without knowing why,* As a couple, they were famous *for their riches and their* [less than enlightened] *uses of wealth.* The Bowers' were living proof of James' written description, *whilst others apparently less the favorites of fortune will be enriched.*

The Bowers' Mansion ca 1865

The project Neely had agreed to undertake was, of all things, designing and overseeing the construction of the extravagant Bowers mansion. It was to be built on a tract of land with spectacular mountain views near the shore of Washoe Lake, 12 miles north of Carson City. When Judge Ralston learned of his cousin's latest enterprise, his sarcastically asked, *how many more heretofore-unknown talents can one man possess?* The Bowers traveled to Europe bringing back all manner of elegant furnishings and art work to appoint their luxurious estate, destined to become the envy of the Sierras.

Two events involving the Ralston family occupied the summer of 1862. The first, the Fourth of July in Virginia City surprised the family. It was truly a gala of great celebration that seemed to be attended by a number of people in excess of the supposed population. The crowd that began to gather at about noon no doubt included the families of nearby miners but also many who climbed the road from Carson City on horseback, by carriage, coach, or the wagon full. The extent of the revelry in the Territorial capital was said to be of a more serene nature than in Virginia City. James shared with Harriet his belief that the more serious nature of Carson's wealthy sparked in their workers a need to use a holiday from work out of town as an excuse to release their pent-up spirit. Harriet had a different view, speculating that the wives of those wealthy men down in the valley never loosened their corsets nor let their hair down long enough to recognize a truly good time. If they did, they would not let their husbands or children partake for fear of social and moral decay. The real reason was likely that Virginia City's number of saloons nearly tripled those of the capital city.

Two weeks before the planned celebration, the city held a contest for the person who could author the most appropriate poetic verse for the occasion. The winner would have the honor of reciting their creation prior to an oratorical presentation in the middle of town. At the stroke of 2:00 o'clock, Harriet ascended the stairs of the temporary platform. She met the polite applause from the women in the crowd in recognition of the contest winner's gender. She waxed poetic

> VIRGINIA CITY.—The Fourth was celebrated in this place with great earnestness. The poem was written by Mrs. J. H. Ralston, and the oration delivered by M. D. Larrowe.

Sacramento Daily Union 7/10/1862

for nearly five minutes followed by more applause mixed with an occasional *hurrah*. This time from everyone within hearing distance in appreciation of her poetic skill. After she rejoined her husband, James whispered to her that in his experience such a raised platform is used for a hanging or to present a medal. He was most pleased she received the latter. Harriet's laughter briefly interrupted the introduction of the featured orator.

The second event of some consequence for the Ralstons was that by late August the candidates for the Nevada territorial delegate to the United States Congress was whittled to four. Among them was J. H. Ralston. James had made a large number of speeches, shook a multitude of hands, and kissed more than his fair share of babies in his territorial *newcomer* role. He needed to convince the voters and even the ballot box *stuffers* that he was a worthy representative. The election was held September 3rd, 1862 and Judge Ralston finished a distant 4th. Thus, in James opinion, likely and forever ending his political career. The outcome was expected and this time there was little hand wringing, sadness, or disappointment in the Ralston household.

Chapter 23

Mark Twain and the Excitement in Austin

Orion Clemens received a letter from his younger brother Samuel in late July of 1862;

My debts are greater than I thought. I bought $ 25 worth of clothing…. I owe about $40 or $45 and have got about $45 in my pocket. But how the hell am I going to live on something over a $100 until October or November…? The fact is, I must have something to do, and that shortly, too…. Now it has been a long time since I couldn't make my own living, and it shall be a long while before I loaf another year.

The younger Clemens had spent the last year in the Nevada Territory and California with unproductive speculative ventures. He had finally begun to discover that this occupation, his dream of riches, the same dream of thousands of other prospectors including James Ralston, would not, so to speak, *pan out*. He decided it was time to fall back on his part time occupation of writing. Sam tried to persuade the Sacramento Daily Union to take him on though, unknown to him, Orion had already made a more productive contact on his behalf in Virginia City. Years later, Sam described what happened next.

I found a letter in the post office as I came home from the hill side, and finally opened it. Eureka! It was a deliberate offer to me of Twenty-five Dollars a week to come up to Virginia [City] and be city editor of the [Territorial] Enterprise.[106]

Just as James had done, Sam took a little more time to swallow his pride and concede failure as a miner. In mid-September, he literally walked to work, because horses cost money. He *hoofed it* from his latest nonpaying mine in Aurora, Nevada, 120 miles north to Virginia City, arriving near the end of September.

I went up to Virginia and entered upon my new vocation. I was a rusty looking city editor, I am free to confess---coatless, slouch hat, blue woolen shirt, pantaloons stuffed into boot-tops, whiskered half down the waist, and the universal navy revolver slung to my belt.

His appearance, though soon modified, was indicative of the general nature of the newspaper. The Territorial Enterprise could not be characterized as a model newspaper of the time. In its three years of existence, advertising and news-based articles could be considered conforming to standards, though they appeared amongst other less newsworthy revelations. The paper had gathered up a collection of unusual journalists, humorists, and poets, many of whom arrived as the result of some sort of twisted fate, including Dan DeQuille, aka William Wright, and now Sam Clemens. J. H. Ralston and the new *Enterprise* editor would meet on a number of occasions in Virginia City as Clemens began a career ideally suited to his disposition, character, and skills. This talent would take him to the literary heights of worldwide renown and financial success.

Samuel Clemens, city editor
from *Roughing It,*
Courtesy of Project Guttenburg

During late 1862, a movement was afoot during the 2nd session of the Nevada territorial legislature to consider taking the steps necessary to achieve Nevada statehood. The movement culminated with the passage of an act on December 20, 1862 that called for a territory-wide vote, yay or nay, as to whether the citizens wanted to become a state. The vote, accompanying the election of delegates to attend a constitutional convention, was scheduled for September 3, 1863. Being elected as a delegate to this convention was a major prize for territory *politicos* and Judge Ralston wanted in on the action. He bided his time as a practicing attorney until closer to the date of the vote.

In late January of 1863, J. Neely and his wife held a grand open house party in Carson City celebrating the completion of their lavishly appointed new home. Judge Ralston and Harriet were invited guests. In the less than formal society of the territory, they both had the pleasing and rare opportunity to *dress to the nines*, he in a tuxedo and Harriet in a lovely sequined red satin gown. The Ralstons and at least one-hundred other guests, many of whom they knew, were greeted by Cousin Neely and Mary at the grand entrance of their extravagant home. After fifteen minutes of obligatory mingling, James saw Samuel Clemens, *dressed to the ones*, standing in a corner savoring a glass of hot whiskey punch. James hoped his presence did not hold the purpose of a tongue-in-cheek account of the event that would appear in the following morning edition of the

Enterprise. Unfortunately, he knew Clemens well enough to know his hope was a practical impossibility.

From a letter dated January 31, 1863, appearing in Virginia City's Territorial Enterprise, February 3, 1863, written by Samuel Clemens, though signed by *Mark Twain*, the first use the famous pen name:

I feel very much as if I had just awakened out of a long sleep. I attribute it to the fact that I have slept the greater part of the time for the last two days and nights. On Wednesday, I sat up all night, in Virginia [City], in order to be up early enough to take the five o'clock stage [to Carson City] on Thursday morning. I was on time. It was a great success...

In the evening, I felt a mighty inclination to go to a party somewhere. There was to be one at [former] Governor J. Neely Johnson's[107], and I went there and asked permission to stand around awhile. This was granted in the most hospitable manner, and visions of plain quadrilles soothed my weary soul. I felt particularly comfortable, for if there is one thing more grateful to my feelings than another, it is a new house - a large house, with its ceilings embellished with snowy mouldings; its floors glowing with warm-tinted carpets; with cushioned chairs and sofas to sit on, and a piano to listen to; with fires so arranged that you can see them, and know that there is no humbug about it; with walls garnished with pictures, and above all, mirrors, wherein you may gaze, and always find something to admire, you know. I have a great regard for a good house, and a girlish passion for mirrors....

I smelled hot whisky punch, or something of that nature. I tracked the scent through several rooms, and finally discovered the large bowl from whence it emanated. I found the omnipresent Unreliable [in this instance, Mark Twain is referring to his creator Samuel Clemens] *there, also. He set down an empty goblet, and remarked that he was diligently seeking the gentle men's dressing room. I would have shown him where it was, but it occurred to him that the supper table and the punch bowl ought not to be left unprotected; wherefore, we stayed there and watched them until the punch entirely evaporated. A servant came in then to replenish the bowl, and we left the refreshments in his charge. We probably did wrong, but we were anxious to join the hazy dance. The dance was hazier than usual, after that. Sixteen couples on the floor at once, with a few dozen spectators scattered around, is calculated to have that effect in a brilliantly lighted parlor, I believe. Everything seemed to buzz, at any rate. After all the modern dances had been danced several times, the people adjourned to the supper-room. I found my wardrobe out there, as usual, with the Unreliable in it. His old distemper was upon him: he was desperately hungry. I never saw a man eat as much as he did in my life. I have the various items of his supper here in my notebook. First, he ate a plate of sandwiches; then he ate a handsomely iced pound cake; then he gobbled a dish of chicken salad; after which he ate a roast pig; after that, a quantity of blancmange [a sweet dessert]; then he threw in several glasses of punch to fortify his appetite, and finished his monstrous repast with a roast turkey. Dishes of brandy-grapes, and jellies, and such things, and pyramids of fruits, melted away before him as shadows fly at the sun's approach.*

After supper, the dancing was resumed, and after a while, the guests indulged in music to a considerable extent.... Up to this time I had carefully kept the Unreliable in the background, fearful that, under the circumstances, his insanity would take a musical turn; and my prophetic soul was right; he eluded me and planted himself at the piano; when he opened his cavernous mouth and displayed his slanting and scattered teeth, the effect upon that convivial audience was as if the gates of a graveyard, with its crumbling tombstones, had been thrown open in their midst; then he shouted something about he "would not live alway" - and if I ever heard anything absurd in my life, that was it. He must have made up that song as he went along. Why, there was no more sense in it, and no more music, than there is in his ordinary conversation. The only thing in the whole wretched performance that redeemed it for a moment was something about "the few lucid moments that dawn on us here". That was all right; because the "lucid moments" that dawn on that Unreliable are almighty few, I can tell you. I wish one of them would strike him while I am here, and prompt him to return my valuables to me. I doubt if he ever gets lucid enough for that, though. After the Unreliable had finished squawking, I sat down to the piano and sang - however, what I sang is of no consequence to anybody. It was only a graceful little gem from the horse opera.

At about two o'clock in the morning, the pleasant party broke up and the crowd of guests distributed themselves around town to their respective homes; and after thinking, the fun all over again, I went to bed at four o'clock. So, having been awake forty-eight hours, I slept forty-eight, in order to get even again, which explains the proposition I began this letter with.

Yours, dreamily,

Mark Twain

James read Sam Clemens' letter with some amusement, noting that he had *almost* accurately described Neely's home. He was thoroughly delighted that in the letter *Twain* had mostly poked fun at his alter ego, *Unreliable*, the real-life Samuel Clemens.

With the help of his closest friends, Judge Ralston began to develop a strategy that would afford him the best opportunity to be a delegate at the prestigious constitutional convention. It became clear to the strategists that James had little chance of being elected from Carson City's county, Ormsby, or the surrounding counties of Washoe, Storey, Lyon, and Douglas. Of the counties remaining, James preferred the central Nevada Territory of Lander County for several reasons. The first being that the overland stage conveniently connected the northern part of the county to his home in Virginia City. Another was that he had heard of some *excitement* over the recent discovery of silver in that area. Alas, the dream had not yet completely vanished. James shared his plan with Harriet stating his political motivation for his temporary move to the fledging mining town of Austin, Nevada[108] in Lander County. He cited the short three-day stagecoach trip to Carson City, though not relating the recent mining activity. This time Harriet was actually glad the family was not moving with him to what she viewed as yet closer to the end of the earth. She did not bother to mention that she too had heard of the new mines in the area. James was on the road to Austin in early May of 1863, promising, for what seemed to Harriet to be a large uncounted number of times, he would write and visit often.

James rented a small house near Austin's main street that served as his living quarters and law offices. He traveled by horseback to nearly every corner in Lander County wherever more than a half-dozen people made their home, campaigning as a delegate from the county to the constitutional convention. During these lonely sojourns, he always kept a sharp lookout for the slightest sign of rich quartz outcroppings, just in case he was still destined to become that illusive silver baron. Once each month he actually kept his promise to Harriet. He occupied a seat on the overland stage from Austin to Carson City, up the mountain to their home in Virginia City. He retraced his steps a week later. Judge Ralston was appointed Lander County's probate judge in July 1863[109]. He replaced a man whose loyalty to the Union was called into question during the Union's dark days of the Civil War. Days that would soon turn brighter when news of General Lee's defeat at the Pennsylvania crossroads hamlet of Gettysburg reached the Nevada Territory.

AUSTIN

Austin residents
1863 10,000
2010 300+

Virginia City

Carson City

MAP INSET

Nevada 1868

Birch Creek
J. H. Ralston
cabin and mine

GENEVA
now a ghost town

SCALE
0   1   2
MILES

As the September 3rd date for the election of the convention delegates neared, Judge Ralston made one last tour of the county. Near the end of the trip, James rode slowly from the desert valley floor up the narrow and winding Birch Creek trail that lead to the newly established mining town of Geneva, Nevada. At a point about two miles below Geneva, James caught the familiar glimpse of rainbow colored light emanating from the boulder strewn far side of the creek's canyon. He dismounted, tied his horse to the trunk of a small pine tree and clambered down the side of the canyon. Using stepping stones, he gingerly crossed the creek for a closer look at what he knew would be a quartz outcropping. On closer inspection of the spot, the now experienced miner knew he had found yet another possible source of rich silver ore. He filled his pants pockets with samples before returning to his horse. Unlike his first brush with possible riches, he calmly continued the journey. After another round of handshakes and a brief political speech at Geneva, he continued the short distance along the side of the scenic ridges of the northern most *Toyabe Mountains* back to Austin. The assay results of his latest find showed high amounts of silver ore though the profitability of mining the quartz ledge would depend, per standard assay wording, *on the length and breadth of the vein*; he bought the land and staked a claim.

Just prior to the convention delegate election, at Harriet's insistence, she, Jackson, and Aurora joined James in Austin to lend him loving support during the ballot counting. In Jackson's recollection of his time in Nevada, he wrote:

One day there was an election, I went to the polls and was handed a ticket to vote for my father who was a candidate for election to the first constitutional convention of Nevada…. Some things made me doubtful if my vote entered the ballot box [tongue-in-cheek, because of this young age]*, but nevertheless my father was elected.*

The happy family celebration that ensued reminded James of his successful post-election parties in Illinois with Jane by his side and with Harriet by his side in Sacramento over ten years before. The three-day family stagecoach ride back to Virginia City was upbeat the entire trip.

Judge Ralston's feeling of overall satisfaction as he entered the convention assembly hall in Carson City was a collection of many feelings rolled into one. He was confident that he could and would provide his knowledge and experience toward the creation of the territory's first ever try at a state constitution. He felt at home in a large assembly of notable and learned gentlemen many of whom he had known well in California, including J. Neely. Lastly, he was overjoyed that after such a long period of time and many failed attempts, he had been elected by a popular vote of the people to act in their interests. This time in completing the most important step in the process of realizing statehood. He was also aware that the territory was on Washington's fast track to be admitted to the Union. It was a matter of *when* the action would be taken, not *if* it would be taken. Harriet made sure that the family attended the Carson City constitutional assembly when they were allowed. Jackson again remembered:

I heard him [his father] speak before the convention in Carson City; about what I am sure I did not then know nor do I now.

There was another familiar face in attendance, Sam Clemens of the *Territorial Enterprise.* After the convention was over, as Mark Twain, Sam authored a letter on December 13th 1863, about selected convention participants describing what Twain called the *Third House.* The *Enterprise* published his letter.

The Third House met in the Hall of the Convention…. On motion …. the rules were suspended, and usual prayer dispensed with, on the grounds that it was never listened to.. . Mr. Mark Twain was elected President of the convention….

Gentlemen: [the President, Mark Twain, speaking] *This is the proudest moment of my life. I shall always think so. I think so still. I shall ponder over it with unspeakable emotion down to the last syllable of recorded time. It shall be my earnest endeavor to give entire satisfaction in the high and bully position to which you have elevated me….*

Mr. Johnson: [J. Neely Johnson speaking] *Mr. President; I wish it distinctly understood that I am not a candidate for the Senate, or any other office, and have no intention of becoming one. And I wish to call the attention of the Convention to the fact, sir, that outside influences have been brought to bear here, that-*

The President: Governor Johnson, there is no necessity of putting in your shovel here, until you are called upon to make a statement. And if you allude to the Engrossing Clerk as an outside influence, I must inform you, sir, that this battery has been silenced with Territorial scrip [money] at forty cents on the dollar….

Mr. Ralston: [Judge J. H. Ralston speaking] *Mr. President; I have but a word to say, and I do not occupy the attention of the House any longer than I can help; and, although I could, perhaps, throw more light upon the matter of our eastern boundary than those who have not visited that interesting but comparatively unknown section of our budding commonwealth, it is growing late, and I do not feel as I had a right to tax the patience-*

The President: Tax! Take your seat, sir, take your seat. I will not be bully-ragged to death with this threadbare subject of taxation. You are out of order anyhow. How do you suppose anybody can listen in comfort to your speech, when you are fumbling with your coat all the time you are talking, and try to button it with your left hand, when you know you can't do it? I have never seen you succeed yet, until just as you get the last word out. And then the moment you sit down, you always unbutton it again. You may speak hereafter, Mr. Ralston, but I want you to understand that you have got to button your coat before you get up. I do not mean to be kept in hot water all the time by your little oratorical eccentricities….

The convention produced a constitution that would be nearly the same one that was eventually passed and submitted to President Lincoln. However, the members of the convention continuously disagreed over political matters and content of little importance. Hence, their thirty days of work was for naught. Seven months later a second convention was convened, the members made short order of their task, and the Territory of Nevada was admitted to the Union as a state, October 31st, 1864.

The Ralston family once again moved, this time to Austin. Harriet, after having the earlier opportunity to become familiar with their new home, still considered it nearest to the end of the earth.

Chapter 24

Death in the Desert

January of 1864 in Austin, Nevada could be described as what seemed to Harriet to be nothing short of miserable. She had grown accustomed to the thinner air at over 6,000 feet from her time in Virginia City. However, the winter wind in Austin seemed to blow through a person unchecked by even the heaviest winter coat. Had Judge Ralston offered to take her and the children back to the warm sunshine of her *Garden of Eden* in the Sacramento Valley, even the seemingly annual flooding of their former home would not raise a hint of complaint. As it was, despite the cold wind and the frigid temperatures, the Ralston family was together again. When often huddled around the warmth of a fire in the parlor fireplace, the dour wintry circumstances seemed to happily fade away.

James was again appointed as probate judge of Lander County, the position he held before going off to the constitutional convention in Carson City. For the last few months, he was also actively involved in the formation of a Masonic lodge[110] in Austin. One of Harriet's favorite pastimes was writing letters and reading the responses. Among the first read, were the Sacramento letters from Lizzie Tilden. The latest news described the antics of the judge's first two grandchildren, Ralston and Charles Tilden. The letters always

Austin Masonic Hall

evoked touching memories of Lizzie's overwhelming need to be a mother, and confirmed their decision to let her marry at such a young age.

Spring had *sprung* in Austin by late April of 1864 and the brilliant colors of alpine wildflowers were everywhere to be seen. The snow-melt from the soaring heights of the northern Toiyabe mountain range began to fill the hundreds of streams in and around town that soon became white bubbling rivulets chasing down the mountainside. At mid-morning, April 28th, 1864, James and Harriet stood on their front porch leisurely enjoying the early onset of spring. This brief respite was set in the town's endless rush of activity caused exclusively by the discoveries of ore in the higher reaches of the mountains.

Toiyabe Mountains near Austin

James' briefly shared his memory just four years earlier, of his journey with Colonel Reese from Carson Valley to Salt Lake. He noted that where Austin now stood was nothing more than another in a series of tranquil desert mountain passes. The view of the pastoral beauty was only disturbed by the happenings around the occasional Pony Express station, the distantly seen wanderings of small colonies of Pahute Indians, and to the south, even fewer Shoshone Indians.

Judge Ralston's self-appointed task for the next few days was to purchase a yoke of oxen for use at the Birch Creek claim[111] he made the previous year. He told Harriet that after he found the oxen, he would take them to the cabin, put them through their paces, and return to Austin no more than a week later. J. S. Whitton[112], a friend and fellow mining stock speculator[113], who had volunteered to help James with his chore, rode his horse to the hitching post in front of the Ralston's porch. The two of them planned to ride the scenic, shorter, and more perilous trail along the side of the mountains to Geneva, about 8.5 trail miles south of Austin. James had heard that a departing miner with no dollars to his name, though with some apparent remaining sense, had oxen for sale in Geneva at a *bargain price*. Harriet hugged James, gave him a kiss on the cheek, and lovingly reminded him to be careful. She received a smiling confident reply that marrying her was the perfect example of his being careful in everything he did. James waved to a still laughing Harriet as the two men reined their horses down the hill toward town.

The Judge and Whitton arrived in Geneva that afternoon and much to James' dismay the miner had no more than an hour earlier sold his oxen. The two men asked around to find out if there were any more of the *beasts of burden* for sale in the vicinity. The only positive reply came from the owner of the general store who had heard of a team for sale at Deering's Ranch about 17 miles east down in the Smoky Valley. James knew it would be near dark by the time they arrived at Deering's, so he told Whitton to return to Austin while there was plenty of light to negotiate the treacherous trail. He would ride on down to Deerings and spend the night. The next morning, if he found some oxen, he would hire one of the ranch hands to help him bring them back up the trail to his cabin. Whitton reluctantly agreed to the plan and the two men parted ways. Judge Ralston arrived at Deering's Ranch just before dark and soon found out that the oxen the ranch did have for sale were purchased nearly two weeks before. The ranch manager suggested that the judge spend the night in one of their houses then ride to his ranch the next morning. James declined the offer boasting that he knew the trail well enough to reach the safety of his cabin. He jokingly added that since he had ridden past the cabin no more than a few hours ago, in the worst case he could re-trace his horse's shoe steps. The judge crossed back over the valley and before he started the climb back to his cabin he thought better of negotiating the trail in the moonless night and set up camp.

What befell Judge James H. Ralston sometime during the night or early the next morning will forever remain a mystery. It is known that he was without his horse that was found wandering in the desert weeks later. What is also known is that whether he fell from his horse and struck his head or, without injury, he suffered some form of

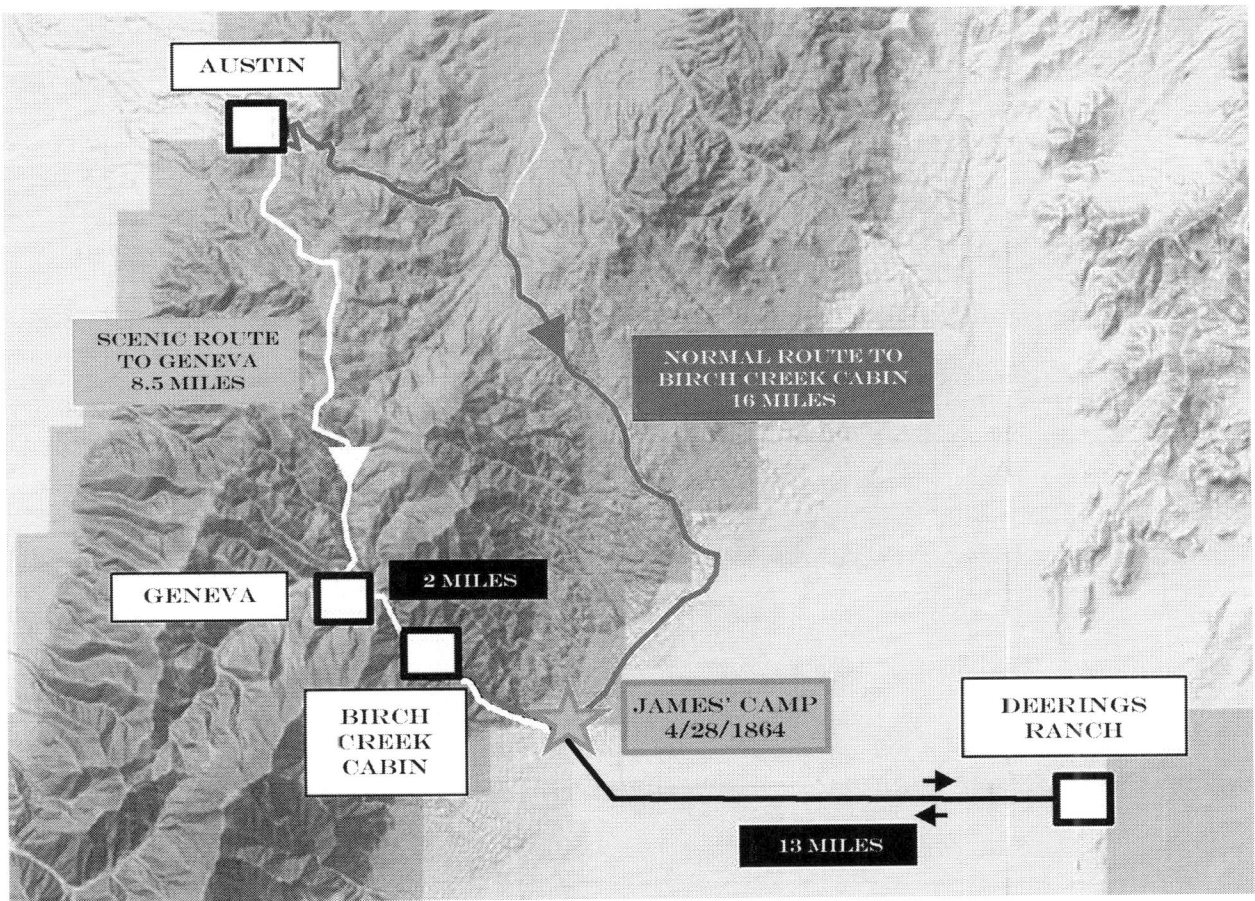

debilitating severe amnesia, his mental faculties abandoned him. Though, as the next ten days would attest, his basic instinct to survive and his body remained dutifully strong.

Since James had told Harriet that he would remain at the cabin not later than Thursday, May 5th, there was no cause for alarm or great concern when he did not return by the following Wednesday. However, after the judge's ranch hand came to Austin that day and reported that the judge had not been at the cabin for over a week, concern spread through town like wildfire. His friend Whitton, in company with others and, separately the ranch hand, went in search of the judge. Whitton's group found the spot on the western edge of Smoky Valley, within two miles of his ranch, where James had camped for the night after leaving Deerings. Whitton returned to Austin reporting no sign of the judge other than the campsite location. On the 10th of May, another group that included Whitton, a Mr. Hawkins[114], Colonel Forman[115], and some Indians, who, unlike the *white men,* were capable of perfectly tracking either man or beast, went to the spot of the camp site to commence another search.

A letter from Harriet to Lizzie Tilden dated May 17th, 1864[116] related the following:

I have written to you, from time to time, a full account of the details concerning the Judge since he left us to go with Whitton in search of oxen for use on his ranch…. We did not know for nearly a week that he had not reached the ranch, 40 miles from here [see endnote 111] *and then his hired hand brought word. Since then diligent search has been made, and we know that he was almost at his ranch; but that at night he must have lost his reckoning, and never again found the right course. He left the hotel* [Deering's Ranch] *so late …. that he had to travel at night to get to where he has evidently camped; and as he was always fearless about traveling, believing that he could not get lost, he has ventured too far, and I fear it was a fatal venture.*

Today word was brought that some Indians had arrived near town who say that "three sleeps" or three days journey from here they saw a man from whom they fled, and who came to their canon [canyon] *for water. A man who understands the Shoshone language has gone out with an Indian to find these others* [this lead turned out to be a prospector who was found and confirmed that he had gotten water at that canyon]. *A party* [Whitton, Hawkins, Forman] *left yesterday with Indians, for white men cannot detect his footsteps. They were going to the point where they lost traces, and would continue on from there…*

I have endured this horrible suspense now for many days, learning first one thing then another, until it is almost unbearable, and I doubt if anything definite is [will be] *known of his fate before the last of the week, the distance and difficulty of traveling is so great. So soon as I learn anything definite I will write, but at present cannot say more.*

The Whitton party left on May 16th and the Indians reached the campsite and were able to follow the judge's footsteps, sometimes in soft ground, through canyons and over rocks apparently searching for water. They went to a point about 25 miles distant from their starting point. The night was fast approaching and the searchers, having nearly consumed all of their water, and the Indians refusing to go any further, were forced to return to Austin on the 17th. While the Whitton party was searching for any sign of the

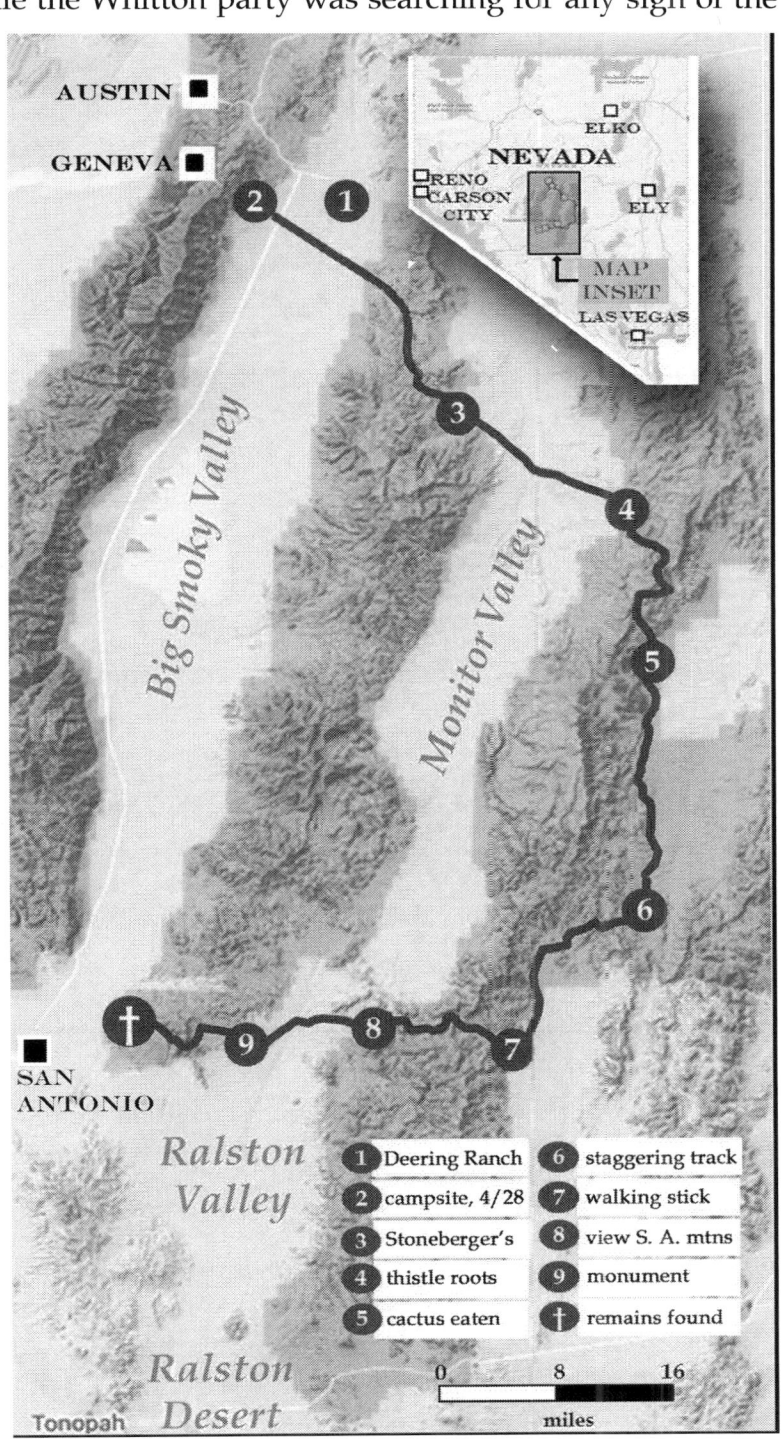

judge, the Austin citizens, led by the Masonic brethren, were formulating a contingency plan to more robustly execute a new search in the event the current Whitton efforts were in vain. A modest sum of money was raised to fund the new search if it was needed. It was.

The new search party led by James Gilson[117], accompanied by J. D. Boyd, W. W. Cole, and an experienced Shoshone Indian guide named *Tom*[118], left Austin on the 18th with a plan to go to the spot near Stoneberger's Creek where the previous group abandoned their search. On the 21st, they crossed the valley [Monitor Valley] southeast of Smoky Valley to a point where more boot prints were found. From a journal kept by Boyd, printed in the *Daily Reese River Reveille*, *5/27/1864*:

Here were evidences where the Judge, having no doubt it was him, had dug with a knife for roots of a thistle.

On the 22nd the search party crossed a rugged mountain traveling in a southerly direction.

At the foot of the mountain we found where he had been sitting down and where were also pieces of cactus partly eaten.

They followed the continuing track for a number of miles south and soon noticed;

The staggering track and the short step indicated that the lost man was severely suffering from fatigue…. At daylight on the 23d we resumed our search …. going southwest. At this resting place we found a stick that the Judge had carried for a long distance as he came. It was standing in the sand as he had placed it…. Our guide told us the lost man had got some pine nuts or other food as he exhibited greater strength…. Our guide was an expert at the business, never failing, and speaking as confidently of all the actions of the Judge …. as if he had been in his company at the time…. He [the judge] *then changed his course west. The Indian said it was a long way to water in that direction. It was the course, however, that would have taken him to where he could have found assistance had he continued on it…. The Judge had evidently been attempting to find some manner of escape from his perilous situation. He had clambered upon high rocks as if to take observations. On the 24*[th]*…. We were now in sight of the San Antonio Mountains. We crossed the valley in the direction of San Antonio…. we were now sixteen miles from known water and nearly out of provisions…. So, building a monument that we could easily find, we returned to Austin* [on the 26th].

We followed the track for upwards of 100 miles, very tortuous wandering. There is every hope and many reasons to believe that Judge Ralston is yet alive and may be saved. His endurance is most remarkable. The party will start in search again today [on the 27th].
From the *Reveille*, 6/2/1864:

Messrs. Gilson and Boyd returned yesterday [June 1st] *from their expedition in search of the missing Judge Ralston, and bring us melancholy intelligence that this much respected gentleman is no more…. His family resides in this city, and their distress, augmented by the most painful suspense, can only be imagined…. Last week we gave an account of their trip. The second trip is as follows:*

The party left Austin [on the 27th] *following the main road south* [in Smoky Valley] *for a distance of 90 miles, then crossed the Smoky Valley at the Indian Wells* [two miles north of San Antonio, now a ghost town, crossing the valley to the southeast] *…. passing Link Barnes' Ranch, and in a few miles found some Indians…. These* [Indians] *told them* [the search party] *that the Judge was dead and directed them to the body. Mr. Gilson, being able to talk the Shoshone language, obtained much information from the Indians….* [the searchers] *were piloted to the place where the remains were. These found but eight miles in an East Northeast direction from San Antonio…. Austin being north* [and] *20* [arc] *degrees west.* [This is not possible if the direction and distance from San Antonio to the site of the remains was at all close to accurate. From San Antonio, latitude 38.4610 N, 117.2937 W, to Austin would be described, in the term used, as North and 9 degrees East. From the site where the judge was found, 8 miles East Northeast from San Antonio, the direction to Austin would be North and 4 degrees East.]

A Shoshone Indian, named Onewada, told Gilson that his *squaw* had seen a white man the day it snowed and he was very weak and tottering. She wanted him to go to camp with her though he did not agree to go. She offered him some pine nuts that he would not take and she said he kept repeating the English words, *my ranch, my house.* Because of the snow and the cold, Onewada and his *squaw* knew the white man would soon die. The Indian told Gilson that when they found his body the next day they decided to burn it to keep it from being eaten by coyotes. Gilson asked the Indian why they did not tell other white men what happened. He replied that he told a ranch hand at Barnes' ranch who did not understand what he was saying. He was too afraid to go to San Antonio because he thought they would accuse him of murder. Gilson removed the judge's spectacles from what remained of the judge's coat and he found a burnt pocket watch near the remains.[119] Based on the information the Indians gave Gilson, he speculated that the judge had died about May 8th, 10 days after he left Austin.

The remains were brought in, together with the coin, spectacles, watch…. The funeral will take place today under the superintendence of the Masons and the members of the bar, both of which bodies he [Judge Ralston] was a most honored member.

The judge wandered an estimated 125 miles in the 9 days before his death though estimates at the time placed the distance at 250 miles. The higher number is not possible with the unforgiving desert terrain he covered and the number of elapsed days. The days and the distance he journeyed are insignificant compared to the persistence, inner fortitude, and the instinct to survive he showed in the near absence of a human's most precious asset, the ability to reason.

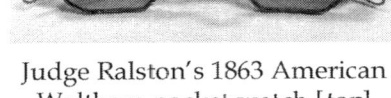

Judge Ralston's 1863 American Waltham pocket watch [*top*] and green shaded glass metal rimmed spectacles [*bottom*].

Both artifacts are in the collection of the Nevada State Historical Society, Reno. Pictures courtesy of NSHS.

A number of days before the last search party returned to Austin, Harriet's tears were spent and she had found a way to accept the worst of all possible outcomes. When she was actually told the news, she calmly thanked the messenger with a polite smile, took a seat in her living room chair, and wearily put her head in her hands. Her worst nightmare of the endless days and sleepless nights of the last month had been that she would never know what happened to her husband and she thanked God for bringing her much needed closure.

She was dressed in mourning black. With one hand in Aurora's and the other in Jackson's, she proudly held her head high as the family walked slowly to the cemetery behind a wagon carrying the flag-draped coffin containing the judge's remains.

The *Reveille*, 6/3/1864

The last sad duties the living owe to the dead were exercised yesterday by our citizens in the interment of the remains of the late Judge Ralston. His body upon its arrival in town was taken in charge by his brother Masons, of which order he had attained the rank of Knight Templar. At an early hour yesterday, the members of the Legal Fraternity met at the Court House and resolved in a body to attend the funeral of the honored deceased. The procession formed in front of the Court House at one o'clock, and headed by the Austin Brass Band, followed by the Masons in regalia, the members of the Bar, Firemen, hearse, the Family of the deceased, citizens on horseback and in carriages, the cortege marched to the [Austin Masonic and Odd Fellows] cemetery. This was the most imposing funeral that has yet occurred in Austin. The worth, position and high esteem, with the melancholy circumstances attending the death of Judge Ralston, gave a solemn and universal interest to the occasion. After the interment, the procession returned, marching to a lively tune, to the Court House, and dispersed.

Austin, Nevada, Odd Fellows and Masonic Cemetery
The cemetery has been *walked* a number of times, the latest in 2014;
the location of Judge Ralston's burial site has not been found.

Afterword

Harriet Jackson Ralston, and Family

A.fter James' death, Harriet, Jackson *Jack*, and Aurora continued to live for about a year in Austin while the judge's estate was settled. Then, she and the children went by ship via Panama to New York and to her father's home in Oyster Bay, NY. There, living with her father, Rev. Aaron Jackson, and her stepmother, Martha Quigley Jackson.

Shortly after Harriet's father died in August of 1868[120], the family moved to Ithaca, where Harriet would continue to pursue her passion for poetry. In early 1869, Aurora contracted scarlet fever while in Ithaca and shortly after she died leaving her mother heartbroken and completely despondent. In his 1941 autobiography[121] Jack Ralston wrote about his sister's death:

While her departure was a course of deep sorrow to my mother and myself …in retrospect, bearing in mind her unfitness for a rough world, perhaps her death brought her eternal relief.

DIED

RALSTON, of scarlet fever. Jan 31ˢᵗ, Mary Aurora Ralston, youngest child of the late Judge Ralston of California.

Funeral services of the above child were held at the house of Mr. Spence Spencer. They were largely attended by the friends of the estimable widow of the late Judge Ralston, including many old school friends and many members of the church of which her late father was pastor a number of years ago.

Harriet accepted an offer from her sister Mary Amelia Jackson Sunderland to move to San Mateo, CA, just south of San Francisco and she and Jackson took a thrilling ride west on the recently completed transcontinental railroad. Jackson attended school for a short time at San Francisco's Boys High School[122]. They returned to Ithaca by train the following year. Harriet and Jackson received a letter from Lizzie Tilden written from Sacramento dated July 5th, 1870.

My Dear Friends,

I received your welcome letter in due time and should have answered it before but have been too sick with remittent fever [a continuously fluctuating body temperature above normal] *to do anything.*

I was pleased to learn of your safe arrival at your former home, and mama's [Harriet] *improved health. I hope you are pleasantly situated and enjoying all the blessings of the season.*

Our little town was quite lively yesterday. There were two processions, both in the morning. It was much cooler than our fourth's usually are, everyone appeared to be enjoying themselves, if the noise they made was any indicator. Not being able to go out, I did not see much of the celebration.

Mr. Tilden's [Lizzie's husband, M. C. Tilden] *health is very poor this summer, the children are quite well....*

We expect to spend the remainder of the summer in the mountains, but Mr. Tilden cannot leave home until after the 19th as he has some land cases to try that day...

I hope you will write often. I would to you if I could write as beautifully as ma does. Hoping to hear from you soon. I close with love to you both.

Lizzie J. Tilden.[123]

Harriet and Jack moved from Ithaca to Rochester, New York in 1872 where 15 year-old Jack worked as a printer apprentice. This was his first exposure to the printing business that would ultimately open a lucrative door to his future.

Harriet knew from early in his life that her intelligent son deserved the opportunity to be formally educated in a profession of his choosing. However, he had not yet decided just what that would be. Based on the experiences she had with her husband in law and politics, she could think of no better place of interest to her, and perhaps her son, than the nation's capital. Jack wrote in his autobiography:

Probably the inclination toward politics came largely because of the career of my father. In all his more ambitious attempts, he registered a failure. Although repeated in the legislature in Illinois and a judge on the bench, he was defeated for Congress. In California, although serving usefully in the State Senate, he failed to be elected to a Supreme Court judgeship. In Nevada he was simply a probate judge at the time of his death. All these events made a deep impression on the mind of my mother, who entertained the hope that although the father had missed, her son might succeed.[124]

In the spring of 1873[125], she and Jack moved to Washington, D. C. where Jack found a job with the Government Printing Office. A year later, Harriet was employed as a copyist[126] in the U. S. Attorney General's Office at an annual salary of $500. During his time in the printing office, Jack attended Georgetown University Law School, earning his law degree in 1876. Jack wrote about the experience:

When 17 and in the Govt. Printing Office, because of the more convenient hours, I attended the Georgetown University Law School for two years. Altho afterwards an excellent institution, it had most incompetent teachers, selected, it may have been, because of religious affiliations rather than scholastic attainments. These two years — eight months in each – enabled us students to be admitted to the bar, and our education to be acquired mostly in practice. Thus at 19 I was entitled to call myself a lawyer.[127]

He was admitted to the bar in 1878 and in 1879 had a law practice for three years in his father's hometown, Quincy, IL, where he lived in his aunt's boarding house. On his return to Washington, D. C., he worked for 8 years as chief counsel for Samuel Gompers, the founder of the American Federation of Labor [AF of L], the labor union comprised of many trades that Gompers headed from 1886 until his death in 1924.

Harriet N. Ralston ca 1880

Late in 1885, Harriet and Jack moved to the new Washington, D. C. suburb of Hyattsville, MD where Harriet built a home they referred to as *Wing Rest.* Jack served on the Hyattsville town council and during this period. Because of her poetic contributions, Harriet became an active member of the newly formed Women's National Press Association [WNPA]. The WNPA, founded in 1882, had for a brief time as its honorary president, Mary Todd Lincoln. The WNPA allowed Harriet to *rub elbows* with many of the elite Washingtonian women of the day including Frances Willard, suffragette and founder of the Women's Christian Temperance Union [WCTU], and Clara Barton, founder of the American Red Cross. In 1894, Harriet joined a number of the members of the WNPA on a trip across the country that included stops in Los Angeles, San Francisco, Salt Lake City, Kansas City, Chicago, Indianapolis, and New York.

Jack married Sara Burns *Birdie* Rankin from and in Keokuk, IA, June 1, 1887. Birdie was formally educated and attended the Conservatory of Music in New York City. Her father, John Walker Rankin was a well-known attorney in Keokuk and served in the 17th IA infantry as Colonel and regimental commander early in the Civil War. Jack and Birdie had no children of their own but in 1899 adopted a son, Jackson Frederick Ralston, his cousin. The behind the scenes story of his cousin's adoption is an interesting one, though not for this book.

In 1902, Jack H. Ralston was the lead counsel representing the United States against Mexico in the first case heard at *The Hague* in the Netherlands that resulted in a substantial monetary settlement in favor of the U. S. In 1903, Jack and Birdie spent six months in Caracas, Venezuela where he was an umpire in a case of Italy vs. Venezuela, resulting in a judgment against Venezuela. These two assignments established Jack in his highly regarded legal career in Washington, D. C.

Harriet continued to make poetic contributions through the first 20 years of the 20th century and Jack, with his long-time Washington law partner, Frederick Lincoln Siddons, continued to be thoroughly involved in the law. On Jackson's 63rd birthday, 2/6/1920, Harriet Ralston passed away, at the age of 91, at Jack and Birdie's Washington townhome.

Jackson wrote a letter to his good friend, and 4th cousin, Opal Viola Ralston, about his mother's last days.

I am sure – tho at the time I did not strangely realize it – that my mother's health has been failing for some time and she in some measure appreciated it. Assisting the straightening up of the house after moving she was at the house of a very good friend and on the Sunday before her death I took her from there to my own house. On the following Wednesday morning she complained of not having slept all night and being seriously ill. This was not in itself so alarming as her constant sleep afterward, only waking at long intervals. The last being at 7 o'clock Thursday evening. After that she sank into a stupor and cerebral hemorrhage followed with speedy death.

Harriet Newell Jackson Ralston 1907

She was in many respects a remarkable woman. Had she realized – could she have been brought to realize – her strong points as a writer she would have attained high pearl. Her flashes of genius showed this. She had a deep emotional nature and this in a literary way as well as otherwise made a strong appeal. She died after a life filled with striking experiences at the advanced age of 91 years.[128]

The Washington [D. C.] Times, 2/6/1920

Mrs. Harriet N. Ralston. ninety-one years old, a resident of the District for forty-seven years, died at the home of her son, Jackson H. Ralston, 1850 Mintwood place northwest.

Mrs. Ralston was born in Waverly, N. Y. In 1853 she married Judge James H. Ralston, who was a member of the Illinois State senate with Lincoln, Douglas, and Shields, and afterward on the circuit bench of Illinois. She came to Washington in 1883, and had lived here and in Hyattsville, Md., ever since.

Funeral Services will be held from the residence of her son at 2 o'clock. Interment will be in Rock Creek Cemetery.

In 1924, Jack retired from his law practice and he and Birdie moved to a comfortable home in Palo Alto, CA. Jackson wrote about his retirement to the west coast.

...I have arrived to the point of my leaving Washington in the month of May 1924. For a long time I had felt no small degree of mental fatigue, something which entered into the very marrow of my being. I had acquired enough money for comfort, altho not great wealth. For this there were two rather adequate explanations. The first was a certain lack of financial skill. I was overly conscious of this and to a great degree relied upon the business judgment of those I considered better qualified... This was a blunder. Their judgment was scarcely as good as my own. The second and more important fact was one entirely familiar to you — that my course of life was not such as to commend me to the good graces of those who had large favors to give. This independence — or carelessness if you will — of results meant the loss of opportunities to gain great wealth. But despite all I found that with fair assurance for the future I could stop and in my own fashion enjoy the latter years of life.[129]

Jackson Harvey Ralston ca 1924
Courtesy Bancroft Library, UC Berkeley, CA

In Palo Alto, Jack continued his passion of pursuing the subject of single taxation, updating some of his previous books about practicing international law, and lecturing at Stanford University. On the 8th of February, 1937, at the age of 79, Birdie, Jack's wife of 49 years and 8 months, passed away from pneumonia. They had traveled frequently together to exotic locations around the world usually mixing Jack's business with their pleasure and he was a lonely man without her.

In 1930 Jack had asked a good friend he had known since his later years in Washington D. C. to edit the first edition of a book he had just completed titled *What's wrong with taxation?*. This friend, Opal Ralston[130], a 4th cousin, was working in the social welfare department for the city of Vallejo, CA. She visited Jack in Palo Alto shortly after Birdie's death to help him recover from the loss of his wife. In early October of the following year, Jack and Opal, 31 years younger, were married in San Diego, CA. Near the end of his life, Jack wrote about his aging condition.

I have indicated that I was obliged to limit straining exertions beyond a certain point. This remains true affecting unusual labors to this time. Little as it [this letter] is, it took strength and from day-to-day, strength and energy seems to ooze out… Health is an important consideration. Death has made some attempts on me, and being disappointed, is just now trying rheumatism for a change. Don't know, of course, how this will work out, altho it so far seems to mean more pain than destruction. We shall see… May I say that if long life is a blessing, I am fortunate in having a wife [Opal] who is determined that I shall enjoy it as delightfully as Nature will permit.[131]

On the 13th of October 1945, at the age of 88, Jack died. He was cremated, his ashes were put in an urn, and placed next to Birdie in a mausoleum at Alta Mesa Memorial Park in Palo Alto. Opal passed away in Mountain View, CA, December 6th, 1972, and her remains were placed next to Jack and Birdie. Before she died, Opal left a perpetual trust for use by the University of California at Berkeley, and at Stanford University Law School to support *The Ralston Prize* to honor the accomplishments of Jackson H. Ralston as evidenced by his activities in international relations.[132]

Note: The Ralston Prize was generously enhanced by Jackson's great-nephew, Ira Randall, Jr., and his wife Winona.

Elizabeth Jane "Lizzie" Ralston Tilden and Family

M. C. and Lizzie Tilden's first child, Ralston Marcellus, nicknamed *Rollie* was born October 28, 1861 at the same time M. C. was practicing law and holding the positon as Sacramento County's Deputy District Attorney. Their second child, Charles Justice was born March 31, 1863. Later that year, in November, Lizzie was in a carriage accident while riding in Brighton Township, she was *badly but not dangerously injured about the head.*

In 1864, M. C. was appointed Sacramento's Justice of the Peace, thus earning the title of judge. M. C. was appointed administrator of his father-in-law's estate. In 1865, he resigned his judgeship and was elected Sacramento's District Attorney. He successfully practiced law in Sacramento for another year-and-a-half when he was elected to a two-year term as Sacramento's City Attorney while still maintaining his law practice, as was the custom of the day.

M. C. and Lizzie celebrated the birth of their third child and son, Frank Neely on May 30, 1868. In 1870, Lizzie who was in her family's opinion an expert with needlework and embroidery, finally won recognition for her hobby at the 17th annual State Fair; an honor she repeated two years later. On the 24th of April, 1871, Lizzie gave birth to their 4th child and first daughter, Laura May.

Beginning in 1876, the fortunes of the M. C. Tilden family turned into what could be called a litany of sadness and tragedy. On January 19, 1876, the joyous birth of twin daughters, Mary Elizabeth and Elizabeth Jeanette, the Tilden's 5th and 6th children was celebrated under a cloud of darkness because of the failing health of their mother. Lizzie had dreams of being a mother from the time in her early teens when she took an active role in caring for her half-brother and sister Jackson and Mary Aurora. She remembered the stories her father shared about her mother and how much Lizzie reminded her father of his beloved Jane, taken from them in San Antonio much before her time. For reasons she could not explain, Lizzie believed her life too would end prematurely and she wanted to live her dream of motherhood to its fullest. Three months after the birth of her twin daughters, at age 31, Lizzie passed away.

Sacramento [CA] *Daily Union, 4/21/1876:*

Death of Mrs. M. C. Tilden. – On Wednesday night [4/19] the wife of M. C. Tilden, Esq., of this city, died in San Francisco. Mrs. Tilden has been relieved by death of great suffering endured with patience during a long illness. Her complaint was dropsy of the heart. Such was her agony that for three months past she has been unable to lie down a moment. Mrs. Tilden was the daughter of Hon. J. H. Ralston, deceased, formerly of the Supreme Court of Nevada [he tried cases there but was not a justice]. Mrs. Tilden was but 31 years old. She leaves six children to mourn the loss of a devoted mother, a woman known beloved in this community for her genial disposition, her gentle manners, and the cheerful influence she shed about her at all times and under all circumstances. She had no enemies but by the tender ties of sympathy and love, and purity of her life, dear friends to her who were held by silken chords but so strong as never to be broken.

In the summer of 1877 four of the six Tilden children joined their father in traveling to Virginia City, NV where he opened a law practice. M. C.'s 16-month-old twin daughters, Mary and Elizabeth were sent to live with Judge and Mrs. Joel T. [Marietta] Landrum at their Sacramento home, on 3rd Street between K & L Street. In November of that year a tragic event was reported from the Landrum home.

Sacramento Daily Union, 11/30/1877:

Sad Accident. A distressing accident, resulting in the death of a little child of M. C. Tilden, took place Wednesday night at the residence of Judge J. T. Landrum. Mrs. Landrum has had charge of the twin daughters of Mr. Tilden since shortly after the death of their mother, which took place when they were but a few weeks old, and has been as a second mother to them. Lately her house has been infested with rats, and Wednesday evening Mrs. Landrum mixed a quantity of strychnine with some mashed potato in a saucer, intending to place it where the rats would get at it. Unfortunately, her husband got the impression that she was preparing the potato as food for the children. During the night the children awoke, and while Mrs. Landrum was attending to the wants of one of them [Elizabeth Jeanette] her husband took up what he thought was food prepared for the little ones and fed the other [Mary Elizabeth]. In a brief time, Mrs. Landrum noticed what he [her husband Judge Landrum] was doing and bade him desist, exclaiming, "Oh, Judge, that is poison, you have killed my baby!"

A gentleman residing in the house was called and dispatched for a doctor, who arrived in fifteen or twenty minutes. Meanwhile Mrs. Landrum had given the child a quantity of castor oil. Before the doctor arrived it [the child] had a spasm. On his [the doctor's] arrival he gave it, mustard and water, to produce vomiting, but the poison had been at work too long, and death resulted in a few minutes. Coroner Wick held an inquest upon the body yesterday, when the jury returned the following verdict : "We do find that her [the dead child's] name was Mary Elizabeth Tilden, a native of California, aged two years in January next, and that she came to her death in the city of Sacramento on the 28th of November, 1877, and that the cause of her death was accidental poisoning with strychnine."

Mary Elizabeth was laid to rest next to her mother in the original Sacramento City Cemetery.

The third death of a Tilden family member, in just over three years, occurred in San Francisco in August of 1879. *Sacramento Daily Union, 8/25/1879:*

Body found — The remains of young Tilden have been found at Oakland and will be brought here today for burial. No further particulars have been received.

Sacramento Daily Union, 8/26/1879:

Charles J. [Justice] Tilden. — The funeral of Charles J. Tilden, son of M. C. Tilden, formerly City Attorney of this city, will take place today. In regard to his death the Virginia [City, NV] Chronicle says: "Charles J. Tilden, second son of M. C. Tilden, lawyer of this city, was drowned in the bay of San Francisco last Saturday [August 16th], as appears from telegrams received this morning by his father. The accident occurred under the following circumstances: Young Tilden was attending the California Military Academy at Oakland, and he and one of his companions, Charles D. Capp, were last Saturday granted a pass to go to San Rafael, to be absent until Monday morning. The boys, not returning on Monday, inquiry was made for them, and it was ascertained that the last that was seen of them, they were in a sailboat on the bay. Since the boat has been found, drifted ashore with the mast broken, a clue has been discovered as to the whereabouts of the young men. They were unaccustomed to the management of a sailboat, and were undoubtedly capsized in a squall and drowned. Charley Tilden was 16 years old, and a very promising young man, the pride of his father, the idol of his brothers and sisters, and the lead cadet of his school. The boys had each been in the school a little over a year and a half, were both in the same class, and had they lived would have graduated next June. They had each been appointed to the office of Corporal, Sergeant and Lieutenant, which latter position they held at the time of the accident. During the last four monthly examinations Charley had averaged the highest in deportment, scholarship, and military efficiency, of any cadet in the school. The citizens of Virginia [City] will sympathize deeply with the family, and particularly with his older brother, Ralston M. Tilden, who still remains at the Academy unaccompanied by the cheerful voice and presence of the loved one, who has been his constant playmate and companion from his birth."

In the spring of 1882, M. C. traveled to Washington D. C. stopping by Portage Co., OH to visit some of his childhood friends and family. In Washington he met with Jack Ralston about the possibilities of practicing law in the nation's capital and gaining advice from Jack as to the political judgeship appointments there. Apparently Marcellus was not attracted to the possibilities and he returned to Virginia City in August of that year. In 1883, attorney Tilden opened a law practice in Carson City and on May 17th, married Miss Meta Maria Woodland in Sacramento. The marriage ended in divorce on August 30, 1884. He returned to Virginia City in October of 1883. M. C. remained in Virginia City until late in 1888 then moved to San Jose, CA where he remained until about 1890.

On July 16th, 1890, M. C.'s oldest son, Ralston Marcellus Tilden[133] was killed in a freak railroad accident in San Jose. *Sacramento Daily Union,* July 19, 1890:

Ralston M. Tilden

A Native Son of Sacramento Who Met Death on Duty.

The remains of Ralston M. Tilden, son of Judge M. C. Tilden of San Jose, but formerly of this city, were interred in the City Cemetery here on Thursday. The deceased had been employed on the railroad, and met his death by being struck on the head by one of the timbers of a bridge which the train was crossing. He had his lantern in his hand at the time, and was knocked down on the top of the car. He was conscious for several hours afterward, and recognized his father and other friends. After being put to bed, however, he became unconscious, and remained in that condition up to the time of his death, thirty-six hours afterward. Concerning the deceased the San Jose Mercury says :

"Ralston M. Tilden, the young man so seriously injured on the railroad Monday evening, died at his father's residence in this city on Tuesday [should be Wednesday] morning at 5:25 o'clock. He became unconscious a few hours after the fearful accident and remained so until his death.

"He was the eldest son of Judge M. C. Tilden, a lawyer of this city, and formerly a resident of Sacramento. He was a young man of much promise, greatly respected by his employers, possessed a cheerful disposition and was beloved by all who became acquainted with him.

"His funeral services were held yesterday afternoon at 5 o'clock at the family residence, 286 San Salvador street, and the interment will take place to-day privately at Sacramento, his former home."

Ralston was the third of Lizzie's six children to be laid to rest with her in Sacramento.

In 1891, forty-five miles north of San Jose in San Francisco, 23 year-old Frank Neely Tilden was a first year medical student at Cooper Medical College[134] located at the NE corner of Webster and Sacramento. In 1893, living at 2109 Bush St. a short walk to the school, he graduated, and the new 5' 7" blue eye brown hair[135] physician was licensed to practice medicine in San Francisco, though he did not stay long. Frank had a wanderlust and in 1894 he was off to the dark continent of Africa to see if he could make a fortune in gold or diamonds, he did not particularly care which.

Laura May Tilden and her father moved from San Jose back to Virginia City by 1893 where she was admitted to the Nevada bar.[136] On July 31st, 1893, the *Sacramento Daily Union* printed an article about her accomplishment:

NEVADA'S LADY LAWYER.

She was born in Sacramento — A Daughter of Judge Tilden. The Carson [City, NV] Appeal of the 23rd says: "Laura M. Tilden, daughter of Judge M. C. Tilden, of Virginia City, passed a most creditable examination in the Supreme Court yesterday morning, and an order was made admitting her as an attorney and counsellor in all the courts of this State. The Judges, in deciding, remarked that she passed the most satisfactory examination of any person that has ever appeared before them.

"Miss Tilden is the first lady to be admitted in this State, and probably the youngest female

Courtesy Nevada State Historical Society

lawyer in the world, , being only 22 years old. The ladies of Nevada owe her a debt of gratitude, for she obtained the passage of a statute by our Legislature last winter giving females all the rights and privileges of males, so far as being lawyers are concerned, which they did not have before. Miss Tilden lived in Carson [City] when a small child, and then had quite a local reputation as an effective and fervent orator. We bespeak for her a bright and glowing future and wish her much success.

"Miss Tilden was born in Sacramento, where her father and mother then resided. She attended the public schools here, and afterward took a course in the State Normal School at San Jose, graduating in the class of '89. Her father is a lawyer, and her grandfather was Judge J. H. Ralston, who came to California in 1849 [actually 1850]. He was a member of the first Constitutional Convention of this State, and was one of the ablest lawyers in California. He practiced law in Sacramento for many years, and is well and favorably remembered by all our old residents.

The young lady comes of the kind of stock that ought to make good lawyers, and Sacramentans will wish her unbounded success.

In 1894, the Tilden father and daughter team moved back to California and established a law practice in their old hometown, Sacramento. The first case Laura tried in California received some attention from the *Sacramento Daily Union*, 1/13/1894:

Unusual interest attaches to the case [Andrew Brechtel tried for theft] *from the fact that Brechtel will be defended by Miss Laura Tilden, the young lady who has just commenced the practice of law in this city. This will be her first case in Sacramento, and if she succeeds in clearing her client, with all the evidence that is said to be available for the prosecution, it will be quite a feather in her cap. Opposed to her will be the gallant and gentlemanly Assistant District Attorney, J. Charles Jones, and it is safe to say that the issue will be fought out on "gentlemanly" lines.*

In July of that year, she was appointed to the Board of Directors of the State Woman's Suffrage Society of California finding yet another avenue to gain recognition for the equality of women. Laura was not quite finished with carrying her suffrage banner to the pages of the newspapers.

The San Francisco Call, 2/9/1895:

VOICE OF THE WOMAN
Raised to Demand Equality With Man.
THEY ALL WANT TO VOTE

…Miss Laura Tilden, an attorney of Sacramento, … declared that women did want to vote, and that a petition now being circulated in Sacramento in favor of equal suffrage was signed by nineteen women out of every twenty to sharing in its [the right to vote] functions. Addressing the men she said: "You are the most ignominious failure so far as government is concerned. It would have been the same in a different way, I have no doubt, if women had managed the government to the exclusion of men. It needs both to make the perfect government. Man when alone tends to vulgarity and brutality; woman to inanity [lack of sense] and vacuity [empty headedness]."

Late in 1895, M. C. and 19 year-old Elizabeth Jeanette moved from Sacramento to San Francisco where the latter began her studies to become a nurse and the former opened a law practice; Laura remained in Sacramento.

As the 1896 New Year began, M. C. and Elizabeth were in San Francisco, Laura was in Sacramento practicing law, and Frank was somewhere near Cape Town, South Africa involved with diamond mining. On the 31st of January, in the obituary section of the *San Francisco Call* a small notice appeared:

Tilden – In this city, January 30, 1896, Marcellus C. Tilden, father of Frank N., Laura M., and Elizabeth J. Tilden, a native of Ohio, aged 62 years, 7 months and 17 days.

Unexpected to everyone, especially to Laura and Elizabeth, and unknown to Frank, their father, Marcellus Crane Tilden had passed away. The *Sacramento Daily Union* finally discovered the death of the long-time Sacramento attorney and published a lengthy obituary in its February 4th edition:

DEATH OF M. C. TILDEN
It Was Unexpected, and Came as a Surprise to His Friends.
His Body to be Brought From San Francisco Today – Interment In This City.

The public were greatly surprised yesterday morning when the San Francisco papers brought the information that M. C. Tilden, the well-known lawyer, had died on the preceding day at his home in that city. It was only a little over a week-ago that he was here for several days attending to cases in the Superior Court in which he was interested, either as counsel or litigant…

Mr. Tilden was in his 63d year, and had led a very active life. He was a practicing lawyer here some thirty years ago, and served two terms as City Attorney when Henry Starr was District Attorney, the latter official then having the appointment of the other.

During the boom days of Virginia City, Nev., Mr. Tilden removed to that place, where he practiced law for several years, when he returned to California and established himself in San Jose, removing to this city some three years ago. He was accompanied by his daughter, Laura M. Tilden, who had been admitted to the bar, and became associated with him in practice here.

Mr. Tilden has another daughter, Elizabeth, and a son who is interested in diamond mining in South Africa. In his younger days, Mr. Tilden was quite successful in his practice and acquired considerable property in this city, some of which he retained at the time of his death.

His funeral will take place here today on the arrival of the 11:20 train from San Francisco with his remains.

Life for the remaining three members of the M. C. and Lizzie Ralston Tilden family moved on. In November of 1896, Frank sailed from Cape Town to Liverpool, England then New York and on his way to San Francisco arriving to be with his two sisters before Christmas. The following year, Frank returned to Africa, Laura continued her practice of law and providing notary public services in Sacramento, and Elizabeth continued her studies at the San Francisco Training School for nurses and following her avid interest in San Francisco's Alpha [women's] Cycling Club.

In August of 1898, Laura married Fred C. Ray in Sacramento, a troubled marriage, and she moved by herself to Denver, CO in the summer of 1900 where she became the first female lawyer from outside the state to be admitted to the Colorado bar. Elizabeth completed her nursing program in September of 1899, and by June of 1900 she had taken a position at the Veteran's Home of California[137] in the beautiful setting of Napa Valley's Yountville. In 1901, Elizabeth returned to San Francisco working at the City and County Hospital. In October of 1900, Frank, traveling with his medical school friend, Dr. William Arthur "Billy" Rowell[138] returned from Africa with a destination, once again, of San Francisco. He and Billy returned to Africa by 1908. In April of 1906, Elizabeth married Ira Edward Randall in San Francisco, where they met when sharing the same boarding house.

Elizabeth received a letter from brother Frank in June of 1909 from Northern Rhodesia [now Zambia] Africa:

Received your letter about a month ago. Have been elephant hunting ever since and have not been near post office. Am in good health…Looks like rubber is the best plan. Can get 10,000 acres of land for 12 cts [$0.12] an acre…Expect to plant about 20,000 trees this year…Think will be *able to make enough on ivory and skins to pay all our* [he and Billy Rowell] *expenses and expense of farm…Will perhaps have enough after three years to take trip to America…Love to yourself and Randall.*[139]

Less than a year later, word was received that Frank was killed by an elephant he wounded in the bush near Fort Jameson, Northern Rhodesia [now Chipata, Zambia].

San Francisco Call, 7/28/1910, Wounded Elephant Kills a California Hunter in Africa

[Special Dispatch to The Call] SACRAMENTO, July 27.— Frank N. Tilden, a Sacramento man, was killed by an elephant while near Fort Jamison, in Rhodesia, British Central Africa, on May 28.

News of the accident reached here today in a letter from a friend to Captain E. L. Hawk, state commander of the Grand Army of the Republic. Frank Tilden was a son of Judge Tilden, well known in this section of California and in Nevada.

The young man had considerable wealth.[140] *He left here before the Boer war and made considerable money speculating in diamond lands. He came back a few years ago, but returned to central Africa with W. A. Rowell of San Francisco.*

Details of Tilden's death are meager, but he wounded the animal and it attacked him, evidently crushing him to death. Tilden is survived by two sisters — Laura Tilden Ray, who is practicing law in Denver, and Mrs. Elizabeth J. Randall of San Francisco.

Elizabeth Randall received a note[141] in November from the Chaplain at Fort Jameson, the Rev. Alexander George De la Pryme[142]:

Dear Madam,

I am writing as Chaplain, to inform you that Dr. Rowell brought in the remains of your late brother, that a suitable coffin was made and covered, and that yesterday morning, with prayers I re-interred in the cemetery all that was left of the deceased. Dr. Rowell took great pains and trouble. The grave will now be perpetuated in consecrated ground[143]*…The Dr.* [Rowell] *in memory has subscribed to our church clock.*

Frank Neely, the 4th Tilden offspring to die accidentally, was laid to rest in Fort Jameson, Africa, 10,000 miles from the City Cemetery in Sacramento.

Laura married Walter Curtis Wilson in Denver in 1916 then she moved to Montrose, CO about 1920 where she again practiced law. On May 31, 1928 she and a friend were driving in the Rocky Mountain foothills near Montrose looking for tracts of land she was interested in buying. Her car left the road, overturned, and she died of injuries she received. Laura was buried in the Sacramento Cemetery, the 5th of 6 children of M. C. and Lizzie Ralston Tilden that accidentally died a tragic death.

Ira E. and Elizabeth J. Tilden Randall

The sixth child, Elizabeth Jeanette Tilden and her husband Ira E. Randall, Sr. lived in San Francisco for a number of years. They had five children, four of whom reached adulthood. Ira passed away in 1939 and Elizabeth in 1948, at the age of 72, after a full family-centered life. They are both buried in the San Francisco National Cemetery, also known as the Presidio Cemetery.

Endnotes

[1] James' birth middle name was *Hervey* as evidenced by his signature appearing on legal documents, primarily land deeds. The few and far-between biographical references to him use the name *Harvey*, though he very rarely used his middle name preferring either James H. or J. H.

[2] A Tragedy in Five Acts.

[3] Joseph Neely [1758-1811] a Revolutionary War veteran married Martha Robertson Johnston [1761-1812], they had a large family and moved from Pennsylvania to Kentucky and lastly to Gibson Co. IN. Two of the Neely daughters married members of the Ralston clan.

[4] Until the formation of Bath County in 1811, the Ralston land was in Bourbon County.

[5] Boone never actually wore a coonskin cap.

[6] The Wilderness Road was the main route early settlers used to travel from Virginia through the Cumberland Gap, to central Kentucky. The road was originally cut in 1775 by Boone and a company of fellow woodsmen.

[7] For more about the *real* battle at the Thames River, aka, Moravian Town, and the fate of Shawnee Chief Tecumseh, read *Tecumseh's Last Stand* by John Sugden, 1985, University of Oklahoma Press, Norman, OK.

[8] In addition to the Ralston children named, the couple had three daughters and two sons that died in infancy, Ruth A. b. 1809, William Hervey [the first son so named] b. 1811, John, Jr., b. 1814, Elizabeth Neely b. 1815, and Roseanne M. b. 1817. Two other daughters were born after 1819 that lived to adulthood, Eliza Jane b. 1822, and Eleanor Marshall b. 1824, for a total of six sons and eight daughters. This information was taken from John Ralston's family bible. One popular biography of the family incorrectly mentions 10 sons and 4 daughters.

[9] William Ralston[1766-1835], wife Nancy McClure Ralston [1772-1844].

[10] Elijah Iles, a highly successful businessman was born in Bath Co. KY, and then moved as a young man to Missouri, near Boonville, then to Springfield, IL. He served in the Black Hawk War where he was a captain commanding a company of volunteers that included *A. Lincoln*. He was also a member of the Illinois state legislature.

[11] Spelled Hindoostan on a map of the time.

[12] The letter is unedited.

[13] Richard Montgomery Young [1798-1861] Born in Fayette Co. KY was an IL circuit court judge, a member of the IL state legislature, the IL Supreme court, and a U. S. senator from Illinois He practiced law in Washington D. C. until his death. He was a close friend, confidant, and mentor of Judge Ralston.

[14] Several people, including James' son, wrote that Joseph Neely was likely the first to arrive in Quincy followed by James. In 1830 when James was being sworn in as an Illinois attorney in Quincy's circuit courtroom, Joseph was found listed on the 1830 census in Vanceburg, Lewis County, Kentucky.

[15] William Alexander Richardson was born near Lexington, KY, attended Transylvania College, attorney, Illinois state representative and senator, U. S. representative and U. S. senator from Illinois, and Governor of Nebraska Territory.

[16] Orville Hickman Browning was born in Cynthiana, KY, attorney, U. S. Senator from Illinois, U. S. Secretary of the Interior. Both he and particularly his wife, Eliza, were friends of President Lincoln.

[17] Archibald Williams was born in Montgomery Co., KY, attorney, Illinois state representative, and senator, appointed by President Lincoln as judge of the U. S. District Court for Kansas.

[18] Unknown to the four was the presence in Beardstown of an elected captain of a militia company from Sangamon County, A. Lincoln of New Salem. IL. Richardson, Browning, and Williams would come to know well the future President of the United States;

[19] Blackhawk identified himself with *his friends*, the British, a friendship that dated back to the War of 1812. He often displayed a British flag in his camp and when his braves went into battle.

[20] The engagement, also called the Battle of Stillman's run named after the leader of the advance detachment, Major Isaiah Stillman, resulted in the death of 12 of the 275 troopers in the unit and an estimated 3 to 5 of the 50 Sauk braves involved in the fight.

[21] Earl Pierce moved to Washington County in southeastern Texas. He died in 1855 but no cause of death is known.

[22] Michigan land was later replaced by land in Missouri.

[23] In 1840, the Masonic Grand Lodge for the state of Illinois was formed and the Bodley Lodge became number 1.

[24] The House of Representatives.

[25] Springfield became the Illinois capital in 1839.

[26] This act called for significant funds to be raised from state bonds to expand the state's infrastructure, mainly railroads, that far exceeded the state's ability to repay. The assumption was that new taxation from increased business activity spurred by the expansion would make up the difference. The Panic of 1837 saw to it this would not happen and it took nearly a generation for the state to recover from the massive amount of debt.

[27] Kelloggs Grove, Illinois, the present location of Blackhawk Battlefield Park, 16 miles west of Freeport, IL, was the site of two skirmishes in the Black Hawk War. Abraham Lincoln's presence at the second skirmish, resulting in several soldier deaths on June 25, 1832 has been verified. President Lincoln would experience far more grief when he gave the Gettysburg address, 11/19/1863, at the dedication of the Soldiers' National Cemetery in Gettysburg, PA. Approximately 3,300 civil war soldiers, both known and unknown are now buried there.

[28] Of the twenty-six murder cases attributed to be defended by Abraham Lincoln, this case marked his only loss.

[29] Sidney Rigdon [1793-1876] a high-ranking official of the Latter-day Saints who fell in and out of Joseph Smith, Jr.'s close circle. He was the president of the church for two years following the murder of Smith.

[30] James W. Whitney [1782-1860] a popular long-time resident of Quincy, a gifted orator and an *agreeable* attorney.

[31] The term Joseph Smith often used meant the geographic center of his church.

[32] Calvin Averill Warren [1807-1881] a native New Yorker studied law at Lexington, Kentucky's Transylvania University and a member of the Ohio bar, moved to Illinois in 1836.

[33] Edwin Alermon Wheat [1813-1895] also a native New Yorker was the city attorney for Quincy, IL and an elected member of the Illinois House of Representatives.

[34] Robert Edward Lee [1807-1870] well known ancestry, a top graduate of the U. S. Military Academy, and at one time its superintendent, army engineer, Mexican American war veteran, revered and iconic Civil War commander of the Confederate Army of Northern Virginia, President of Washington and Lee University.

[35] Money for the boats was finally paid in 1852, 8 years following the death of Joseph Smith. Legal fees for the multi-year affair amounted to over one-third of the original cost of the boats. The supreme irony was the fact that the steamboat sank in an accident on the river less than eight months after the purchase and never fulfilled its intended use.

[36] Originally called the Equal Rights party on its formation in New York City.

[37] James lost the election to John Todd Stuart, [21,726 – 19,562] ,an early law partner of Abraham Lincoln and a favorite cousin of Lincoln's wife, Mary Todd Lincoln.

[38] Calvin Warren availed himself of the act and, after declaring and gaining a judge's approval for bankruptcy, reacquired his own assets at the bankruptcy sale for pennies on the dollar. When James discovered his partner's activity, the partnership ended. When congress discovered the widespread abuses of the new act, it was repealed in 1843.

[39] The same attorney hired by the U. S. Government in the effort to force Joseph Smith to repay the note issued in payment of the Robert E. Lee boats.

[40] The armed militia of the Mormons in Nauvoo directly commanded by Brigham Young.

41 William [1819-1892] married a Mormon woman, Mary Esther Wood, and resided in Warsaw, IL, where, among other real estate ventures, he built then sold the [Fort] Edwards House in 1849, the premier hotel on the Mississippi for a number of years. He briefly moved to Leavenworth, KS returning to Warsaw during the border wars between Kansas and Missouri, then permanently settled back in Leavenworth after his beloved wife died in 1858. He was a leading businessman in Leavenworth where he was involved with Missouri river freight hauling, land ventures, and a practicing attorney.

42 Nauvoo House was an intended hotel that was never fully completed or used as such. Later, the bodies were disinterred and buried under an outbuilding at Joseph's Nauvoo homestead that overlooked the river. The current monument in remembrance of Joseph, Hiram, and Joseph's second wife Emma Hale Smith is not located at their actual burial site.

43 After the debt was settled, the land did indeed remain in Emma's ownership.

44 Based on the journal kept by Brigham Young during this period, the Mormon leadership was well into the execution of a plan for a mass migration of Nauvoo saints to the west.

45 The Nauvoo temple burned in 1848 from a fire of suspicious origin and in 1850 straight-line winds of tornadic force further damaged the temple ruins.

46 *Texians* was a term the Mexicans used, the natives of the area preferred to be called *Texans*

47 A military quartermaster is responsible for providing all equipment, materials, and supplies, including pay, needed by the troops to complete their assigned duties.

48 Edward Everett [1818-1903] was the namesake of his cousin Edward Everett [1794-1865] a prominent politician, pastor, educator, and orator from Massachusetts. The elder Everett was a Massachusetts representative, senator, its 15th governor, minister to Great Britain and, on the death of his good friend Daniel Webster, temporarily filled the office of Secretary of State. He may be best known as the orator who spoke for nearly two hours at Gettysburg in 1863 preceding President Lincoln's brief two-minute but timeless address.

49 San Antonio's first city cemetery, on the site of the present Milam Park soon became too small for the growing city, and by the early 1850's, most of the burials were moved to new cemeteries east and further west of town; Jane's gravesite has not been found.

50 Captain Ralston wrote several letters to his superiors outlining his plans and the costs for restoring the mission buildings. In one letter James significantly understated but pinpointed the need for the work when he wrote, *the improvement of the Alamo might become a subject of some importance.*

51 Within a year after James left San Antonio in December of 1848, the army, under the direction of then Alamo quartermaster, Major Babbitt, completed Ralston and Everett's planned work leaving the chapel's appearance as it does presently.

52 In the late spring and early summer of 1850, storms that brought torrential rains that flooded Sacramento lost little energy moving over the Sierras to the high desert. In a 200-mile stretch of the California Trail from the lower basin of the Humboldt River to the higher Carson River valley [see inset on the map *To California ca 1850* on page 80.] flooding had made the much-needed grazing grasses used by the wagon train oxen and cattle inaccessible. The lack of food for the animals had substantially slowed wagon train progress that in turn resulted in dangerously low human food supplies.

53 Also published September 11, 1850 in the Sacramento Transcript under the heading, *Starvation on the Plains-Interesting Report.*

54 The date J. Neely provided in his August 18th report to the committee.

55 According to the Sacramento Transcript, J. Neely left the Carson River valley on the 13th.

56 Likely paraphrased from *The Reasoner, Vol. 6, March 7, 1849, p. 159.*

57 The next day the Sacramento Transcript printed a retraction correcting the name to J. H. Ralston.

58 Nathan Page Sunderland [1825-1909].

59 A. Cook Campbell [ca 1824-1865].

60 George Washington Riley [ca 1825-1899] stock broker and family friend of Samuel Clemens

61 Ships anchored a good distance from the river and passengers were ferried in smaller boats to Chagres village. In 1848, a railroad was begun to span the isthmus that was completed in 1855 at a cost of over 8

times the original estimate. For a time it was the most heavily traveled rail in the world based on passenger miles.

[62] The same location J. Neely Johnson first stopped.

[63] Courtesy of the descendants of James H. and Jane Alexander Ralston.

[64] At the time, James Best Dodd [1807-1872] was the head of the Mathematics and Natural Philosophy department of Morrison College, a unit of the prestigious Transylvania University in Lexington, the alma mater of J. H.'s brother Joseph.

[65] The nativity of St. John the Baptist, celebrated annually on December 27th for Roman Catholics and Protestants.

[66] John Charles Fremont [1813-1890] The pathfinder, led expeditions in the western United States, served as a major in the Mexican American War and was California's military governor. He was one of the first two senators from California in 1850 and defeated as a candidate for the presidency in 1856. He was briefly the Commander of the Western Armies during Civil War, lost his gold claim fortune in a failed railroad venture after the war, was appointed the Governor of the Arizona Territory, and died penniless in New York City.

[67] Jessie Ann Benton Fremont [1824-1902] was instrumental in her husband's high regard helping him write the popular accounts of his expeditions and in later years his most ardent and outspoken political supporter; a women truly ahead of her time. She died in Los Angeles.

[68] Although an overland route was established for mail in 1851, it was not until the late 1850's and early 1860's that companies such as the Pony Express made that route practical.

[69] Gold was also transported in this manner from California to the east coast.

[70] Joseph Augustine Benton [1818-1892] Came by ship to California in 1849 and was a highly regarded preacher in Sacramento. He moved to Oakland where he became the president of Pacific Theological Seminary. His wife, Mary Park Benton, finally moved to California in 1855. She was one of only two female professional artists in the state at that time.

[71] Tom Sunderland was defeated as the Whig candidate for district attorney.

[72] The other democratic contender was David C. Broderick of San Francisco who minted gold coins containing less gold than their face value; his $10 gold piece contained $8 worth of gold, he, pocketing the difference. Weller was elected senator.

[73] Virgil Young Ralston, see *Afterword* at the end of the book for more about him.

[74] From the diary of Enoch W. Conyers of Quincy, IL, a pioneer to the coast, July 4, 1852.

[75] In 1861, Edward F. Aiken purchased 175 acres from J. H. Ralston he named Glen Orchards. In 1872, the Glen Orchards nursery was described as being located 1 mile east of East Park and 3 miles from the post office. In 1902, East Park was named McKinley Park and its present location is shown as East Park.

[76] On the present site of Manhattan's Bryant Park behind the New York Public Library.

[77] Thomas partnered with Ferris Forman [1808-1901] who was born in NY. He was a good friend of Judge Ralston, lived in Vandalia, IL, and was the U. S. Attorney for IL at the time James was in the IL state legislature. He was a Colonel in the Mexican American War, came to CA in 1849, and worked with J. Neely and Judge Ralston in the relief of emigrants in 1850. In 1860, he was the CA Secretary of State under Gov. John B. Weller. Weller and Forman formed a law practice in Austin in 1864. He later went for a time to IL, then returned to CA. Col. Forman died in Stockton, CA.

[78] Joshua Soule [1781-1867] was born in Bristol, Maine, and became a member of the Methodist Church at age 16. A year later he was licensed to preach, and 26 years after, he was ordained as a bishop of the Methodist Episcopal Church. In 1846 he was named the bishop of the newly formed southern division of the church, headquartered in Nashville, TN. He is interred at Vanderbilt University.

[79] Mary Barron Ewing [1831-1881] married W. C. Wallace, 12/6/1853, in Lexington, MO.

[80] Mary Doty Barnes [1806-1878] moved from Sacramento to Santa Rosa, CA in 1855 where she was the principal of a Napa Valley school for girls. She married Thomas L. Barnes, from Sonoma Co., in Sacramento in 1861, by Rev. J. H. Benton. She is buried in Ukiah Cemetery, Ukiah, CA.

[81] The bill was enacted as the Kansas-Nebraska Act.

82 William Tecumseh Sherman [1820-1891], an 1840 West Point graduate was in Monterey, California near the end of the Mexican American War. His exploits during the Civil War are legendary and he was one of the few Union generals considered to be close to General Grant. After the war he was promoted to General of the Army retiring in 1884. He was a much sought after speaker and at one time was considered a presidential nominee until he was quoted as saying *I will not accept if nominated and I will not serve if elected.* He died in New York City in 1891 and was buried in St. Louis, MO.

83 Mary Esther Wood Ralston [1826-1858], of Mormon faith, married William in Quincy, IL in 1845. Her mother, Phebe Pack Wood Herrick lived at the time in Fairmont, MO, about 240 miles northeast of Leavenworth. Mary passed away during that visit.

84 William's children, James Hervey Ralston [1846-1932], Mary Eliza *May* Ralston Dill [1851-1933], Josephine *Josie* Ralston Clark Johnson [1854-1929], Jessie Lena Ralston Nelles [1856-1939].

85 Mercury, mined from cinnabar ore used in refining gold.

86 Edwin McMasters Stanton [1814-1869] was appointed by President Buchanan as U. S. Attorney General in 1860, and Secretary of War by President Lincoln in 1862. Though a strict, brusque, and intolerant leader, he nonetheless gained Lincoln's confidence in the execution of the Civil War. On Lincoln's death the quote, *Now he belongs to the ages [or angels]* is attributed to Stanton who vigorously directed the apprehension and biased prosecution of the accused assassination plotters. His opposition of President Johnson's reconstruction policies nearly resulted in Johnson's impeachment. He died four days after he was appointed a justice of the U. S. Supreme Court.

87 One investment was the Natoma Water and Mining Co. formed in 1852 to bring water to Sacramento from the south fork of the American River.

88 Frank Farmham Taylor [1830-1899] an attorney by trade and a painter by pleasure was born in New York. He had been in Sacramento for just a few years before joining Judge Ralston, engaged most recently as a moneylender. The partnership only lasted until early October.

89 James Blake [1814-1893] was an English born physician and surgeon who studied at University College in London. In 1847 he was Professor of Anatomy at St. Louis University and joined Captain Howard Stansbury's troops for much of the captain's expedition to Utah in 1849 as a doctor and geologist. He had a medical practice in Sacramento for 12 years beginning in 1850. He moved to San Francisco where he was a Professor of Obstetrics and Mid-Wifery at Toland Medical College and was a founding member of San Francisco's Academy of Sciences. He died in Middletown, Lake Co., CA.

90 Horace Greeley [1811-1872] newspaper editor and founder of the Liberal Republican Party. Founder and editor of the New York Tribune, he championed the working man. He died shortly before the electoral college results confirmed his landslide loss to Ulysses Grant in the 1872 presidential election.

91 Duane Lee Roy [Leroy] Bliss [1833-1907] arrived in California in 1850 and immediately went to the gold fields with limited success. In 1854, with a partner he bought a hotel in Trinity Center, CA later moving to Sacramento. Bliss went to Virginia City, NV in 1860 where he eventually made a fortune supplying lumber to the mining companies working the Comstock lode. In later years he created a vacation retreat for the wealthy at Lake Bigler, officially named Lake Tahoe in 1945. A California state park, D. L. Bliss, and nearby Bliss Mountain are named in his honor.

92 A year later arrangements were made for burying Lucia Mary and her sister, Bellzora Matilda next to their mother at Lone Mountain Cemetery in San Francisco.

93 Washoe was the name used for the Nevada portion of the Utah Territory, prior to becoming the Nevada Territory.

94 Actually incorporated as the Central Overland California and Pikes Peak Express Company in early 1860, the first rider arrived in Sacramento from St. Joseph, MO on April 14th of that year. It officially ceased all operations in October of 1861 with the first operational transcontinental telegraph.

95 John Reese [1808-1888], a Mormon, gained his rank as an officer of the Mormon military arm. Reese and his brother Enoch established a store, J. & E Reese and Co., in Salt Lake City. In June of 1851, he and several other Mormon faithful traveled from Salt Lake to the Carson Valley to establish a trading post to supply the legions of gold seekers. This first permanent settlement in Nevada became known as Genoa,

located in the eastern foothills of the Sierra Nevadas 16 miles south-southwest of Carson City. Eight years later Reese accompanied the Army topographical engineer, Captain James Harvey Simpson, in documenting a 288-mile shorter central Nevada desert route from Salt Lake to Carson City. During the expedition, Simpson named the central Nevada Reese River after the Colonel.

[96] Pah Ute, Pahute, or Paiute American Indians, also referred to as *root diggers*.

[97] Howard Egan [1815-1878] A Major in the Mormon Nauvoo Legion, came from Illinois to Utah in 1846 worked for the Overland Stage and Pony Express. He wrote a diary of his many experiences, *Pioneering the West, 1846-1878*.

[98] Edward Creighton [1820-1874] a successful businessman, financier, and cattleman. In early 1861 he worked for the Pacific Telegraph Co. surveying the telegraph route between Omaha, NE and Sacramento that became operational in October of 1861. Creighton University in Omaha Nebraska is named for Edward and his brother John.

[99] Estimates: 3.2 million combatants [10.4% of the total American population], 750,000 dead [23.4% of the combatants], 64% of the dead died from disease. There is no solid estimate of the number of soldiers surviving at least one battle wound or injury, but general estimates range from 30% to 55% of the total combatants. In other words, a Civil War soldier's chances of dying or being wounded/injured were approximately 6.5 out of 10. Sources: *Civil War Trust* and *Wikipedia*.

[100] From Virginia City, NV, Atwill and Company Mining Agency registrations to 7/30/1861, J. H. Ralston.

[101] Courtesy of the descendants of James H. and Jane Alexander Ralston.

[102] Lord, Eliot, *Comstock Mining and Miners*, Government Printing Office, 1883, pp. 198-200.

[103] J. P. O'Brien, *History of the Bench and Bar of Nevada*, Bench and Bar Publishing Co. San Francisco, 1913, p. 31.

[104] Lemuel Sanford *Sandy* Bowers [1833-1868] Born in Illinois, came to Nevada Territory in 1856 where he and a partner filed a 20-foot mining claim on the Comstock Lode. His wife to-be bought his partner's portion of the claim. He is buried in a plot behind his mansion.

[105] Alison *Eilley* Oram[Orrum] Hunter Cowan Bowers [1826-1903] Born in Scotland and immigrated to America about 1843, arriving in Nevada by way of Illinois. She is buried next to her husband.

[106] Mark Twain [Samuel L. Clemens], *Roughing It*, American Publishing Company, Hartford, CN, 1879, Chapter 42.

[107] December 29th 1868, Samuel Clemens wrote a letter to Jervis Langdon, the father of his to-be bride Olivia [Livy], using Johnson as a reference. *I wish to add to the references I gave Mrs. Langdon, the following: Hon. J. Neely Johnson, Carson City, Nevada. He was one Governor of California some ten years ago, & is now Chief Justice of the Supreme Court of Nevada, if my memory serves me. He has known me about seven years – he & his wife – we were next-door neighbors – & his house is always my home, now a days when I am in Carson, & has been for a year or two past.*

[108] Austin, NV was founded in 1862 after the discovery of silver in nearby Pony Canyon. The town became the seat of Lander County in September of 1863.

[109] Thompson and West, *History of Nevada with Illustrations and Biographical Sketches of the Prominent Men and Pioneers*, Oakland CA, 1881, p. 463.

[110] After being initially under the jurisdiction of California as Lander Lodge # 172, after Nevada achieved statehood in 1864, the order became Lander Lodge # 8. The Masons still meet in the Main Street building finished in 1868 as a meeting place for the Masons and the Odd Fellows that is listed on the National Register of Historic Places in Lander County. In addition to the role of housing Austin's fraternal organizations, the ground floor was also used as a roller skating rink and the second floor for Lodge meetings and dances. The strength of the second floor is assured by a patented cable-supported floor that provided a certain *bounce* for dancing.

[111] Nevada State Journal 9/3/1952: The exact location of the Judge's ranch is not clear, records indicating it was 15 to 40 miles [southeast] from Austin. It is generally believed now to have been an old ranch, up the canyon of Birch Creek, some 16 miles on the frequented route [south-southeast] from Austin.

[112] James S. Whitton [1838-1921] was born in Rochester, Vermont and came west about 1860. In 1864 he was a major shareholder in the Lander County, Constitution Gold and Silver Mine. He moved to Eureka Nevada where his occupation was a *moneylender*, and in later life to Idaho, where in 1895, he was summarily acquitted in the stabbing death of William Loucks. He died in San Diego, CA.

[113] J. H. Ralston was a minor shareholder in the Lander County, Indus Tunnel and Mining Co.

[114] Although not verified, this may have been Harry Hamilton *H. H.* Hawkins [1830-unknown] born in Missouri, who, in 1864 was on a tax list in Smoky Valley, NV [near Austin] and was later the owner of a newspaper in the now ghost town of Belmont, NV, 80 miles SSE of Austin.

[115] *See endnote 77.*

[116] *Sacramento Daily Union*, 5/20/1864.

[117] James W. Gilson [1838-1872] was born in Plainfield, IL and with his brother Samuel were Pony Express riders. After his time in Nevada, he and his brother farmed and mined in Utah. The hydrocarbon *Gilsonite,* also called asphalt, is named for the brothers who first discovered the substance at their Utah mine. James was a rough and tumble frontiersman noted for carrying a repeater rifle, two revolvers around his waist, a small pistol in one boot, and a knife in the other.

[118] *Tom,* as the Shoshone Indian was called, had several run-ins with the law over his repeated actions in *borrowing* horses that he neglected to return. In fact, because of his documented tracking ability, he was released from incarceration in May specifically to assist the Gilson party in their search for Judge Ralston. Later that year in August, he was again being sought for his proclivity of horse thievery and inciting discontent among a colony of Shoshones north of the stagecoach station and smelting operation at San Antonio, NV. Sources: *Daily Reese River Reveille*, 5/28/1864, *Sacramento Daily Union*, 9/5/1864.

[119] The estimated location where Judge Ralston's remains were found: 38.486879 N , 117.122381.

[120] *Queens County* [New York] *Sentinel*, 9/3/1868.

[121] Courtesy of Bancroft Library, UC Berkeley with special thanks to Martin "Marty" Hansen.

[122] Founded as Union Grammar School in 1854, now Lowell High School, it is the oldest high school in continuous operation west of the Mississippi.

[123] Letter courtesy of the descendants of James H. and Jane Alexander Ralston.

[124] Courtesy of Bancroft Library, UC Berkeley, special thanks to Martin "Marty" Hansen.

[125] Freedman Bank records, Washington D. C., 4/30/1873.

[126] For most of the 19th century, offices that needed copies of various documents employed a copying clerk or copyist that sat on a high stool in front of a slanted work board and tediously hand-wrote the needed copies. These were much sought after jobs that required a political appointment and a number of well-known and previously affluent women held these positions. Harriet's appointment was received from the state of Nevada, 6/30/1874, at a starting salary of $500 per year; a position she held for nearly 20 years.

[127] Letter written by Jackson Ralston, 5/7/1945, to Chief Judge [of the Washington D. C Municipal Court] William E. Richardson. Courtesy of the descendants of James H. and Jane Alexander Ralston.

[128] Courtesy of the descendants of James H. and Jane Alexander Ralston.

[129] William E. Richardson letter, 5/7/1945.

[130] Born in 1885 to a Quaker family in Farmland, Randolph County, IN. She was reared by her uncle and aunt and she was formally educated at Western College for Women in Oxford, OH, now the Western Program at Miami University. She worked for the Playground and Recreation Association headquartered to New York when she first became acquainted with Jackson circa 1918. In 1928, she moved to San Francisco where she worked for an investment brokerage firm. She went to work for a time with the American Red Cross in Washington State and returned to Berkeley, CA where she completed a degree in social work at the University of California in 1934.

[131] William E. Richardson letter, 5/7/1945.

[132] Past recipients include, Jimmy Carter, Pierre Trudeau, Warren Christopher, and Shirin Ebadi.

[133] Before his death, Ralston had a son with Sara Jane Hartigan.

[134] Eventually became Stanford University's Department of Medicine.

[135] Frank's physical description from the 1892 San Francisco voter registration list.

[136] There is no evidence Laura was formally educated in the law, likely learning the trade from her father.

[137] Established in 1884 it was taken over by the State in 1897. At that time there were 55 steam-heated buildings, electric lighting and a running water and sewer system. The 910-acre grounds had a successful dairy farm and was the home for 800 veterans of the Mexican, Civil, and Indian wars.

[138] Born in San Francisco in 1868, he graduated from Cooper Medical College as a physician in 1892. Dr. Rowell died in Alameda, CA in 1951.

[139] Letter courtesy of the descendants of James H. and Jane Alexander Ralston.

[140] There was nothing found that would support the statement that Frank had considerable wealth. In fact, his letter to Elizabeth suggests just the opposite.

[141] Courtesy of the descendants of James H. and Jane Alexander Ralston.

[142] Born in 1871, graduated from Cambridge University Trinity School 1889, ordained as a Catholic priest, died in England, 1935.

[143] Frank was buried in the churchyard St. Paul's Church in Fort Jameson, the church was built in 1906.

Made in the USA
Columbia, SC
07 December 2022

72948117R00120